These volumes bring transpersonal psychology into a more contemporary era and expand its application into new approaches for healing and growth. It is a pleasure to see new thinking that extends the seminal insights of transpersonal psychology into such areas as social action, diversity, and inequality, to connect the inner with the outer world, and to locate personal transformation in a context of social transformation, indeed as the most powerful form of social action. This is a much needed contribution to the field.

Brant Cortright, PhD
Author of *Psychotherapy and Spirit:*
Theory and Practice in Transpersonal Psychotherapy
Professor of Psychology, California Institute of Integral Studies

Drs. Kaklauskas, Clements, Hocoy, and Hoffman have pulled together an impressive display of talented Transpersonal Psychology writers who present the complexities of the theory and practice in a way that the reader can readily understand and grasp. The writings are applicable for numerous issues, conditions, and settings and will be a valuable resource that will enhance the teaching, learning, research, and practice in the field.

Nina W. Brown, EdD, LPC, NCC, FAGPA
Professor and Eminent Scholar

This collection literally has it all from scholarly reviews of the intellectual and cultural origins of transpersonal psychology through relevant research and moving personal experiences to contemporary cutting edge applications. It clearly demonstrates that transpersonal is alive and well as it passes from middle age to elderhood. Timely, yet timeless.

David Lukoff, PhD, Past Co-President Association for Transpersonal Psychology and the Institute for Spirituality and Psychology

This book takes the reader on a journey across time, cultures, and perspectives, arriving at a fully contemporary view of transpersonal psychology. A mindful look at impassioned living, this scholarly collection explores the crossroads of Human Science and Spirituality, and is a must read!

Donna Rockwell, PhD, President Elect, Society for Humanistic Psychology (American Psychological Association Division 32)

Shadows and Light is a stunning collection of essays that enables the reader/ seeker to take a deep dive into a richly imagined framework for transpersonal education. It is a timely and elegant offering of contemplative-based theories, research, and practices. I predict it will be heralded as a triumph in the field!

Gaea Logan, LPC-S, CGP
Executive Director, Founder, *International Center for Mental Health and Human Rights* - Social Responsibility Award Recipient, Group Foundation for Advancing Mental Health

This collection is filled with compassion and curiosity, hope and humility. By integrating contemporary research, multicultural and social justice perspectives, and the vitality of relationships with self, others, and the world, the essays and talks provide refreshing energy to psychological perspectives on growth, transformation, and finding one's place in this often challenging world.

Pat Denning, PhD, & Jeannie Little, LCSW
Founders, The Center for Harm Reduction Therapy

Shadows & Light:
Theory, Research, & Practice in Transpersonal Psychology

Volume 2: Talks & Reflections

Francis J. Kaklauskas
Carla Clements
Dan Hocoy
Louis Hoffman
Editors

University Professors Press
Colorado Springs, CO

Book Copyright © 2016

Shadows & Light: Theory, Research, and Practice in Transpersonal Psychology (Volume 2: Talks & Reflections)

First Published in 2016, University Professors Press.

ISBN 13: 978-1-939686-88-6

University Professors Press
Colorado Springs, CO
www.universityprofessorspress.com

Front Photo by Charles Kershenblatt
Cover Design by Laura Ross

Dedication

To the faculty, students, alumni, and staff at Naropa University and Saybrook University who have carried the torch of transpersonal psychology into the 21st century.

Contents

Acknowledgments

We would like to thank all the authors who gave their time, effort, expertise, and wisdom to this collection. We appreciate the encouragement of the staff and other faculty at Naropa University and Saybrook University in completing this collection. We also owe a great deal to the many creative, thoughtful, and passionate individuals and communities that forged many of the ideas and perspectives presented in these volumes, as well as the many students and clients who helped to inform this effort. We also would like to thank our families and friends for their continual support and patience throughout this process.

Chapter 1
The Importance of Curiosity:
In Transpersonal Psychology, in
Spiritual Development

Charles T. Tart[1]

I participated recently in an intensive meditation practice, and Jeff Warren introduced the session with a word that I have seldom heard used or given very much importance by many, perhaps all, meditation teachers I have received instruction from. The word is *curiosity*. I have been thinking about curiosity for years, as it's one of the main reasons I have been interested in meditative and similar practices: curiosity about my mind, about other people's minds, about how minds work, about how they can work better, etc. Of course, that is just one motivation among many: I certainly would like to reduce my suffering and reach "enlightenment" (whatever that is). Hearing Jeff Warren use the word *curiosity,* though, stimulated me to write about curiosity, Buddhism, and modern psychology. I thought more deeply about my own curiosity and became curious about what brought me into transpersonal psychology and related fields. This is something that I haven't shared often, and it is nice to share it here. This will be in the style of personal storytelling

---

[1] This talk was taken from Charles Tart's personal blog entries on http://www.paradigm-sys.com and edited, arranged, and minimally added to by Francis J. Kaklauskas. These blog entries are deliberately written in an informal style as the emphasis is on sharing ideas that may be valuable, but which Professor Tart no longer has time to develop in his usual scientific and scholarly manner.

rather than didactic, academic lecturing, as I think it will more effectively communicate some points that way.

Becoming A Transpersonal Psychologist

To my conscious knowledge, there were two major forces in my becoming a transpersonal psychologist. The earliest was my childhood religion, Lutheranism. My parents weren't religious but my maternal grandmother, Nana, who lived in the apartment downstairs from us, was very much so. Grandmothers, as many of you may personally know, are sources of unconditional love. She took me to church and Sunday school. We had a special bond, and I naturally felt that what was good enough for her in religion was good enough for me! As a child and early teenager, then, I was quite devout and followed the practices and explored the beliefs of being a Lutheran and a Christian.

The second major force was science. As early as I can remember, I loved everything connected with science. As a teenager I read about science all the time, including a lot of "adult" books. In my basement I created chemical and electrical laboratories, became a ham radio operator, built my own equipment, and planned to be a scientist or engineer.

The teenage years are a time of starting to question what you've been taught and to think for yourself. I became aware, as most idealistic teens do, of the apparent hypocrisy of adults. Some of those church people were not living what they preached! Worse yet, I knew enough science by then to realize that most, if not all, religious ideas and beliefs were quite nonsensical from the point of view of science—just old superstitions. How could I reconcile this with the deep religious feelings that had begun in my childhood?

From an adult perspective, I know many teenagers go through similar conflicts between science and religion. A common "resolution" is to go to one extreme or the other: religion is all nonsense and materialistic science is right, or religion is the ultimate truth and science can be ignored when it's inconvenient. I put "resolution" in quotes, for as a psychologist, I see this extremism as usually an incomplete and often psychologically costly way of dealing with the conflict; too much suppression of parts of our nature are involved.

Luckily the Trenton City Library was my second home, and it had many books on spirituality, religion, psychical research, and parapsychology. My curiosity found a thousand ways to be stimulated, and sometimes fulfilled. I discovered in reading that many intelligent people had gone through conflicts similar to mine, and the founders of the Society for Psychical Research had come up with a brilliant idea. Instead of a wholesale rejection of all religion and spirituality and adoption of materialism in whatever form was then scientifically fashionable, why not apply the *methods* of science—the insistence on accurate data collection, logical theorizing, testing of theories, and the collegiality of full and honest sharing of data and theory—to the phenomena of religion and spirituality? Why not examine and refine the data and devise more adequate theories? I was inspired by this idea, and it has been the central theme of my professional work and personal life ever since. Look at the data of spirituality,[2] see how to observe it more accurately, create and test theories about it, share these with colleagues, and slowly work our way toward a spirituality based on as many observable/experienceable facts as possible.

Of course there are deeper reasons, but let's not stray too far from my (relatively) conscious mind...

Psychic Experiences: A Reality Underlying Spirituality?

My more active probing of possible realities underlying spirituality began when I was a sophomore at MIT, studying electrical engineering. I conducted my first parapsychological experiment using hypnotic suggestion as a (hoped for) way of producing out-of-body experiences (OBEs), so my subjects' "minds" or "souls" might leave their bodies temporarily and see and accurately describe a target locked in the

---

[2] I switch now to talking about spirituality rather than religion, using spirituality to refer to the primary kinds of transpersonal experiences individuals have that, when turned into theories, beliefs, and dogmas, become "religions." Religions are more the province of social psychologists.

basement of a distant house. Looking back, the experimental design wasn't bad for a teenager, although I didn't have an objective way of evaluating the data I hoped to get—a qualitative description of an unusual target (nor did the field of parapsychology as a whole at that time). I didn't formally write the results up until many years later (Tart, 1998), by which time I had carried out five others studies of OBEs.

While at MIT I met other students interested in parapsychology, and we formed a student club to talk about it and ask speakers to lecture. One of those speakers was Andrija Puharich, whom Eileen Garrett (one of the world's most famous spiritualist mediums and head of the Parapsychology Foundation) had told me about. Puharich was a physician-researcher who not only claimed to have a way of making quantitatively measurable (hits above chance in a matching test) telepathy work better or to block it, but was doing it with electrical devices—Faraday Cages. Invented by renowned British physicist Michael Faraday, such a cage is an all-metal enclosure that keeps electromagnetic waves from penetrating to its inside. What could rouse the curiosity of students of electrical engineering and physics more than this? Some of us visited Puharich's laboratory in Maine and thought his work seemed basically sound. He gave a lecture on his findings at MIT for our club, and I was intrigued enough (and needed the money!) to ask him for a summer job. So I saw some of his research up close for three months in 1957.

I was young and, of course, rather naïve so didn't fully realize that, in spite of being rejected by mainstream science, the few parapsychologists around did not all band together in a friendly way to present a united front to irrational criticisms. There was a parapsychological "establishment," centered in Professor J. B. Rhine's laboratory at Duke, and Puharich was definitely not part of that establishment; he was a "bad boy." I had already met Rhine when he came to lecture in Boston several times and had corresponded with him. I wanted to switch from electrical engineering to psychology to prepare for a career in parapsychology. MIT had no psychology programs at that time, but Rhine helped me transfer to Duke as a psychology major and had indicated he would find a part-time job for me in his laboratory.

However, once he discovered that I had spent the summer working for Puharich and would not admit I was foolish to have done so, he decided I did not have sufficient discrimination to make a scientific parapsychologist, and the promised job disappeared. I was, a friend told me, put on the list of people to be discouraged from visiting Rhine's lab. I was a "bad boy" now myself, in a minor way. And discovering that curiosity might have lip service paid to it by an otherwise pioneering scientist, J. B. Rhine, but that there were strong social and psychological forces channeling it into approved directions, away from non-approved directions.

Still an idealistic young man, I was naturally miffed over this treatment, although as I matured I realized I would probably have acted the same way as Rhine in a similar situation. If I had devoted my life to making a case for my field, based on very careful, methodologically sophisticated research, I would discourage wild young people from getting involved and undermining my work with questionable work of their own!

On the other hand, J. B. Rhine had given a talk to the entering freshmen women and invited any of them who were interested in parapsychology to visit his lab. So there I was reading books in the Parapsychology Laboratory's library (I did not accept Rhine's ban) when this beautiful young woman came in and asked me, "Do you believe in ESP?" More than 50 years of marriage later, Judy tells me I still use the same response I did with her way back then: "It's not a matter of *belief*, it's a matter of *evidence*..." I said with a subtle but certain air of snootiness. So Rhine was the proximate cause of far more happiness than unhappiness for me, and he did decide after another 20 years or so that I had enough discrimination to make a good parapsychologist...and the next 50 years were quite interesting....

Curiosity about the female mind was, of course, a big factor in dating and getting married, and I'm still trying to figure out the female mind. Wonderful, puzzling, delightful, frustrating...

And just to put a cap on these beginning threads of my career pursuing my curiosity, Puharich became even more of a "bad boy" to the parapsychological establishment by getting involved with things like

UFO studies, while I became a part of that tiny parapsychological establishment. Puharich eventually got too far out for me with this ("What? I have some rigid conservative beliefs? Me?"), but it's a shame that his basic finding, that Faraday cages may amplify or shield psi, have been ignored, as they may be a key to a major advance in getting reliable psi in our laboratory work. As far as I know, I'm the only one who did even a partial replication study of his work, with supportive results (Tart, 1988). Two former students of mine are now starting to continue this work with Faraday cages.

As I have gotten older I would like to think that I have stayed curious about the many questions that are very difficult to answer, to re-question any answers I *think* I may have found, and to question the answers others promote with certainty. Despite my curiosity and uncertainty about most things, and my immediate knowledge of how little I actually know, others often see me as an expert, and I often receive inquiries from others looking for answers about parapsychological and spiritual matters.

Can I illustrate using words to stimulate curiosity and possibly help understanding without getting too caught in them?

Defining the Non-Material

As an example, recently a colleague emailed me that he was on a Quixotic quest for a definition of the non-material. He elaborated that it seems like defining or describing consciousness itself is Quixotic in that everyone seems to recognize it when they see it (I assume you, dear reader, have consciousness yourself and can recognize that simply by turning your attention inward for a moment), but have no clue what it specifically is. I think some folks would find my response interesting. Words can stimulate and really help curiosity, and can also derail us and drive us kind of crazy.

The Email on Defining Non-Material

Dear Colleague, Yes, that makes consciousness just like pornography, like the Supreme Court Justice Potter Stewart, who said he couldn't really define pornography, but he knew it when he saw it. So for some fun off the top of my head, without going to any authorities like the Oxford English Dictionary, I did an exploration myself about how I may go about defining such ideas at this point in my life.

I like to look at what is implicit or assumed in questions and ideas, so let's start with the assumption that we ought to be able to "define" the "non-material."

At one extreme we can get into a rigid kind of arrogance: We humans are the smartest things in the universe and we can define everything! We can make everything make sense in terms of our human conceptual systems—with the usually unvoiced corollary that if we can't satisfactorily define it, it doesn't exist and/or isn't important, so let's ignore or suppress it. I'm all for giving things a good try—but also think it's a good idea to practice a little humility and remember that we may not be smart enough to figure everything out. And/or maybe we're just temporarily stuck and a new approach will arise later, or a new tool will be developed to work on the problem. But I won't be surprised if we run into some things we never make any progress in explaining properly.

At the opposite extreme, I have no interest in the ideas of those who claim a priori that we cannot know about X and *should not try*. That's an uninteresting recipe for failure. As Henry Ford is reputed to have said, "Those who think they can and those who think they can't are both right."

So we may not be smart enough to ever "define" the "immaterial," or maybe just not smart enough to do it now, but I'm pretty sure there's something there of interest and importance.

Now on to "define." To me that means come up with a verbal (or special language, like math) formulation about a phenomenon, X, that makes "sense," that makes it fit "logically" into the rest of our *valued* knowledge base. As with the implicit aspects above, there's an implicit assumption that we ought to be able to do this and that our current knowledge base is correct enough and expandable enough to handle X. To which I have the same *maybe* as above.

I get a lot of headaches, and I'm also good at using language fairly precisely, but if you ask me to exactly define "what" or "where" my headaches are...well, damn it! They move around, some qualities change, and have lots of qualities I just can't find satisfactory words for! Yet I know it when I have a headache, it's certainly real—and it's not like pornography!

So if I say something is "non-material," without making any absolute or final statement, I'll make a pragmatic one, given what we/I know currently or reasonable extensions of that knowledge. It is important to remember that such a statement is subject to change if the right new data comes along.

Let me try to illustrate with respect to *psi*, the general term now applied in parapsychological research for acquiring information about or affecting observable processes when there is no reasonable explanation in terms of what we know about the physical world. If I ask you to tell me the order of a deck of thoroughly shuffled, ordinary playing cards on a table in a locked room next door, for example, you ordinarily have to use known physical energies like light to determine this. Or if I ask you to watch, via video, a machine in that locked room throwing dice, but I want you to make more threes come up than would happen by chance, you have to apply physical energies to the dice to affect them. If you are too correct in calling the cards or affecting the dice just by wishing, determined by statistical analysis, we talk about psi. We could call your correctness with the cards the form of psi we call clairvoyance or, if someone in that locked room is looking at the cards, telepathy. If you significantly affect the outcome of the dice rolling, we call that form of psi psychokinesis (PK).

As an example, I would say that psi is "immaterial" or "non-material" compared with our current knowledge of electricity or reasonable extensions of that knowledge; it just doesn't show the kinds of qualities electricity does. Translating that into pragmatic decisions, I would say that if someone says they want to take all of what little money currently supports psi research and put it into buying more sensitive radio receivers to detect psi: "That's almost certainly a waste of time, you can't have the money." When I say psi is "immaterial" in the larger sense of the term "material," I'm saying that what we *currently* know about the physical world and reasonable extensions of it does not offer any satisfactory explanations of psi. My criteria of "satisfactory" would be both that the physical theory of psi makes conceptual sense in terms of our physics database *and* allows someone to build a material gadget, working according to known physical principles, that would significantly amplify psi[3]: The old-fashioned prediction-and- control criteria for judging scientific theories.

At present we have some odd and occasional correlations of psi with physical variables (e.g., local sidereal time, geomagnetic weather, a possible Faraday cage effect), but they don't really make "sense" of it as far as I can see. Note that I don't buy into what philosophers long ago termed *promissory materialism* here either. I'm not much for untestable faith that *someday* they will explain psi in terms of physical principles. Maybe, but that's faith, not science. Someday is always in the future, and you can never prove that someday it won't happen, or that someday it won't all be explained by invisible, tiny green angels.

Note, too, that by saying psi is "non-material" by present knowledge standards, I'm not saying it does not obey any laws or that we can't figure out how it works or what it means someday. That is, I have no "supernatural" theory of a non-understandable god meddling to change things sometimes—although I'm not arrogant enough to say that I'm so smart myself that I can declare there are no beings more intelligent or powerful than me.

The pragmatic bottom line for me is that I'm not saying don't look for physical correlates or explanations of psi—I love those attempts. I'm a nerd and fascinated by technology!—but I am saying don't sit back and fail to investigate what the actual characteristics of psi (or other transpersonal phenomena) are because you assume "they" will explain it all someday in terms of physics.

This is exactly the same position I have about consciousness in general. Yes, the brain is heavily involved in what we ordinarily experience as our consciousness, but don't ignore those characteristics of consciousness that don't readily fit into a physical, neurological model; get on with investigating them on their own terms.

---

[3] You may wonder, then, if the Faraday cage effect is real, does it mean psi is electrical in nature? Probably not, given other factors, but it may cut down ordinary noise in our physical brains which thus allows us to pay better attention to faint psi signals.

So "immaterial" pragmatically means real phenomena that do not follow known physical laws and which should be investigated in a variety of ways until we find some that make a new kind of sense out of them. And of course it's more complicated than this. But enough! See how you've overstimulated my brain/mind first thing in the morning? With best wishes, Charley[4]

(End of email on defining the non-material)

Curiosity as Blessing and Curse

Even after writing the above email, my curiosity about and musings on defining *immaterial* and *consciousness* have not, of course, ended. My interminable supply of curiosity has been a gift for me, albeit not an unmixed blessing—it gets me in trouble sometimes—and one that can be extended to contemporary spirituality and psychology. Later in my life, for example, I increasingly developed a somewhat dedicated routine of Buddhist practices. But as someone raised as a Christian, I have a strongly conditioned idea that to be a "good" member of a religion you are supposed to believe all aspects of it. In that sense, I'm not a "good Buddhist" or a "dedicated Buddhist." While I have great respect for this tradition and make it one of my main sources of practical guidance in life, I don't have a blind faith that all aspects of Buddhism are true. Many followers of Buddhism act as if that's the case, of course, although Gautama Buddha, in his Sutta to the Kalamas,[5] warned people not to take

---

[4] After my response I did go check in with an authority, the *Shorter Oxford English Dictionary,* and here is the essence of each definition rather than the whole thing: **material:** an adjective—of or pertaining to matter or substance; formed or consisting of matter; corporeal, and **immaterial:** an adjective—not material; not consisting of matter; spiritual.
[5] A translation by Gates (1989) that I like is:
Do not believe in anything simply because you have heard it.
Do not believe in traditions because they have been handed down for many generations.
Do not believe in anything because it is spoken and rumored by many.
Do not believe in anything simply because it is found written in your religious books.
Do not believe in anything merely on the authority of your teachers and elders.
But after observation and analysis, when you find that anything agrees with reason, and is conducive to the good and benefit of one and all, then accept it and live up to it.

any of his teachings on faith but to thoroughly test them to see *if they indeed made sense and worked for them.* Using one's curiosity, and being pragmatic about it. I also am someone who is very scientifically oriented. I realize that we humans make observations and have experiences and then we come up with intellectual explanations, theories to explain them. It's one of the most important aspects of being human. I'm sure that Buddhism, indeed probably all religions, started with powerful and moving transpersonal experiences, but then people invented theories, then called *doctrines* in a religious context, to make acceptable sense of them. As a scientist, though, I have the pragmatic, working belief that *all* theories are tentative, working hypotheses, never *The Truth*. They are the best we can do intellectually at the time with the data we have, but it's important not to get overly attached to them because new data/experiences/understandings coming in may show that they are inadequate and need modification or replacement. This has manifested many times in the history of modern science. All that was important in some field of study was perfectly understood, everyone felt very smart and smug, and Bang! Data came in that required an overthrow of the reigning paradigm and a new one had to be formed. Thomas Kuhn (1962) documented this so well in his work on the history of science.

My Curiosity and Buddhism

I regard the doctrines and belief system of Buddhism, indeed of all religions, as theories and practices that undoubtedly have some usefulness and truth value, yet are probably inadequate and need revision in other ways. It's more complicated than formal science, though, as most people in a religion are really strongly attached to doctrines at an emotional as well as an intellectual level. Questioning any of the religion's doctrines is generally not valued, indeed may be considered heresy. People who think of themselves as scientists may forget the tentativeness of their theories also, believe their science has found *The Truth*, and get emotionally attached to these apparent truths. What makes this transition from science as a method, leading to working hypotheses, to the ossification of believing we know all the important truths is that the people to whom it happens generally don't know it's happened; they continue to think they are open-minded scientists. But, believing that the methods of essential science can help us clarify many things in the spiritual area, I respect doctrines but ask questions. Hopefully my questions are always based on a desire to be clearer about what's more or less useful and not just an emotional reaction to what I don't like.

I find that a lot of Buddhist ideas and practices make sense and work for me. I can see in my own life experience that I've come to understand my mind better and live a somewhat kinder and wiser life. As to more metaphysical aspects, such as psychic blessings from the Buddhas and bodhisattvas, I hope that those are real. I would be glad to receive them, and will be happy to treat them with respect. I, and most of us, can use all the help we can get! But I don't know whether the Buddhist worldview and formulations are ultimate truths or just good theories given the present state of our empirical knowledge. Perhaps not fully adequate theories, so I can and do ask questions, and continue being curious.

I also believe (I should say I *treat as a useful working hypothesis*, to follow my own advice above) that the implicit and explicit background of the Buddhist worldview, in common with any spiritual system's detailed worldview, may basically inhibit curiosity. I worry that some believe that Gautama Buddha figured out *everything* of importance, pointed out the *one* important goal in life—the cessation of suffering—and mapped out the *best way* to get to that goal by becoming enlightened in a Buddhist style. Consequently, some may believe there are no other important questions, so why waste your time on anything that isn't following the traditional Buddhist path as much as you can? There may be technical questions on using the methods most effectively, or adapting them to a particular individual's strengths and weaknesses, but there are no basic questions.

This is the reason why I have long technically characterized Buddhism and other spiritual systems not as spiritual *sciences* but as spiritual *technologies.*[6] A scientist, in principle, can be curious about anything and everything. A scientist is initially educated in certain basic principles and findings considered fundamental to her field, but may well go on to question these basic principles and find them erroneous or in need of revision. A technician, on the other hand, is trained in the application of basic principles, in applying them in an effective technical and practical manner, not in questioning these basic principles.

Of course, a lot of people socially designated as scientists actually behave as if they were technicians, never really asking any fundamental questions, but just creating and implementing small, technical improvements *within* the worldview they were already given. This valuable work is essential and important to the progress of any field of science. When a field of science is dominated by a theory that has implicitly or explicitly been accepted as the Truth and habitually molds thinking and action, the famous historian of science, Thomas Kuhn (1962) called this *normal,* paradigmatic science. But this scientist/technician distinction is useful. If you're working in a spiritual tradition that already knows all the important answers, no basic curiosity is needed. But we may want to be curious about that, especially if we are transpersonal psychologists, dedicated to expanding spiritual knowledge, not just applying it.

Similarly, I am curious about curiosity in contemporary psychology. In the late 1800s, when psychology began differentiating itself from philosophy, one of its primary methods was *introspection.* This was basically a method of examining inner experience, and some of the early psychologists wrote about having "trained observers" examine and report on their experience. Unfortunately, psychology failed to establish itself as a useful discipline with this approach. There was simply too much disagreement among the results from various laboratories as to what was observed in the mind and why these things were observed. Introspection became discredited as a method, and

---

[6] Note that I am not downplaying the immense value of accomplishments on various spiritual paths but, if you believe in progress, as I do, accepting any worldview and spiritual goal as final, ultimate Truth, may seriously discourage you from looking for alternatives that might even be more valuable, and certainly a part of reality.

replaced by behaviorism. Behaviorism produced much more objectivity. Did a person do external behavioral act A or not? You could get perfect agreement among observers about that. But this left out the whole interior side of human experience.

As I have written about elsewhere (Tart, 2005), with the wisdom of hindsight we can see many reasons why this introspective approach didn't work. There was no understanding of the importance of individual differences, for example, but rather a naïve belief that each of us possessed what we might call a "standard mind," so anyone's observations and experiences could give basic insight into the way a standard mind worked. I assume there is some really basic core to mind at some deep level, but the semi-arbitrary qualities added on top of that through enculturation and personal experience may keep it quite hidden. There was also no understanding of the vital importance of *experimenter bias*, an issue still largely avoided even in modern psychology as we cling to the idea of being "objective observers." Most important, "trained observers" usually meant people who might have had 10 to 20 hours of training on how to report a particular aspect of experience. With our current familiarity with meditation systems from Buddhism and other spiritual disciplines, however, I've heard Buddhist teachers estimate that it generally takes at least 5,000, if not 10,000 hours of disciplined practice to become a really good observer of one's own experiences. This 10,000 hour figure has been applied now in many fields as a foundation for real mastery (Gladwell, 2008). Thus, the fact that untrained, introspecting observers did not produce reports which agreed with one another is hardly surprising (Tart, 2005).

In the last couple of decades, psychology, particularly clinical psychology, has discovered that aspects of meditative practices can be therapeutically helpful in relieving a variety of conditions. But note that we have a close parallel to what I said about Buddhism above—namely, we have an overall belief system, our culture's beliefs, about what is normal and how a normal mind should operate. Meditative methods are now seen as an adjunct to other forms of therapy that are designed to help patients' minds operate in accordance with our views of normal. It's wonderful that aspects of traditional meditation systems have been adapted in ways that reduce human suffering, but a general curiosity is not there. The exciting question, for me, is what would happen if we developed a lot of people trained in spirituality, mediation, psychology, and related fields and then tasked them, in the sense of essential science, to investigate *all* aspects of experience, *all* aspects of reality? Not simply those that help people be "normal" and get rid of their specific kind of suffering. Could we develop a new introspective psychology that actually worked? Could we expand upon what we currently know and open new doors to new areas of study and knowing.

For me, curiosity is the heart of science, psychology, and spirituality. At their best, these fields search for truth, or at least a deeper and fuller understanding of ourselves, others, and our world. Curiosity embodies all our senses, our mind, brain, and spirit. Everything we see and all things unseen. What do we think we know, how do we think we know it, what else may also seem true, and what may we be overlooking? Curiosity has filled my life with confusion at times, but also vital life energy. I humbly suggest you try it.

References

Gates, B. (1989). Reflections on the Suttas. *Inquiring Mind, 6*(1), 4.

Gladwell, M. (2008). *Outliers.* Boston, MA: Little, Brown and Company

Kuhn, T.S. (1962). *The structure of scientific revolutions.* Chicago, Il: University of Chicago Press.

Tart, C., (1988). Effects of electrical shielding on GESP performance. *Journal of the American Society for Psychical Research, 82*, 129–146.

Tart, C. (1998). Six studies of out-of-the-body experiences. *Journal of Near-Death Studies, 17*(2), 73–99.

Tart, C. (2005). Future psychology as a science of mind and spirit: Reflections on receiving the Abraham Maslow award. *Humanistic Psychologist, 33*(2),131–143.

Chapter 2
Beyond Buddhism:
What We Need to Lose to Save
What We Love

angel Kyodo williams[1]

Thank you so much for having me here. Often after I have finished talking, people are interested and ask questions about my history, my earlier life, how I came to practice. I think I can start there briefly, and I think it will be particularly relevant to this talk.

I am a stone-cold New Yorker. Like really in the thick of New York City and one of the outer burrows. Forgive me—anybody that lives in the outer burrows—but we would call them bridge and tunnel. So I grew up in Queens, Brooklyn, and Manhattan. I was kind of like a downtown snob and in those days I was hip, too. Anything above 14th street, and I would get a nosebleed. I was very much living a life of a hip, mixed race, queer woman of color. You know, parties that ended at 4 a.m. then you started to go out to the next party.

And as happens to many of us, I eventually ran into a wall—a wall that was made up of my own places of confusion. Where the world stopped making sense to me. My grandfather passed away, and he and I were very close. I just couldn't make sense of anything and you know how grief does that to you. Everything that you knew about the world

---

[1] From a talk given as a Lenz Scholar at Naropa University on March 18, 2105; transcribed and edited by Francis J. Kaklauskas.

just comes completely undone.

So simultaneously I ran into a book called *Zen Mind, Beginner's Mind* (Suzuki, 1970) in Tower bookstore, and it started to help me put some pieces together. This little Japanese man who was, you know, all the way across the country in California, knew something about my life. He knew something about how to help me make sense of my life. It was striking.

I made a practice space in a closet because that is where you did things that no one should know about. I was out as queer but I had to keep the meditation thing in the closet. When I had the opportunity to go on a trip to the West Coast, I visited San Francisco Zen Center and I got my first meditation cushion. Eventually I got it out of the closet and would bring it up to Yonkers to sit with Bernie (Glassman). I eventually found my way to the Village Zendo.

And there I was. At that time, I was hip and cool. I was actually the first black woman to own a cyber café. That is what we called them back then. I was really sort of living in some way someone's idea of a dream. I had my own business, or it had me. It was a very cool place with lots of spoken word going on by famous poets, and well-known jazz artists would sneak off their contract and come and perform. All the groovy people in the world were there. It was cool like that.

But then I started doing this Zen thing. One year we had a legendary New Year's Eve party. People talked the whole next year and asked, "Are you going to have the party again this year?" I said, "Of course, we're going to have the party." The following year came, and we were all ready to have this party. But I was at a crossroads because my Zen community was having a sesshin, a silent retreat. Suddenly I was faced with being hip and cool and all in the know and part of the black digerati—one of the cool kids. It was everything I knew about myself and everything I knew about who I was. It was who I constructed myself to be. I was either going to go to the party and be that person that I had so carefully constructed, or I was going to go to a cold-ass house in the snow that had no heat and walk around basically in circles seeing nothing but a bunch of white folks' feet (laughing). Anybody know the sesshin? That sound like it? Easy choice—right?

So I remember someone was on the phone when I was at the café, and they had already placed me at the party. And I thought, "Oh!" This image of myself was fading and I couldn't see myself at the party anymore. Through my practice, the idea of myself was starting to come apart. In that moment I knew that, on the one hand, I could go to the party and have the benefits of that part. I could be the center of the attention.

Or I could go and attend to my heart.

So I went into this cold house and walked in circles around several white folks. As strange as they were and as strange as it seemed, I could be with a different group of people that New Year's Eve. That was my moment of giving up something in order to save what I loved.

And I think that Buddhism is at a crossroads in that kind of way. It has to look really deeply at itself. You know we can't fix the past, right? And so there's no real point in looking back and saying we should have done this or we should have done that. But we can only go forward. We're in a moment in which mindfulness is on the rise. We barely have meditation anymore. We have mindfulness. There is technology and mindfulness. There is mindfulness in schools. There is mindfulness in end-of-life care. And there is just mindfulness everywhere. And we all know that it's a code word for the part of the dharma that people can take in—for now. That's okay. We take what we can and meet the situation as we can in the way that we are in this moment. There is a kind of lens on Buddhism. It's a little small right now while people largely focus on mindfulness, but it will get bigger.

People will come. And they'll investigate and they'll wonder, like what is this about? We'll have to have an answer. So we sit at this crossroads with opportunities. Can we say we are about the dharma? How we find it in this country, in this culture, in this place at this time. We can't judge other places and other times because things have to fit the conditions. But in these conditions, we can either go down the road of expressing the full and complete dharma that has a place for everyone. The radical dharma that has a place for everyone. Full and complete. We can live up to its full promise.

Or we can go down the road of irrelevance, and we can just be another preoccupation: a kind of entertainment and a bit of amusement. Someplace for people that have too much to do and too much to spend to put their attention and time. Embodying not the true heart and essence of the dharma but rather peddling it as yet another expression of the fundamental illnesses of this country—that illness being that we are masters at forms of oppression—masters of oppression despite being in the midst of actually having opportunities to work with our diversity. We're not like other countries that are actually dominated by particular groups, worldviews, and beliefs. They don't have the opportunity to come into contact with true difference like we do. We have the opportunity to welcome that difference. Not even because we want to, but because we are committed.

You don't have to want to. I don't really care whether you want to or not. But if you want to say that you're committed to liberation, it means you have to let everyone in. We don't have the luxury of liberation for the sake of liberation. At this time, liberation for the sake of all beings is the only liberation that is worthy of who we are. Not liberation for those of *us*, the people that are in our clubs. Not liberation for the people that look like us and talk like us—who wear the same outfits and hold their bodies like us, who express their emotions like the ways we express our emotions. Not liberation for the people that make us comfortable and feel at ease. Not liberation for the sake of people that do not upset our view.

Liberation for all beings.

Ubuntu. All beings. I don't want to complicate liberation for all beings, but to actually mean liberation *with* all beings. And to complicate it further, say liberation *as* all beings. Because we're not separate. We are not separate. Ubuntu. The phrase essentially means because you are, I am. This is the phrase that is most repeated in Buddhist texts. Most often repeated if you believe these are the words of the Buddha. He tried to basically drum it in people's heads. When this arises, that arises. Because this is, that is. This being that becomes. I like that translation better. When this arises, that arises.

This not being, that does not become. When this ceases, that ceases. The this and that are you and I. We rise and we fall together. And the delusion of constructive privilege has hidden that from our view. It is an illness within our communities that we should all feel. We should feel fiercely upset that this extraordinary dharma is being corrupted to a system and a construct that has done so much harm to so many people. Not the least of which is ourselves.

I read this article recently that talked about Ambedkar and Gandhi. Ambedkar was in charge of drafting the Indian Constitution. In one way he was contemporary with Gandhi, but in another he wasn't, because he was born an untouchable. But through a series of events and convergences he happened to be positioned so that people recognized his brilliance. He demanded that the constitution be drafted in a way so everyone would have equal rights. But others were very hesitant because they felt many in the Brahman class would not accept it, and the next step was to just have the constitution accepted. In some way, he was the Malcolm to Ghandhi's Martin. In the end, the constitution remained limited. Ambedkar pushed very hard, but others felt that because many Hindu accepted the concept of untouchability, the untouchables would have to wait.

Ambedkar was brilliant and actually studied many religions, both rooted in India and beyond. He concluded that Buddhism was profound in being able to accept all people equally. He wasn't foolish or naïve, and he knew that there had been a history of expressions of Buddhism that were corrupted by human failing. But in the texts themselves, we must accept all people. This is the answer.

And so he went on to lead a masked conversion of untouchable people from being out in the cold. From being marginalized, from being born into a place in which one accepts one's place as less than others. He essentially re-birthed them into full human beings. He did it with this precious teaching. How dare we manifest it in any other way than a full, complete, open-hearted teaching that insists upon liberation for all?

What is it that we have fallen in love with in the idea of Buddhism that is keeping us from allowing it to be fully expressed? What is it that we have to give up? In our identity? In our sense of privilege? In who owns what? Who gets to interpret what? Who gets to have a voice? Who has a voice? Even if we are not Buddhist, how can we not love this stunningly beautiful, complete teaching.? It lets us all know that there is a place for you. And all of us in our awkwardness, our confusion, and our sense of ill-belonging can come and find a home here. How could we cast anyone out into the cold? Of course, we're not doing it by law.

So that's why we have to do the work of really looking into what is it that we're doing and how is it that we're showing up. What is it that we feel like we own that is hindering this full expression of love? I imagine that if you look deep enough, you'll discover that it means that you are hindering something in your own being.

But when we feel free in ourselves, we don't hold onto stuff. It's just a natural law. If we're not fixated on ourselves, we don't have anyone to defend. In these times, in these conditions, a Buddhism that is not engaged is a Buddhism that has failed. So not only do we have to do the work within our communities, we actually have to reach out and extend ourselves beyond our comfortable little seats of practice and practice where it matters. Because out in the world is where all beings are. We can't wait for them all to come into our little centers.

We have to unhook ourselves from this kind of obsession with the coolness of Buddhism in the same way that I had to unhook myself from the coolness of me. In order to actually step into it, I had to unhook myself from my own coolness. I had to unhook myself from my blackness, from my femaleness, from my queerness because they were getting in the way of me actually being able to drop into my practice. That's not PC to say!

I still have my blackness, queerness, etc., but I was able to find roots in my own being. I learned to let go of all the rigid identities. But anyone who asks us to put our identities aside because it's disrupting our comfortable little seats and our comfortable little communities should be turned away. They need to go back to examine what it is that they have to work with, because we don't defend from the seat of freedom.

Because freedom sees possibilities, we see possibilities. We don't see someone that is going to come to disrupt; we see someone that is going to come and help us to learn. We don't see someone that is not going to fit in; we see someone that is going to help us to grow. We don't try to make them fit in the center, but the center reaches out to the margins. Instead of us changing them, we are going to be changed by the presence of real difference and by the acceptance of real difference. That's the way it should be. It's how we stay alive.

So here is what I know. I know that communities and the people that are upholding a static view of the dharma are suffering. They may not be entirely aware of it yet, but they are suffering. And often when we are not experiencing the impact of other people suffering, it is difficult for us to actually be in relationship with that person's suffering. But I want to invite that experience in whatever way you find yourself in that experience.

Our constructs can divide us from one another. They keep us separate from one another. They keep us from loving one another and from seeing one another. Everyone deserves our compassion and deserves to be seen. We may try to avoid others that make us uncomfortable; but when you take a moment to observe the situation, you recognize that it is in your effort to not relate to them that you are actually the first one that disappears. You have to disappear yourself. And conversely in seeing them, we are seen. Not by them. That is not the point. In choosing to see people that are suffering or that we deem "other," we begin to see ourselves.

I don't like to be exceptionalist about Buddhism. I truly believe that and know that there are many different cultures, particularly cultural indigenous teachings that have a shared understanding of our interconnectedness. I don't mean interconnectedness as people, I mean interconnectedness as things—as dharmas. As that which exists.

And we have a planet that is in crisis from our lack of understanding and living into our connectedness. We have countries that are at war and children that don't eat. Black men and black girls being shot in their beds. We feel helpless, but we're not. We have this teaching to stand in and to root in, but we must express it. We must manifest the full complete dharma. Without holding on to other people needing to buy Buddhism. That's just another club. You don't have to be Buddhist in order to manifest the dharma. Get beyond Buddhism. You know, Dr. King would talk about the love that does justice. When we get beyond our fixed idea of a self, of a doer, there is no one to do. There is no one to do justice. There is just—love is justice. Love is justice.

Someone said to me earlier, what do I say to people that feel like the idea of social justice is something they don't want to deal with. I ask, if they object to love. Justice is love. Expressed in society. Between people. Right here. Justice is love beyond the privacy of your own body.

So the moment that you are acting outside of just your own little thoughts, the love that you have, and the love that you say you believe in, and the love that you invest in expresses itself with justice. It's how you know when you see injustice or when you see yourself participate in injustice. It's how you know you are not loving yourself. When you don't interrupt injustice, you're not loving yourself, see, because your love can't exist in a bubble. Or just in here (points to her heart). You actually don't even know that it's love until you get it out there (points outward). And that's hard work (laughs) I know.

References

Suzuki, S. (1970). *Zen mind, beginner's mind*. New York, NY: Weatherhill.

Chapter 3
Beautiful Darkness

Jeanine M. Canty

Make direct wishes of kindness and love to both yourself and to all that is with you in the darkness, especially toward what you fear. (Coleman, 2006, p.145)

I love my blackness. And yours. (DeRay McKesson, activist, Black Lives Matter Movement, as cited in Mock, 2016, para. 25)

Our relationship with darkness is manifold. Darkness resides within our inner and outer spheres, metaphoric of what we do not see within our psyches as well as in the material world. Darkness is the space where what is not yet known is birthed. It is a place of discomfort as well as a place of blessings. Here lies creativity, the feminine, death, rebirth, the mystery. Within darkness the transpersonal domain flourishes. Yet our society has developed an unhealthy relationship with darkness. It is not cherished, but rather is feared and often demonized. This view of darkness fears wilderness, the irrational, the primal, the dark other, the female body and the numinous—breeding separation from nature, racism, disembodiment, patriarchy, and a host of oppressive behaviors and systems. Here, the dark is seen as the opposite of light, a fight between good and evil. This binary view is destructive, separating us from the deepest sources of life. The universe is primarily comprised of darkness. When we relearn to embrace the dark—tending a beautiful darkness—we restore our most sacred connections.

There is a deep irony with the infatuation popular culture has with monsters and the battle between light and darkness, a duality of good and bad, right and wrong, winners and losers. Movies and television shows bombard us with vampires, werewolves, witches, ghosts, zombies, and all sorts of characters that elicit our fear. This seems to be no small metaphor for the fear our society is gripped with, yet we need not stuff ourselves with imaginary fears when we live in a world with so many genuine and obvious ones. In the context of our interlinked crises—from the collapse of our natural systems, social injustice, economic insecurity, widespread violence, addiction, and trauma—our world is choking on fear. The mess we have collectively created is so great that we are too afraid to look at the suffering and the large shadows we have cast. Many people choose to live in denial and in darkness, the darkness of not seeing or feeling.

Our Western society and worldview has us living within a sterilized reality. We like things in well-ordered boxes of right and wrong, me and not me, rational and irrational, white and black. This translates into the stereotyped image of the "American dream," where one is raised in a nuclear family within the suburbs, is educated in a particular discipline, becomes employed in a specialized expertise, chooses a political party and perhaps a sports team, and raises a family within the suburbs. This stereotyped lifestyle is synonymous with whiteness. Views are tidy, choices are clear, and spaces are neat. Yet no one can connect to soul within this reality. Issues of soul reside within darkness. Here is where creativity, death, the feminine, and the numinous are encountered. The Western reality uses fear as a boundary from soul. It fears its inner contents, the unknown, the mysterious, the wild, the uncontrollable, the mystical, the feminine, the cultural other. Darkness has become the unspoken enemy.

In truth, darkness and light are not in opposition to one another; rather they are in deep relationship. The Taoist symbol of the yin and yang depicts a circle where dark and light mirror one another, with each holding the seed or spark of the other. This wisdom of balance between dark and light is seen in the seasons where the spring and fall equinoxes are a time of balance between daylight and dark, while summer is the time of abundant light and winter of extended darkness. Metaphorically, summer is seen as the time of adolescence, fire, creativity, procreation, and play, while winter is a time of maturity, the elder, barrenness, cold, death, and letting go. While the balance between dark and light is important to see, there is actually more darkness within the universe than light, and mystical traditions counsel that lightness comes out of darkness. Mystical wisdom comes from firsthand experiences with darkness, emptiness, the void. Our Western society suppresses these experiences, teaching us to fear both inner and outer darkness. This cuts us off from soulfulness and the wisdom we need to engage our truest callings.

Dark Matter

...billions of dark matter particles pass through each of us every second. (Randall, 2015, p. 3)

Dark matter underlies everything. It shapes the structure and will determine the fate of the cosmos in a way that we do not, and perhaps cannot, understand. (Sheldrake, as cited in Fox & Sheldrake, 1996, pp. 137–138)

Although I have little expertise in science, new physics, or new cosmologies, I am fascinated by dark matter. Recently, the scientific community became excited by the evidenced discovery of gravitational waves. While these waves were predicted by Albert Einstein a century ago, this was the first time scientific technology could actually measure their existence (Radford, 2016). An important significance of this discovery is the new potential to detect dark matter. Lisa Randall (2015) states, "Dark matter constitutes 85 percent of the matter in the Universe while ordinary matter—such as that contained in stars, gas, and people—constitutes only 15 percent" (p. xiii). Dark matter, which is different from either black holes or dark energy, is quite elusive stuff. Essentially, it is all around us; it pervades everything, yet we cannot see it. Large concentrations of dark matter result in "substantial" gravitational pulls "leading to measurable influences on stars and on nearby galaxies" (Randall, 2016, p. 3). Hence, this new ability to measure gravitational waves is somewhat revolutionary.

Perhaps what is most fascinating about dark matter is how very little is known about it, although proportionately it makes up most of reality. This is a humbling reflection, in contrast to a dominant positivistic Western worldview that prides itself on being knowledgeable about most things. It is ironic that the current age is often upheld as an age of reason, enlightenment, scientific revolution, and evolutionary development, yet, in truth, we know so very little. Moreover, society often holds a binary view of light as knowledge and dark as not knowing. The Dark Ages are seen as a time of the past, a time of ignorance and fallibility. This view of light and dark in opposition to one another—where light is good and dark is bad—has resulted in a split in awareness in which darkness is shunned.

We literally swim within a world of darkness that is unfamiliar. Darkness has so much to teach us and perhaps holds the seeds of transforming our current worldview to one that comes back into balance with the interdependent wisdom of dark and light. Rupert Sheldrake explains that light waves themselves are actually made up of equal quantities of light and dark, or "positive" or "negative" light, and even our visual process of seeing occurs because of the blackness within the eye (Fox & Sheldrake, 1996, p. 132). It is darkness that allows us to see. Sheldrake (1991) states, "Just as the conscious mind floats, as it were, on the surface of the sea of unconscious mental processes, so the known physical world floats on a cosmic ocean of dark matter" (p. 95).

Darkness is also metaphoric for our psychological unconscious—both of the individual and collectively. Our psyches contain much content that we are not aware of and, to our detriment, are afraid to explore. Much of this content has to do with our emotional and metaphysical selves, the work of soul— dark matter indeed.

Fear of the Wilderness

Deeply seeded in the psyche is the image of evil darkness in
wilderness. (Harper, 1995, p. 194)

The fables told to children often translate the values held by a society. Many of the classic fairy tales that generations of folks grew up with forewarned of the perils encountered in the wilderness, including scary animals, witches, wolves, and poisoned fruit. The victims were usually the weak—children and pretty, vulnerable young ladies. The basic storyline cautioned: Do not venture alone in the dark forest for bad things will happen.

Stephen Harper (1995) warns that through much of "the history of civilized society" wilderness has served as "the object of projection for many a dark shadow" (p. 194). Harper explains that we place unto wilderness those aspects of ourselves and the world that we do not want to see, resulting in a deeply repressed society. Our fears are placed within the darkness of the forest, of wilderness and its associations. The result is that many people are afraid of what lies in wilderness—both outer and inner—and avoid these realms and demonize things associated with these domains. We have unnatural fears of what is natural: wild animals, spiders, caves, dark bodies of water, and peoples who are nature-based. We are most fearful amidst the combination of wilderness and the dark. This translates to urban and suburban culture as well, where nighttime is seen as an unsafe time with innumerable threats, particularly for children and women.

Anyone who has spent considerable time in wilderness knows that this is a place of direct experience. It is hard not to enter into relationship with the natural world when immersed in the sensuous and varied shapes, smells, colors, and sounds. The contour of the ground we walk on is not static; we must continually pay attention to what is going on for both pleasurable experience as well as for survival. Laura Sewall (2012) counsels that "the skill of attention is a devotional practice" (p. 266) that brings us into the present moment.

When in the present moment within nature, we have firsthand experiences in which we rely on relationships with what surrounds us, as well as our inner wisdom. This often breaks our normal patterns of the conditioned mind where meaning comes from an indoctrinated worldview. For many, this is a sacred experience as wisdom comes forth from our direct experience, and we learn new ways of relating that employ to our full selves. Harper (1995) terms this *the instinctual self,* an identity that has been repressed within modern society. Harper advocates, "It is crucial to reclaim our wildness, because this is where vitality lives (p. 195).

Fear of Other: Whiteness and Blackness

> Even though we are told that the evil one masquerades as an angel of light, and that God dwells in the welcoming darkness, we persist in this connection of light and white with goodness and holiness. The outcome is that those who live in dark skins become shadows in the world. (Holmes, 2002, p. 103)

> ...that it's one hundred percent pure. Like pure granulated sugar, pure white bread. Meaning unsoiled, unsullied, undamaged, unconnected with dirt. So white people are "pure" and clean. And black people are "'dirt.'" (Anthony, 1995, pp. 270–271)

This fear of wilderness by Western culture is also associated with fear of darker skinned peoples. In the statement above, Carl Anthony (1995) challenges his interviewer's association with purity, pointing out the problematic connections our society often holds with viewing purity as related to whiteness and, hence, viewing blackness as unclean or soiled. This one point spurs a host of both conscious and unconscious underpinnings of a society that is still deeply embedded within racist paradigms. Whiteness is a constructed identity, originally created to divide a diverse constituency of people including free blacks, indentured servants, Native Americans, poor laborers, and many others who threatened the status of the wealthy owning class in the American colonies during the late 1600s. By legally creating whiteness, solidarity between diverse races and classes was broken as poor, working class whites and even indentured servants received a host of privileges by claiming whiteness, while those who were not white were subject to a series of exclusionary laws and practices (Anthony, 1995; Smith, 2007). This legal exclusion resulted in over 300 years of institutional racism against darker skinned peoples and systems of oppression that persist today. The Black Lives Matter movement speaks to the overt oppressions still facing African Americans and other communities of color, with disproportionate racial profiling and police brutality, including deadly shootings and large-scale imprisonment.

Carolyn Merchant (2005) also links the fear of nature, the fear of the dark other, and the concepts of pure and soiled within white identity. Her connections include the relationship between the enslavement of African peoples and the damage that was done to the land through cultivation, as well as the creation of national parks coinciding with the removal of Native Americans from these wilderness areas. She states, "At the same time that parks and wilderness were being reconstructed as white and pure for the benefit of white tourists, Indians were characterized as dark and dirty" (p. 382).

The creation of whiteness to formalize institutional racism is also grounded in European demonization of blackness. Barbara Holmes (2002) explores the theological underpinnings of European Christianity that "...taught us that light is blessed and darkness is demonic" (p. 102). Merchant continues along this vein, describing how "Europeans associated blackness with witchcraft, Satan, beasts, and putrid, decaying matter" (p. 384). Clearly, there are deeply buried associations within Western culture around darkness and blackness that have bred not only fear but hatred. This loathing has been exploited to keep people separated from nature and other people, as well as from their inner self and spirituality.

The Dark Mother

...everyone's genetic 'beautiful mother' is African and dark...she is the oldest divinity we know. (Birnbaum, 2001, p. xxv)

Along with wilderness and peoples of color, women have also suffered from Western culture's fear of darkness. The female body and the feminine identity have been associated with a negative darkness. Ecofeminists narrate how the body of the earth is often viewed as feminine and how humans have been destroying this divine female body for centuries (Griffin, 1978; Merchant, 2005). Women, like the earth, are givers of life. New life emerges from the dark womb of the female body. The feminine is often associated with emotions. We live in a society that often fears these domains and is quick to shut down our feelings in other than private settings. The feminine is also associated with the realms of the mysterious, and through history women have held roles as sacred healers and wisdom keepers. These roles have been demonized with the image of scary witches.

The documentary, *The Burning Times* (Read, 2007), depicts the horror of the European Witch Burnings that started in the 15th century and lasted over 300 years during which "hundreds of thousands of people—mostly women, mothers, and healers—would be hanged, drowned, or burned in town squares all across Europe for nothing more than seeing life from the old elliptical, nature-based perspective" (Glendinning, 1994, p. 59). The witch burnings eventually spread to areas around the world, and some historians estimate the number of deaths to be in the hundreds of thousands and even millions (Read, 2007). The persecution of women and nature-based peoples is far from over. We are living in the heart of a patriarchal world.

Each of us is born from the dark womb of our mother. From the dark womb of the universe, everything emerges. In reciprocity, after death our physical bodies return to the earth. The feminine is associated with both birth and death. Many cultures hold the archetype of the Dark Mother. She is Kali, Hecate, Ashanti, Isis, Athena, The Black Madonna, Spider Woman, Persephone, Lilith, Durga—the names for her go on and on within our ancient traditions (Birnbaum, 2001). The mystery of birth and death surrounds the Dark Mother. This wisdom has been omitted from much of modern religion and spirituality, another suppression of darkness.

Chthonic: The Dark Night of the Soul

> Darkness can allow transformation to occur. Seeds benefit from darkness in their hulls and can drink from it for many long years before becoming beautiful plants when they finally burst into the light. (Bliss, 2009, p. 180)

The birth process of plants is a beautiful example of the wisdom of darkness. A seed germinates in the dark, rich soil. The dark soil is literally where roots form. Bliss (2009) reframes the term *endarkenment* as the process of turning food waste into "fertilizer to feed my soil" (p. 180). The word chthonic comes from the Greek word "*chthonios* meaning 'in the earth'" (Clements et al., 1999, p. 34). In the gardening world, this represents the time between planting the seed and the emergence of the sprout. It is a time of not knowing, for even though the intention and action are in place, the outcome is not assured.

"In English, chthonic has come to mean 'dark, primitive, and mysterious' or 'of the underworld and its gods and spirits'" (Clements et al., 1999, p. 34). Within the transpersonal realm, the descent into the underworld is often called the dark night of the soul. It is a descent into the unknown, an unraveling of the self that, once again, has no assurance of creative rebirth.

> How many Mystics in their spiritual journey have spoken of 'the dark night of the soul'? Brave enough to let go of accustomed assurances, they let their old convictions and conformities dissolve into nothingness, and stood naked to the terror of the unknown. They let processes, which their minds could not encompass, work through them. It is in that darkness that birth takes place. (Macy, 1995, p. 255)

While the term dark night of the soul, is most associated with St. John of the Cross, the dark night of the soul is a cross-cultural tradition—a rite of passage. Metzner (2010) describes this as the "descent into the depths," "lower world or underworld journeys" from the world's most ancient shamanic traditions (p. 234). It is a metaphoric death of the old self, where the individual steps away from their familiar identity, descends into the dark mystery—a time of liminality between worlds— and eventually emerges into a new identity that carries a larger gift for the world. The time between worlds is one of entering into darkness. Bache (2000) explains, "What dies in the dark night is our deep attachment to living as a separate, private self, cut off from each other and from the universe at large" (p. 92). Here darkness represents our fears, buried emotions, deep pain, confusion, mystery, the sacred.

Matthew Fox resurfaces a mystical understanding of "the Godhead," that "which all things begin," as residing within darkness (Fox & Sheldrake, 1996, p. 138). He brings up another name for the dark night of the soul, "*the vianegativa*" where "illumination comes at the end of the bottoming out in the darkness experience" (p. 139).

There are many narratives across traditions that speak to the importance of the dark night of the soul. The essence is that in order to gain wisdom and align with our truest callings for the world, we must dip into this darkness, facing our fears, allowing a death of our selves. When we encounter the wisdom of darkness, the void, a death, the winter of our soul—we step into our maturity, our adulthood. Our current society's fixation on lightness, endless summer, and eternal youth bars this descent into darkness, leaving us in perpetual immaturity.

Reframing this descent into the dark night of the soul as both positive and essential is needed to transform our society and to usher in an age of soulful wisdom. Joan Halifax (1993) employs the term *fruitful darkness* for this, where "we can see into the depths of suffering, our own and that of others, and in seeing, in understanding, we harvest the fruits of compassion" (p. 214). Fox counsels us that "...divinity comes in a shadow"(Fox & Sheldrake, 1996, p. 141) and Shepherd Bliss (2009) names the gift of going through the journey of darkness as "sweet darkness" (p. 179).

Emptiness

> ...in emptiness there is no form, no feeling, no perceptions, no mental formations, and no consciousness. There is no eye, no ear, no nose, no tongue, no body, and no mind. There is no form, no sound, no smell, no taste, no texture, and no mental objects... (Tenzin Gyasto, 2005 p. 60)

Returning to the idea of the Godhead—the mystical space of darkness where all things originate (Fox & Sheldrake, 1996, p. 138)—many traditions relate this space to one of emptiness, or the void. Barbara

Holmes (2002) beautifully conveys that "There is a darkness that is the dwelling place of God, an enveloping comfort to the comforter, a place where the God of consciousness can pause" (p. 102). The Buddhist name for this place of void or emptiness is "sunyata" and "also expresses the ultimate" (Von Essen, 2007, p. 122). The quote above from what is known by Buddhists as "The Heart Sutra" or "Prajnaparamita" describes this space of emptiness where all of our faculties and perceptions drop. It is difficult to imagine that all our modes of awareness cease to exist.

Whether this place is entered through meditation, rites of passage, wilderness sojourns, and/or through truly experiencing our fear and sadness, it seems the pathway is immersion into our direct embodied experience rather than the abstract mind. These points of entry all parallel the world of darkness that is so deeply repressed in our society. In essence, this repression cuts us off from the most sacred form. It is a mystical journey as opposed to a religious one, for it involves submersing into our authentic experience in order to enter the sacred.

Beautiful Darkness

For some time, I have been contemplating beautiful darkness. When we allow ourselves to fall into the deep darkness of the present without filters, the unknowable manifests. This plunging into darkness and release of all that binds us allows us to momentarily dip into the origin of all being. This darkness is the source of all creation. We are emptied into darkness. One definition of beauty is a "quality giving intense aesthetic pleasure" (Stein & Su, 1980, p. 75). The moments of resurfacing from darkness are often the most beautiful. Our souls are reset. We have reclaimed a numinous experience, and we are filled with beauty.

The modern experience avoids emptiness. We are afraid of being alone and are encouraged to spend most every moment employed in some sort of activity. Our downtime often involves stuffing ourselves with television, the computer, alcohol, drugs, co-dependent relationships, mental fantasies, and fears. This stuffing of our selves serves to avoid our feelings, our fears, and our boredom. These dark places are shunned. Many do not even consider that connecting to this darkness could actually transform our selves and world. Out of darkness come our mystical selves, our soul callings.

At the start of this writing, I mentioned the fascination pop-culture seems to have with monsters. Our television shows, movies, and fiction books are filled with an assortment of horrifying characters. On some level, these monsters seem like our fears parading before us. Perhaps we secretly long for them to devour us, to break through the barriers that prevent us from entering darkness. Perhaps all of the negative ways we stuff ourselves are also secret longings to experience pain, or to suffer, so we may gain entry into the dark. Our suppression of darkness has created an age of darkness where we are scared of what is sacred and instead persist in devouring our planet, perpetuating racism and misogyny, and avoiding our highest callings. It is time to hug these monsters, to see they are distorted and abused aspects of ourselves that are calling out for witnessing and love. A world without darkness is a world without beauty. When we cross the threshold of embracing our darkness and that of the whole, we will drop into a beautiful darkness that has the power to heal and create anew.

> I think we are starved for darkness today. (Fox & Sheldrake, 1996, p. 153)

> Those of us who hunger for the light are beginning to taste the wildness of darkness, and swallow it—taking the night, quietly into our bodies. (Abram, 1997, p. 7)

References

Abram, D. (1997). Returning to our animal senses. *Wild Earth*, Spring 1997, 7–10.

Anthony, C. (1995). Ecopsychology and the deconstruction of whiteness (Interviewed by T. Roszak). In T. Roszak, M. E. Gomes, & A. D. Kanner (Eds.), *Ecopsychology: Restoring the earth, healing the mind* (pp. 263–278). San Francisco, CA: Sierra Books.

Bache, C.M. (2000). The eco-crisis and species ego-death: Speculations on the future. *Journal of Transpersonal Psychology, 32*, 89–94.

Birnbaum, L. (2001). *Dark mother: African origins and godmothers*. Lincoln, NE: Author's Choice Press.

Bliss, S. (2009). In praise of sweet darkness. In L. Buzzell & C. Chalquist (Eds.), *Ecotherapy: Healing with nature in mind* (pp. 174–184). San Francisco, CA: Sierra Club Books.

Clements, J., Ettling, D., Jenett, D., & Shields, L. (1999). *Organic inquiry: If research were sacred.* Unpublished manuscript.

Coleman, M. (2006). *Awake in the wild: Mindfulness in nature as a path of self-discovery.* Novato, CA: New World Library.

Fox, M., & Sheldrake, R. (1996). Darkness. In *Natural grace: Dialogues on creation, darkness, and the soul in spirituality and science* (pp. 131–160). New York, NY: Doubleday.

Glendinning, C. (1994). *My name is Chellis & I'm in recovery from western civilization.* Boston, MA: Shambhala Publications.

Griffin, S. (1978). *Woman and nature: The roaring inside her.* San Francisco, CA: Sierra Club Books.

Halifax, J. (1993). *The fruitful darkness: Reconnecting with the body of the earth.* New York, NY: Harper Collins.

Harper, S. (1995). The way of wilderness. In T. Roszak, M. E. Gomes, & A. D. Kanner (Eds.), *Ecopsychology: Restoring the earth, healing the mind* (pp. 183–200). San Francisco, CA: Sierra Books.

Holmes, B.A. (2002). Race, cosmology, and inclusion. In B. A. Holmes (Ed.), *Race and the cosmos: An invitation to view the world differently* (pp. 94–114). Harrisburg, PA: Trinity Press International.

Macy, J. (1995). Working through environmental despair. In T. Roszak, M. E. Gomes, & A. D. Kanner (Eds.), *Ecopsychology: Restoring the earth, healing the mind* (pp. 240–259). San Francisco, CA: Sierra Books.

Merchant, C. (2005). Ecofeminism. In *Radical ecology: The search for a livable world* (pp. 193–222). San Francisco, CA: Routledge.

Metzner, R. (2010). *The unfolding self: Varieties of transformational experience.* Ross, CA: Pioneer Imprints.

Mock, J. (2016, February 25). Vested interests: Why DeRay McKesson matters. *Advocate.* Retrieved from http://www.advocate.com/current-issue/2016/2/25/janet-mock-why-deray-mckesson-matters

Radford, T. (2016, February 11). Gravitational waves: Breakthrough discovery after a century of expectation. *The Guardian.* Retrieved from https://www.theguardian.com/science/2016/feb/11/gravitational-waves-discovery-hailed-as-breakthrough-of-the-century.

Randall, L. (2015). *Dark matter and the dinosaurs: The astounding interconnectedness of the universe.* New York, NY: HarperCollins.

Read, D. (2007). The burning times. In *Women and spirituality: The goddess trilogy* [video recording]. New York, NY: Alive Mind.

Sewall, L. (2012). Beauty and the brain. In P. H. Kahn & P. H. Hasbach (Eds.), *Ecopsychology: Science, totems, and the technological species* (pp. 263–284). Cambridge, MA: MIT Press.

Sheldrake, R. (1991). *The rebirth of nature: The greening of science and god.* New York, NY: Bantam Books.

Smith, C. (2007). *The cost of privilege: Taking on the system of white supremacy and racism.* Fayetteville, NC: Camino Press.

Stein, J., & Su, P.Y. (Eds.). (1980). *The random house dictionary.* New York, NY: Ballantine Books.

Tenzin Geyasto. (2005). *Essence of the heart Sutra: The Dali Lama's heart of wisdom teachings.* Somerville, MA; Wisdom Publications.

Von Essen, C. (2007). The mystic ladder. In C. Von Essen (Ed.), *Ecomysticism: The profound experiences of nature as spiritual guide* (pp. 120–146). Rochester, VT: Bear & Company.

Chapter 4
Befriending Our Voices[1]

Laurie Rugenstein
with Todd Thillman

> Voice makes human nature audible,
> reveals contradictions and defenses,
> allows limits to be felt and overcome.
> Our voice is the muscle of our soul.
> (Pikes, 2004, p. 1)

I remember the fun I had as a young child singing on long car trips, imitating animal sounds, and simply making silly sounds with my voice. I later learned that it was not acceptable to engage in such unbridled vocal expression. Genuine, spontaneous emotional expression through sound was considered "unladylike," and I learned to contain and control my voice. I also learned that singing in public was something that was reserved for the few who had *talent*, usually meaning that their voices sounded like the currently culturally accepted standard for singers. How many of us have been shamed at a very early age by being told to "stand next to Mary and just mouth the words" in a school choral performance? How many have been robbed of their ability to engage in free vocalization?

As we become older, we receive messages telling us to limit our vocal expression to a relatively narrow range that is culturally

---

[1] I dedicate this chapter to my wonderful teachers, Don Campbell, Ethlyn Friend, Carol Mendelsohn, and Saule Ryan. I also express my gratitude to the students who have participated in the Contemplative Voicework class at Naropa University. This work would not be possible without them.

acceptable. We learn to use words to communicate in a way that actually covers over authentic emotional expression. When we limit our vocal expression, we lose touch with aspects of ourselves. Our diminished self-image is reinforced as we construct boundaries between that which we identify as sounding like "me" and sounding like "other." This loss is the loss of an essential part of ourselves.

As an adult I (LR) set out on a journey to find what was lost, to rediscover and befriend my authentic voice. I discovered that I could explore my inner landscape through vocal toning, and I could express my deepest feelings and connect with others through singing and other forms of vocalization. I learned that the human voice has the potential to form a bridge between inner and outer experience and between the physical and non-physical realms. This chapter retraces the steps of my own journey to rediscovering my authentic voice and describes a course entitled *Contemplative Voicework: Sounding the Body-Mind* that I created for counselor trainees and have been teaching for many years at Naropa University. One of my students describes his experience in this course later in this chapter. Throughout, voice work is shown to be a practice of transformation.

My Journey

I had my first experience with free vocalization when I was a graduate student in music therapy.

> A group of ten of us lay on the floor in a darkened dance studio waiting to make our sounds. This was something very different for me. There were no rules, no melody, not even a pre-determined form to use as a framework for improvisation—nothing but the space to let the sound emerge. I felt naked and exposed. What unexpressed feelings lay within me? Was I ready to release them with other people in the room? I took a deep breath and timidly let a soft sigh escape. The sigh became louder, giving voice to the weariness and stress that were close to the surface. My sound blended with the sound of others, and I let go

of my self-consciousness. The sound evoked images of buzzing bees, roaring jet planes, primitive rituals, and angelic choirs. I felt exquisite pleasure in moving in and out of the sonic tapestry we were creating, sensing my body spinning with the strangely beautiful, spiraling harmonies. This experience was merely an introduction, but it awakened a yearning for more exploration. (Rugenstein, 1992, p. 210)

I was quite moved by my introduction to free vocalization, and, eventually, my own exploration in two areas of voice work came together and led to the development of a course for graduate students in counseling.

Vocal Toning

After graduation I began working with Don Campbell (1989), a musician and author who had a strong interest in vocal toning. Vocalization in the form of chanting or toning on elongated vowel sounds has been a core element in many spiritual traditions, including Sufism, Judaism, Hinduism, Christian Gregorian chants, and indigenous people's spiritual practices (Campbell, 1989; Gardner-Gordon, 1993; Goldman, 1992; Hale, 1995; Khan, 1983). Influenced by his own experiences with vocal toning and the work of Laurel Elizabeth Keyes (1973), Don developed an independent study course that provided students an opportunity to engage with the power of toning without being aligned with a specific religious or spiritual tradition. He stated,

> Exploring the inner world through vibration is the most easily available and grounded way to learn of the spirit. It does not require study, travel, or devotion to a guru. It is clearly held in each breath, each heartbeat, each utterance. To enter into the initiation of sound, of vibration and mindfulness is to take a giant step toward consciously knowing the soul. (Campbell, 1989, p. 12)

Toning involves repeating an elongated vowel sound. Sometimes vowel sounds are changed through the course of a practice or exercise.

Toning can be done individually or in a group. Individual toning deepens one's relationship with oneself—one's own voice and body—while in-group toning can create strong feelings of community and connection. Through this practice, we can become increasingly aware of deeper feelings and body sensations, and even enter a trance-like state. Toning allows us to enter other states of consciousness that are outside our everyday experiences. Different vowel sounds have been related to different chakras in the yogic traditions and different body parts in the Western tradition (Gardner, 1990; Goldman & Goldman, 2005). The limited quantitative research to date has shown such practices to have positive impacts on physical and mental health, while qualitative research and case studies report dramatic changes ranging from recovery from physical illness to improvements in mental health (Snow, 2011).

I was fortunate to serve as mentor to more than 300 students who participated in Don Campbell's toning course over a period of five years. This gave me the opportunity to hear many voices and to learn a great deal about the experiences students had as they explored their own vocal landscape.

> Their voices were often tentative at first, but after several consecutive weeks of toning, richness and resonance began to develop. Their voices became more fully embodied and integrated. One woman, a Jungian analyst, described her toning as "a means to Sonic Individuation. (Rugenstein, 1992, p. 211)

It became evident that toning was also serving as a form of sonic mindfulness practice. Students' awareness of their voices increased. They reported not only on the sound of their voices, but also on the vibration they felt in different areas of their bodies, the energetic and emotional states they experienced, and images evoked by the sound.

As I engaged in my own daily practice with toning using extended vowel sounds, I began to notice not only how the toning affected my emotional and physiological state, but also how these states were reflected in very subtle changes in the sound of my voice. My voice was serving as a barometer for my internal state. I found that I was able to carry this awareness into my counseling sessions, and it helped me pick up on clients' vocal nuances and use my own voice as a more effective tool in supporting my clients' process.

While I learned a great deal about my own voice and the vocal expression of others through my work with vocal toning, something was still missing. I longed for the freedom and excitement I had experienced with the free vocalization exercise we had done in the music therapy class in graduate school. The opportunity to study with members of the Roy Hart Theatre fulfilled this longing.

Alfred Wolfsohn and the Roy Hart Theatre

I was introduced to the work of the Roy Hart Theatre when Naropa University faculty member Ethlyn Friend came into a classroom where I had been teaching and began a voice lesson with a student. I was hearing those wild and free sounds I had heard many years earlier in my music therapy class! Here was a way I could reconnect with that part of myself!

I learned that Ethlyn used teaching approaches from the Roy Hart Theatre. I wanted to learn more about this way of working with the voice, so I began studying privately with her. I also took classes with Carol Mendelsohn and Saule Ryan, teachers Ethlyn brought to Naropa from the Roy Hart Theatre in France. I was hooked and knew I wanted to follow this path. Eventually, I was able to go to the Chateau de Malerargues in France and immerse myself more deeply in this work. It became evident from sessions with teachers from the Roy Hart Theatre that voice work is not simply about the larynx and breath. It is a full-body experience. The teachers encouraged authenticity and emotional involvement with vocal expression. They also introduced improvisation through play, the fertile ground from which improvisation arises.

The Roy Hart Theatre grew out of the work of Alfred Wolfsohn, who served in the German army during World War I, spending much of his time in the trenches where he witnessed horrific suffering. He felt that he lost both his soul and his God during this time. After the war Wolfsohn experienced severe "shell-shock" and was haunted by the sound of the screams of injured and dying men he had heard in the trenches. He was sent to a sanatorium, but the doctors and psychiatrists were unable to help him heal from his psychic wounds (Braggins, 2012).

Wolfsohn had done some singing before the war, and he thought studying singing again might give him some purpose in life. While most of his singing lessons focused on conventional vocal techniques, one of his teachers sometimes encouraged him to make sounds expressing the troubling feelings he held within. He gradually found a path to recovery through his vocal expression. This expression was very different from primal scream therapy in that Wolfsohn believed that healing took place through exploring the entire range of vocal expression, including the tender, the vulnerable, the sensuous, the painful, the playful, the beautiful, and the powerful (Newham, 1997). He believed that the voice was "first and foremost the direct expression of the soul" (Pikes, 1999, p. 51).

As Wolfsohn regained his soul, his faith in God, and his spirit, he began investigating ways in which singing could be used to help others do the same. He studied the psychological literature of the 1930s and found that his discoveries about the voice seemed to be particularly aligned with the work of C. G. Jung. Wolfsohn believed that Jung's archetypes—such as the animus, anima, and shadow material—could be expressed through the human voice. He felt that the voice could be a vehicle for integrating the personality and incorporating feminine and masculine elements, as well as gender fluidity (Braggins, 2012). He worked with his students to expand the range of vocal expression available to them with the intention of the voice becoming an expression of their whole being. He learned that singing with this "unchained voice" provided "a means of recognizing oneself, and of transforming this recognition into conscious life" (Pikes, 1999, p. 34).

Wolfsohn, who was Jewish, fled to England when the Nazis came into power in Germany. After the end of World War II he began teaching singing lessons in London. In 1947 Roy Hart, a young South African, became one of Wolfsohn's students. Hart went to London to study at the Royal Academy of Dramatic Art but felt that something was lacking in his training. He found that something in his singing lessons with Wolfsohn. Hart left the Royal Academy and continued studying with Wolfsohn until Wolfsohn's death in 1962. Hart carried on Wolfsohn's work and formed the Roy Hart Theatre in 1968. Members of this group continued teaching and giving performances, using Wolfsohn's approach to the voice. Hart also connected with the transpersonal aspect of the voice work.

> For Roy, the psychological elements of his work did not exclude religious elements such as "energy" and "spirit." Early on in his work Roy said that "there is a voice which is pure energy," meaning that it has a divine, perhaps even unhuman element. (Pikes, 1999, p. 106)

Hart died tragically in an auto accident in 1975. However, the work was so compelling that others carried it on after his death, and Wolfsohn's approach is still taught internationally (Braggins, 2012).

Developing Vocal Training for Counseling Students

It seemed that the things I had learned through my exploration of the voice and vocal expression could be helpful for students learning to become psychotherapists, and I developed a course to introduce students to this work.

The Voice in Psychotherapy

How do vocal toning and the voice work developed by Wolfsohn relate to psychotherapy? Psychotherapy is a communication process, and the voice is a medium through which much of this communication occurs. While part of the client/therapist communication relies on words, much more of it is nonverbal (Norman, 1982). Mehrabian (1972) broke down the nonverbal components of communication into tone of voice and other nonverbal expression, including facial expression, eye movement and contact, body posture, and movement, and use of space. He found that words accounted for only 7% of the meaning, while the tone of voice conveyed 38%. The other nonverbal forms of expression, such as body movement/position and facial expression, accounted for 55% of communicated meaning. While all forms of nonverbal communication are an essential part of the therapeutic relationship, tone of voice, including pitch, loudness, tempo, and rhythm, is especially important.

Many psychotherapy students lack vocal awareness. While they may be attuned to subtleties in vocal tone that convey messages lying beneath the words their clients speak, they are less aware of using their own voices to support the wide range of emotions they encounter in clinical work. For example, vocal tone is crucial in conveying empathy. Rogers (1957) stated that, "The therapist's tone of voice conveys the complete ability to share the patient's feelings" (p. 99). How can psychotherapists become more aware of the role that vocal tone, or prosody, plays in a therapeutic relationship? Also, how can they become more fully integrated themselves?

Developing vocal awareness can begin with the exploration of one's own voice. Vocal toning is a way to form a more intimate relationship with our own voices and learn to hear that which is usually outside our conscious awareness. As we listen to our own voices, we begin to hear subtleties that reveal our physical and emotional state, including the functioning of our autonomic nervous system (Porges, 2011). Attuning to our own voices in this way helps us better attune to clients' voices and use our voices in a way that best supports the therapeutic process.

Improvisation/Play in Psychotherapy

As psychotherapists, we constantly incorporate improvisation in our work. There is no script. We are not entirely sure what will happen next in our interactions with clients, and we need to be able to respond to whatever arises in the moment. Engaging with play is an essential element in developing improvisational skills. Brown (2009) suggested that play shapes our brains, helps foster empathy, and helps us enter into social relationship with others. According to Brown, "When people know their core values and live in accord with what I call their 'play personality,' the result is always a life of incredible power and grace" (p. 12).

Nachmanovitch (1990) wrote extensively about the relationship between play, improvisation, and creativity. He stated,

Our play fosters richness of response and adaptive flexibility. This is the evolutionary value of play—play makes us flexible. By reinterpreting reality and begetting novelty, we keep from becoming rigid. Play enables us to rearrange our capacities and our very identity so that they can be used in unforeseen ways. (p. 43)

It is interesting to note that Rogers (1961), founder of person-centered counseling theory, believed that one of the characteristics of a fully functional person was to have a flexible, constantly evolving self-concept. It seems that play contributes greatly to this flexibility.

Contemplative Voicework Course Design

The course I created, Contemplative Voicework, was designed with the intention of providing a container in which students could explore their own voices, learn to embody their voices, and express authentically in relationship with others through play, sounding, and singing. This section describes several aspects of the course.

Students do homework toning on different vowel sounds each week as a kind of "sonic mindfulness" practice and then journal about these toning sessions. This fosters more awareness of the voice and how it reflects their mental, emotional, and physical condition. Each class begins with group toning on the vowel sound of the week. Students experience the difference between hearing only their own voice while toning alone and hearing their voice as one of many—part of the tapestry of group sound.

The group toning is followed by physical exercises and stretching to loosen the body and prepare for vocalizing. Each class then focuses on a different aspect of voice work done within the context of play. The first few classes involve group work so students do not feel too exposed as they begin this exploration. Later, the classes move to dyad work, and, finally, each student presents a song to the class. These are sung a capella, and students are encouraged to incorporate movement and authentic emotional expression in their presentation.

Some of the classroom activities are games such as making animal sounds. Newham (1994 spoke of how people in preverbal cultures embodied the nature of an animal and then used sound and movement to communicate their experience of the animal to others. Young children often imitate animal sounds in their vocal play, and it seems like a natural thing for humans to do. These sounds also help us extend our vocal range beyond the limits we usually place on it. Swooping wolf howls take us into our higher register, the mewing of kittens invites exploration of soft, vulnerable sounds, while the lion's roar puts us in touch with vocal power.

Other games involve taking on the voices of different imaginary characters to explore the archetypes, such as animus/anima as expressed through voice. In these games, students often experiment with shadow vocal qualities—sounds they consider to be "not me." This helps develop a wider range of expression and helps students become more aware of the countertransference that comes up in response to certain vocal qualities. Students also learn that the voice can accommodate the tension of opposites and be "both/and"; as such, the voice can be a medium for psychic integration.

The final song presentation challenges students to sing in front of the group. Not only do they sing, but they also use the song as a vehicle for authentic emotional expression, making the song truly their own. This can be a scary experience; however, students often state that they feel fully alive and empowered following these presentations.

Students "workshop" their songs in class before the final presentation. During the workshop time students receive feedback from the instructor and other members of the class. This feedback includes suggestions for moving the body in various ways to change the somatic experience, slowing down the tempo of the song, singing with different vocal qualities, or singing in different pitch ranges. The intention of the workshop experience is to open the students to more possibilities for authentic emotional expression during the song presentation.

Student Reflections on the Course

Students have commented on several ways in which this class has contributed to their personal growth and their effectiveness as psychotherapists. Some of the areas cited in students' comments include greater sensitivity to emotional expression, understanding more about their shadow aspects, greater ability to improvise and take risks, and increased ability to let go of judgment of self and others. The following is a brief summary of some of the students' observations.

Students commented on their understanding of how the voice can be a naked, authentic expression of who we are in a given moment. They became aware of how the voice reflects a wide range of emotions, including freedom as well as constriction. They were much more attuned to what is conveyed by the voice that may not be spoken in words. Students noted that being vulnerable and expressing raw feelings in the presence of others in a safe container allowed them to be more aware and accepting of their own fragile places. They found this helped them become better attuned to the fragile places in their clients and transmute vulnerability into authenticity.

Students also discussed how the improvisational nature of the class exercises helped them learn how to get out of their own way, let go into the moment, and just play. They were often surprised by the creativity that arose when they let go of thinking and planning. Students were able to understand how having a strict agenda in a therapy session might inhibit their ability to respond to what arises in the moment.

Another area on which students commented is developing awareness of vocal qualities that may be part of their shadow, qualities to which they may have an aversion. When working with clients, this awareness could be helpful in dealing with negative countertransference that may arise in response to certain vocal qualities. They also found that they were able to accept their voices as they were and release judgment about how they should sound. Releasing judgment about their own voices helped them be more accepting of others.

During the song presentation at the end of the class, students commented that they were able to use the song to convey something authentic about themselves, rather than sounding like a singer they might admire. They talked about how freeing this was, how it led to greater awareness of their bodies as they sang, and how it enabled them to transcend self-consciousness.

Todd Thillman's Experience in the Contemplative Voicework Course
The following is Todd Thillman's description of his personal experience in the course. At the time he was a first year student in the MA program in Clinical Mental Health Counseling at Naropa University.

Toning. I have spent most of my life paying attention to and being curious about sound. From an early age I was drawn to sounds of varying kinds. I would play with sounds, trying to recreate the varying tonal patterns. As an adolescent, I began to be aware that my voice could affect others. To this end, I have always been curious to learn more about how sound influences us spiritually and psychologically. This impetus drew me to the Contemplative Voicework class.

As part of this class, we practiced toning. This practice involved making specific vowel sounds. In many ways this practice is a type of meditation in which we used the sound as the focal point of our attention. I began by noticing the felt sense of the sound in my body. I felt different parts of my body resonating as I made the sound. At first I would notice the vibration in my throat and chest. As it continued, I would notice more subtle versions of it in my limbs and extremities.

Another aspect of the toning practice was to notice other sensations or thoughts as they arose. This was the part that surprised me the most. On several occasions, toning seemed to shine a light on emotions that I was consciously or unconsciously ignoring. It was as if the sound I was making had the ability to bypass whatever my mind thought I should be focusing on and get straight to the heart of what was needing my attention. I often experienced these feelings as tenderness or rawness around my heart. They would usually start out subtly, almost on the periphery of my consciousness. However, as I focused the sound and my attention on this area of my body, the feeling would become more intense and poignant.

Sometimes the feeling was just there, seemingly unattached to any specific story or memory. At other times images or thoughts from incidents in my past began to arise in my mind. I would find myself suddenly thinking about past experiences that I had not thought about in a long time. There were times a surge of sadness would rise up, and I would find tears streaming down my cheeks. This had a cathartic effect that would last several minutes and then gradually dissipate.

Often after the toning practice I would begin a more formal meditation practice. One particular time, I had a quite profound experience. As I settled into my meditation practice, I allowed the quiet to sweep over me, my mind and body slowly relaxing and unwinding. I could feel the tension of the morning draining into the earth under my cushion as I recognized places where I was holding energy. I felt the tender, raw sensation around my heart that had been awakened only moments earlier when I was toning. As I touched this feeling, I noticed questions arising in my mind. Why was sound having this affect on me? What was going on? The sound seemed to have a wisdom or knowing to it because time and time again it honed in on places in my body that I had been neglecting or ignoring. Sometimes it would simply point to what was present for me and amplify it. I also experienced times when it seemed to reach into my unconscious and bring forth old traumas that needed to be healed. How was this possible? Doesn't knowing imply some level of consciousness or aliveness? Could sound be alive? Or was it simply a vehicle through which some form of deeper, spiritual intelligence communicated?

I let these questions ruminate for a moment and then they slowly dissolved without leaving any trace of an answer. I went back to focusing on my breath and trying to notice what was happening in my body. For a moment, I languished in the stillness. Then another thought arose in my mind, "I love the silence." As if on cue, I then heard the consistent low-level ringing in my ears—tinnitus. "Well, so much for the silence," my mind began. It dawned on me that because of the tinnitus true silence was an impossibility for me.

I then began to ponder: What is true silence? Is there any such thing? If I did not have tinnitus, could I experience silence? As I contemplated this, I first thought about my breath. It appeared to be rising and falling silently but actually it was making sound. I am not able to always hear it but that doesn't mean it is silent. The same is true for my heart and the flow of blood through my body. Both of these are always creating sound whether I hear it or not. What about the other electrical impulses that are happening within my body, such as neurons firing? Do these make noise?

What I started to realize was that the whole idea of silence was really a fallacy. There are varying levels of volume, and certain things that I will or will not be able to hear. However, silence, when understood as the absence of sound, was impossible. If there was no such thing as silence, that implied sound was always present. This discernment then gave rise to the premise that sound was one of the basic elements or aspects of life. It was something inherent in all living things and potentially, it could be argued, even in inanimate objects. It seemed to be as fundamental as carbon, the elemental building block of all physical phenomena.

As this new awareness floated around inside of me, I sensed I was sitting on the edge of a precipice. It felt as though I had brushed up against a profound understanding of something, and yet there was nothing that I understood. I experienced an unusual combination of vulnerability and joy. I also noticed a strong desire to have an answer. However, the message I kept getting over and over again was that I needed to just be with this. There was no way yet to fully grasp what was glimpsed; it needed time to ferment in my system, my awareness, and my being.

Part of what I did realize, though. was that toning was having an effect on me. Another important insight about this effect was that my voice was a crucial part of this equation. My unique tonal patterns seemed to create an avenue for some kind of wisdom to be expressed. If sound can serve as a means for spiritual wisdom to be accessed, the voice is the direct conduit to this sound. Voice gives life to the sound, making it audible for all who will listen. It has the ability to shape, affect, and alter the sound. In this way, it is vital to the expression of the wisdom.

Workshopping my song. Having spent many years studying and being involved with theater, I have always loved musicals. Long before I ever saw some of the big musical theater productions, I heard the scores and bought the CDs. I loved how the music would invoke a myriad of feelings in me. I would sing along with the music and secretly dream of one day being able to express myself as beautifully as these professionals. When the opportunity to choose a song for this class arose, I immediately thought of a few of my favorite musicals. The song "I Dreamed a Dream" from Les Miserables quickly came to mind.

When I listened to this song, I often felt tears arise. I never associated the feelings with something specific in my life, but I knew it had a strong effect on me. When contemplating using it for this project, I felt skeptical because it is about a woman's experience of failed dreams and thus sung traditionally by a woman. However, when I looked beyond the literal words, I realized the song was about a very human experience, one that I could easily relate to. In the end, I decided to follow my heart, to venture into the unknown, and choose this song for the project.

I really had no idea of the extent to which this choice was going to affect me. In the beginning, my hopes were twofold and fairly simple. First, it would offer me the chance to sing a song that moved me. Second, it would give me the opportunity to finally perform a musical theater piece in front of others. What was unexpected, though, was that the journey would also include an incredible opportunity to touch an old trauma. Little did I know that this song was going to serve as a gateway and catalyst to unearthing a difficult moment from my past, and in so doing offer an opportunity for emotional expression and some resolution. In the following paragraphs, I will describe this trek, some of the insights that arose, and how this may apply to my development as a counselor.

When I first brought the song to class, my primary concern was to remember the words. As I fumbled through singing it to the group for the first time, I remember not feeling very connected to it emotionally. I was very caught up in my mind, concerned more with memory and performance. After the first run-through, I was asked to choose a line in the song to begin workshopping. I chose one that particularly tugged at my heart. The line in the song was, "As they tear your hope apart."

The instructor then asked two other students to join me in front of the class. One stood on my right side and the other on my left. She asked them to each take one of my arms and, as I sang the line over and over again, to pull in opposite directions like they were tearing me apart. It took several repetitions before it started to crack the walls around my heart. I felt the feeling rising slowly at first, but then it moved much more quickly and, like a dam breaking, I suddenly found myself overcome with emotion and tears. There was no reference point to the sadness welling up through me in that moment. As I kept trying to sing the song, the same thing would happen over and over. While I was crying, I remember wondering if this was connected to something specific in my life, but I wasn't able to notice any direct link to anything at the time.

A few days later, I met with my therapist for a previously scheduled visit. I shared with her about how the song seemed to have triggered something in me. She asked me if I wanted to explore this situation in more depth, and I agreed. Almost immediately, I started thinking about a traumatic incident that happened when I was seven or eight years old. My parents had been having a big fight. They were in the family room and I was sitting on the couch, watching TV in the adjoining living room. The fight continued to escalate as they both shouted at each other. Suddenly, my father shoved my mother to the floor, picked up a small end table, held it high in the air, and threatened to kill her if she didn't "shut the fuck up!" I was sitting only a few feet away and was frozen in fear as I watched this unfold.

As I began to relive this moment, I felt a strong sense of anger arise within me. I shared this feeling with my therapist. She affirmed and encouraged me to work with this new feeling. She suggested I go back to that moment and, either as the younger or older me, do whatever I wanted in that situation. In my mind's eye, I rose up from the couch, shoved my father off of my mother, and yelled, "No! This is not appropriate! Now walk away!" I then turned to my mother and told her, "Stop egging him on like that! You are just as much at fault in this situation! You go away as well!" I immediately felt a sense of power coursing through my body.

My therapist and I talked about the significance of this situation and the actions I had "re-taken." She asked me about the meaning behind the line from the song, "as they tear your hopes apart," and shared her impression that it seemed I was being torn apart by my parents. I agreed with her sense of the situation. To me, the hopes and dreams that were being torn apart had to do with my ideas around love and how people who loved each other treated one another. The song was acting as a catalyst or an access point to this old wound.

With this glimpse of what had arisen for me, I was curious to keep working on the song and see what else would arise. At home, I practiced singing the song in different "operatic" voices. This was a technique we had learned in class. The different voices invoke various qualities of one's personality to rise to the surface that may not normally come through. For this practice, I played with the voices of "Antonio" (tenor) and "Miriam" (alto). They had differing results.

One of the characteristics the Antonio voice invokes in me is strength. It was helpful for me to call upon this sense of strength as I sang the song. I felt more able to face the feelings of pain and injustice that the song brought up for me. The Miriam voice embodies more of the emotional struggle for me. By summoning this character, I allowed the pain of the situation to rise more fully and to affect the words as I sang them.

When I workshopped the song for a second time in class, I chose the section of the song that represented the emotional climax for me. The lines were, "I had a dream my life would be so different from this hell I'm living, so different now from what it seems. Now life has killed the dream I dreamed." I was amazed at how quickly the emotion rose up in me. Previously, it had taken several repetitions to penetrate my heart, but not this time. When singing it, I almost immediately felt a lot of anger, and with it a strong sense of power. I could feel the energy coursing through my veins, causing my hands to shake.

The instructor encouraged me to physically act out what I was feeling and to stomp around the room as I sang these lines. Adding this somatic component intensified the experience for me. This time, as I sang the verse I could feel a grounded strength in my voice that I had never experienced before. I was able to sustain notes in a completely new and different way. Most important, I had found a way to clearly express feelings that had been locked away for many years.

As the time neared for our final presentation in class, the performer in me rose to the surface. I wanted this last rendition to be stage worthy. However, each time I practiced the "performance version," I felt frustrated and unhappy because it was never good enough. Finally, as I rehearsed it again on the day of the class, I realized that I had not been listening to my heart and that I needed to offer the stage to someone else—the little boy who had never been given the opportunity to share how he felt. As soon as this thought crossed my mind, I knew it was what I needed to do.

When I got up to present that evening, I shared my new insights with the class about who I needed to let sing. The older, performer side of me stepped back, and I offered the stage to the little boy part of me that had been silent for so many years. Almost immediately, the tears began to stream down my face. I took my time with the song, and I could feel the poignancy of each and every line. I just allowed each part of the song to arise out of how I was feeling in that moment. It was not easy exposing such a tender, wounded side of myself. In the end, this rendition turned out to be the most honest and sincere version I had ever sung.

I had fairly simple aspirations when I originally chose this song to perform. What actually arose from the experience, however, left me feeling completely surprised. I had no idea this was going to be so personally transformative. I feel as though I have stumbled upon an incredible tool for self-healing and been given a wonderful gift.

The implications of this course on the field of counseling seem quite broad to me. First, it gives me another contemplative practice that can help illuminate aspects of myself. As a counselor in training, it is imperative to the people I may one day serve that I have a strong understanding of my own wisdom and neurosis. Prior to helping someone heal from a wound, I have to be able to make that journey myself. How can I be a witness to another if I have not also walked on that path?

Another important aspect of this training is that it taught me to listen more carefully. Listening is a vital tool for a therapist. As I have become more aware of my own subtle vibrations, I am more cognizant of the faint tonal shifts in others' voices. Sometimes these slight variances in communication offer a wealth of information about how a person is doing or what is not being addressed directly.

Finally, there is the opportunity for these practices to be used to help people acknowledge, touch and possibly work through difficulties in their lives. This was certainly the case for me. I was able to use the toning and the singing practice as an authentic means of expression—a way to give voice to something that had happened to me years ago, and in so doing to serve as a catalyst for forgiveness and healing. Based on my own journey and witnessing my classmates' shifts, it is clear to me that contemplative voice work is a valuable clinical tool, which can be quite transformative.

Conclusion

I (LR) believe that, like me, students in the Contemplative Voicework class have come to know their voices through direct experience. Our voices can lead us inside, helping us explore the inner landscape, revealing emotions and experiences that may have been hidden from conscious awareness. Our voices can also provide us with a means for expressing and integrating these aspects of ourselves. It is crucial for those of us who practice psychotherapy to develop self-awareness and compassion for ourselves so we can help our clients do the same. As demonstrated in Todd's story, when we engage in vocal expression we are able to transmute long-held limiting beliefs and energetic patterns and move to a place of greater self-acceptance.

Campbell (1989) stated that there are "a variety of channels through which the human mind can perceive dynamic dimensions outside normal consciousness" (p. 20). The voice is one of these channels for experiencing the transpersonal. When we approach voice work with contemplative curiosity and a heightened sense of listening, we are drawn into an exploration of the inner landscape of vibration, somatic sensation, and embodied emotion. Through authentic vocal expression we are able to connect with that which is larger than ourselves. The voice is a natural medium through which the spirit and soul are expressed (Campbell, 1989).

Pikes (2004) addressed the many dimensions of the voice in the following statement: "Voice is the resonance of inner states—it reflects bodily and psychic impulses; it reverberates movements and emotions; it evokes and provokes the memory and imagination, reminding one of elemental and animal origins, expressing spiritual aspirations" (p. 1). As we engage in the exploration of our own voices, we can open to our vulnerability, access a full range of emotion, and, ultimately, discover our spirit and soul.

References

Braggins, S. (2012). *The mystery behind the voice: A biography of Alfred Wolfsohn.* Leicester, UK: Matador.

Brown, S. (2009). *Play: How it shapes the brain, opens the imagination, and invigorates the soul.* New York, NY: Avery.

Campbell, D. (1989). *The roar of silence: Healing powers of breath, tone & music.* Wheaton, IL: Quest.

Gardner, K. (1990). *Sounding the inner landscape.* Stonington, ME: Caduceus Publications.

Gardner-Gordon, J. (1993). *The healing voice: Traditional and contemporary toning, chanting, and singing.* Freedom, CA: The Crossing Press.

Goldman, J. (1992). *Healing sounds: The power of harmonics.* Rockport, MA: Element Books.

Goldman, J., & Goldman, A. (2005). *Tantra of sound.* Charlottesville, VA: Hampton Roads Publishing.

Hale, S. (1995). *Song and silence: Voicing the soul.* Albuquerque, NM: La Alameda Press.

Keyes, L. E. (1973). *Toning: The creative power of the voice.* Santa Monica, CA: DeVorss & Company.

Khan, H. I. (1983). *The music of life.* Santa Fe, NM: Omega Press.

Mehrabian, A. (1972). *Nonverbal communication.* Chicago, IL: Aldine-Atherton.

Newham, P. (1994). *The singing cure.* Boston, MA: Shambhala.

Newham, P. (1997). *The prophet of song: The life and work of Alfred Wolfsohn.* Boston, MA: Tiger's Eye Press.

Nachmanovitch, S. (1990). *Free play: The power of improvisation in life and the arts.* New York, NY: G. P. Putnam's Sons.

Norman, S. L. (1982). Nonverbal communication: Implications for and use by counselors. *Individual Psychology, 38*(4), 353–359.

Pikes, N. (1999). *Dark voices: The genesis of the Roy Hart Theatre.* Woodstock, CT: Spring Journal.

Pikes, N. (2004). *What is the "whole voice"?* Retrieved 7/21/2004 from http://www.thewholevoice.com/pages/pg1.htm

Porges, S. (2011). *The polyvagal theory: Neurophysiological foundations of emotions, attachment, communication, and self-regulation (Norton Series on Interpersonal Neurobiology).* New York, NY: W. W. Norton & Company.

Rider, M.. & Haas, M. (1997). *The rhythmic language of health and disease.* St. Louis, MO: MMB Music.

Rogers, C. (1957). The necessary and sufficient conditions of therapeutic personality change. *Journal of Consulting Psychology, 21*(2), 95–104.

Rogers, C. (1961). *On becoming a person: A therapist's view of psychotherapy.* London, UK: Constable.

Rugenstein, L. (1992). Becoming a sound woman. In D. Campbell (Ed.), *Music and miracles.* Wheaton, IL: Quest Books.

Snow, (2011). Healing through sound: An exploration of a vocal sound healing method in Great Britain. Doctoral dissertation, Concordia University, River Forest, IL.

Chapter 5
Taming the Tyranny of Time

Tina R. Fields

One winter, I backpacked into a remote canyon with my students and fellow faculty of the Audubon Expedition Institute. It was snowing. As it grew dark, we sat closely together and ate the modest supper we had cooked on backpacking stoves. We had no fire. It was so cold, dark, and wet that there was nothing else to do; after cleaning up everybody just wanted to go to bed. As we laid out our sleeping bags, I turned to my colleague and wondered, "What time do you suppose it is?" When he saw the face of his watch, he groaned. "You don't want to know." "Tell me," I replied. And he said, "It's 6:30." We laughed, a bit horrified. Only 6:30 pm, and here we were, people between our early 20s and mid-40s, all going to bed. "We have no life," we only half-joked. This was in January. I slept an average of 11 to 13 hours per night that month, and the next month too. And even though we were living outdoors 24/7, often in snow and other "bad" weather, I've rarely been healthier or saner.

Living outdoors, fully exposed to the temporal cycles of the planet for that long was a very interesting, unusual, and eye-opening experience for a modern, middle-class North American. Yet this is, of course, an experience that most humans have had for millennia, and that other animals and plants have every day.

The stress of ever-increasing pressure to rush that characterizes industrial growth societies is having detrimental effects on the health of individuals, communities, and the planet. This chapter illustrates the need for change and introduces alternative cultural modes of perceiving and interacting with time. Its final section offers simple, practical exercises based on these models, as viewed through the lenses of transpersonal psychology and ecopsychology, for experiencing time as sacred rather than as a tyranny.

Hurry Sickness

"Clock time" is a relatively new concept, and therefore involves a considerable mental adjustment. For most of our tenure as a species, humans have related to the temporal world in terms of seasons, not nanoseconds. Everyday transportation is now mind-bogglingly faster than foot travel. And, of course, the increasing speed of communication brings attendant demands for a swift response. Whereas 100 years ago a correspondent might wait six months or more for a response to a written letter, now some e-mailers become anxious and even angry at a delay of 15 minutes. Such a rapid shift in demand load begs the question of whether we humans are hardwired to successfully deal with this ever-increasing speed of life.

The English word "haste" has the same etymological root as the word "violence" (Merriam-Webster, 2016; Dictionary.com, 2016). The truth of this connection can be witnessed playing out every day—for example, in road rage. A thwarted desire for speed invokes internal emotional violence, which sometimes then gets expressed externally to tragic ends. Consider the internal experience of a leisurely drive to view the turning autumn leaves for pleasure versus the desire to get home fast during rush hour traffic. Frustrated commuters are certainly not focused on seasonal length changes. Their internal clocks are set to much faster measures, such as the interval jokingly referred to by a Los Angeles professor as the "honkosecond": the brief time elapsed between the moment a traffic light turns green and the car behind you honks their horn (Levine, 1997, p. 152).

More and more studies show how performance actually suffers when people try to take on too much in any given timespan. For example, Loh and Kanai (2014) reported, "Individuals who engage in heavier media-multitasking are found to perform worse on cognitive control tasks and exhibit more socio-emotional difficulties" (Abstract, para. 1).

With the possible exception of a few very advanced yogis, people cannot actually multitask at all. Rather than conducting multiple tasks simultaneously, what actually occurs is repeated task switching. And it takes time for the brain to switch focal direction.

Ironically, the attempt to swiftly multitask rather than focusing on repeated performance of one task at a time results in slower brain response and therefore slower achievement of those tasks (Meyer et al., 1997). Better to focus on one thing at a time and do it at a pace compatible with animal life. According to a summary of current psychological research on multitasking, recent studies suggest that "...even brief mental blocks created by shifting between tasks can cost as much as 40 percent of someone's productive time" (APA, 2006, para. 2).

This is especially obvious in the aged, who need more time to conduct each task. Fitch (1985) notes, "When older people are allowed more time to perform, they are generally able to do as well as younger people" (p 104). However, they often will not be granted the time needed. They rarely get the opportunity "to slow down without being considered a nuisance" (Fitch 1985, p. 104). This phenomenon is, of course, not limited to the elderly, either in concern or effect. In fact, it is possible that the stress of constantly rushing too much to meet societal demands of speed can lead to premature signs of mental aging. As one early study showed, "When things move too quickly, one's performance—and just as important, one's motivation—drops precipitously" (Kastenbaum, 1971, as cited in Fitch, 1985, p. 104). As I will soon show, mood and even physical health suffer when trying to meet a continuously overwhelming task burden in a "timely manner."

As the uncertain global economic climate has brought a new norm of pushing to do more work with fewer personnel, time pressure has become a major stressor. Most U.S. citizens, blue- and white-collar workers alike, have less leisure time now than 40 years ago (Schor, 1991). A tense, manic quality has come to characterize daily life due to what social scientists have termed a "time-compression" effect (Goodhew & Loy, 2002). Symptoms range from workaholism to burnout, chronic sleep deprivation, depression, anger, latchkey children, and little time for soul-restoring interaction with family, friends, or nature.

A survey conducted by the National Recreation and Parks Association found that 38% of U.S. citizens reported "always" feeling rushed (Mowen, Graefe, Barrett, & Godbey 1992), up from 22% in 1971 (Goodhew & Loy, 2002). And this time pressure keeps people from engaging in the activities that could serve as an antidote. "Don't have enough free time" was found to be the greatest barrier to participation in outdoor recreation (Hornback, 1992, p. 19). In Japan, the strong workplace ethic has made taking vacations rare and speed a virtue, sometimes to the extent that basic bodily needs are ignored. Witness the modern Japanese saying "hayameshi, hayaguso, geinouchi," which means, loosely translated, "to eat fast and defecate fast is an art" (Levine 1997, p. 172). Even though mistakes are an inherent part of trying to go too swiftly, many people perceive their inability to keep up with the increasing number of demands—which appear faster and faster—as a personal failing, thereby leading to low self-esteem and less enjoyment of life.

Chronic time urgency not only leads to loss of emotional resilience and short-term cognitive abilities; it can also carry notable detrimental long-term physical effects. *Hurry sickness* is becoming an accepted medical concept, recognized as a possible cause of such widespread killers as heart disease (Ulmer & Schwarzburd, 1996; Dossey, 1982).

Recognizing it therefore becomes important. After examining several scales for Type A and coronary-prone behaviors, Levine (1997, pp. 20–22) identified ten behavioral areas that appear as symptoms of time urgency:

1. Concern with, and awareness of, clock time. Frequently consults watch (vs. the other extreme, forgetting the time or the day of the week).
2. Speech patterns. Frustration with those who take a while to get to the point. Frequent interruptions. Fast speech.
3. Eating habits. Being the first person finished eating at the table. Rarely takes time to eat three meals a day in a relaxed manner.

4. Walking speed. Fellow walkers ask the person to slow down or to stay with them.
5. Driving. Excessively annoyed in slow traffic. May honk or make rude gestures at slower drivers to speed them up.
6. Schedules. Addicted to setting and/or maintaining schedules for each activity. Punctuality may become a fetish.
7. Compulsive list-making.
8. Nervous energy. Becomes irritable if must sit for an hour without doing something.
9. Waiting. Gets more annoyed than most people if have to wait in line for more than a couple of minutes. May walk out of restaurants, banks, stores.
10. Alerts. Friends and family warn to take it easier, slow down, become less tense.

Trying to do two things at once is also frequently noted in coronary-prone personalities (Friedman & Rosenman, 1959), so I'd add that as an eleventh area.

Nearly everyone in industrial growth societies exhibits time urgency in some ways, of course. Further, some of these behaviors may simply be personal or intercultural characteristics. But a person exhibiting strong concern with time and speed in most of these areas, or being particularly extreme in even a few areas, according to Levine (1997) would probably be classified as a "time-urgent personality" (p. 21). When such thoughts and behaviors become extreme and habitual, they can progress into dangerous territory. In their 1996 work on treating time pathologies, Ulmer and Schwarzburd identified three symptoms that warrant a diagnosis of hurry sickness, which Levine (1997) paraphrased:

1. Deterioration of the personality, marked primarily by loss of interest in aspects of life except for those connected with achievement of goals and by a preoccupation with numbers, with a growing tendency to evaluate life in terms of quantity rather than quality.

2. Racing-mind syndrome, characterized by rapid, shifting thoughts that gradually erode the ability to focus and concentrate and create disruption of sleep.
3. Loss of ability to accumulate pleasant memories, mainly due to either a preoccupation with future events or rumination about past events, with little attention to the present. Focusing on the present is often limited to crises or problems; therefore memories accumulated tend to be of unpleasant situations. (p. 22)

A recent Yale University study showed that every stressful life event actually causes the brain's gray matter to physically decrease. The area most affected is in the medial prefrontal cortex, the part of the brain that regulates not only blood pressure and glucose levels but also emotions, desires, impulses, and self-control (Ansell, Rando, Tuit, Guarnaccia, & Sinha, 2012). So once begun, a road rage, racing-mind, or anxiety/addiction pattern may be harder to overcome. Yale neurobiologist Rajita Sinha states that the 2012 study by Ansell et al. illustrates the need to "find ways to deal with the emotional fallout" of such stress (as cited in an interview with Hathaway, 2012, para. 6)

Medical concern about the negative effects brought on by hurry is not a phenomenon limited to the modern industrial growth society. Describing the three basic foundations of human illness in her people's cosmology, Comanche healer Sanapia named this as the first cause: "Things in rapid and erratic motion, or rapid and erratic motion itself are intrinsically dangerous to the human body" (Jones, 1972/1984, p.97).

The increasing speed of life in the industrial growth society clearly poses a problem that needs to be addressed. People don't always have the power to change the situation they find themselves in, but they do have the power to change the attitude from which they meet such challenges. This issue is being addressed in the context of transpersonal psychology and falls under the aegis of a much larger discussion about the role that consciousness—specifically consciousness about time—plays in issues of health and sanity.

Physician Larry Dossey (1982) presents remarkable clinical data showing that by changing their view of time, people have been able to positively affect the course of disease. In the next sections of this chapter, I will offer alternate cultural views of time and practical ideas to experiment with in everyday life, stemming from the perspectives of transpersonal psychology and ecopsychology.

Other Modes of Time

Linear Time

Please take a moment to consider how you generally think about time and how it works. In Western industrial growth society cultures, the story of human lives is told as a linear progression along a series of events beginning with birth, then growing up, having experiences, and incrementally aging. Extending this timeline, each person is also placed in a genealogical family lineage along centuries, with ancestors coming before and descendants coming after. Time passes in more or less equal chunks measured in seconds, minutes, hours, days, weeks, months, years, decades, and so on. Like kilometers on a map, intervals on the clock are equal and constant and, with a few exceptions, calendar intervals are too. Because of this, we can place our location in time similar to the way we orient in spatial dimensions. Conceptions of time can even fuse with spatial distance: When asked how far away a place is, the response might be, "around three hours." All of the sequences can basically be predicted in detail, and we are taught to perceive time as moving in a line, measured by the calendar and clock. This is known as *linear time* or the *terminal model of time* (Wallace 2005) since in this view time's arrow is seen in spatial terms, shooting ever onward toward the future until everything ends.

You may be surprised to discover that this is not the only way that people think about time. Time perception is based not only on physics but also on anthropology and psychology. Following are two additional mental models of time besides linear time: *cyclical time* and *eternal time.*

Cyclical Time

The concept of cyclical time or circular time basically pays primary attention to cycles. In this mode, like a wheel, the world goes through a given span, and its momentum eventually slows down, decays, and dies. But the pattern doesn't stop there; the wheel then arises again to repeat the pattern in a new and changed way. Examples of calendars based on this cyclical model include the Mayan calendar (Wallace, 2005) and the Hindu concept of Yugas. These cover enormous cycles of time that are calculated to play out over hundreds, thousands, or even millions of years. The pattern is really more of a spiral than a proper circle, because what comes around again does not necessarily involve the same beings or events; only the pattern repeats.

Although cyclical time is a very old view and not the model of time consulted on smartphones every day, all contemporary people still experience it in the recurring bodily rhythms of hunger and sleep, and in the cycle of the earth's days and seasons. The sun and moon rise and set each day; the moon waxes to full and fades away to black; spring follows winter and then is followed in turn by summer and fall. These are cyclical events on which agricultural peoples base their livelihood. Even though the currently used Gregorian calendar lays this pattern out in a line, with January at the beginning and December at the end, we still think of these time changes as a cycle of events, and we don't typically question whether this periodicity will continue, whether Christmas will indeed come again this year.

The farther away from the equator, the more dramatic the seasonal changes. Particularly in such regions, seasonal cycles correspond with changing psychological states such as extreme depression that arises in autumn and peaks in winter due to the long, dark days (a.k.a. seasonal affective disorder) and recovers in spring. Another example is suicide rates reaching their highest, surprisingly, around midsummer (Roenneberg, 2012).

Eternal Time

The third model is *eternal, fixed,* or *steady-state* time. I prefer the term eternal since fixed can imply stagnation, whereas this model of time also describes a kind of flow. Eternal time holds the idea that everything that ever was and ever will be is in this moment, and all whens are essentially the same at the core. This concept is often a little more difficult for Westerners to grasp because it is so alien to the way we are raised to think about time. Contemporary Christians touch on the idea of eternal time through the religion's conception of the afterlife in a semi-eternal Heaven or Hell, but still the concept of linear, terminal time holds sway in everyday experience during this embodied lifetime.

A fine example of eternal time can be found in the Australian Aboriginal peoples' view, in which the traditional patterns of interactions between people, animals, and spirits continue without end (Wallace, 2005). "What happened in the past is happening now, and will go on unchanged forever" (Roberts & Mountford, 1971, p. 11). Life takes place in *dreamtime*, a sacred landscape created by ancestors of mythic dimensions long ago, and which is still accessible today. Before European contact, Aboriginal people believed that their children's spirits originate in many different places, then enter their chosen mothers' bodies to begin life as human beings (Roberts & Mountford, 1978). So people are who they are from time immemorial, and everything around—lizards, rocks, waterholes, and even the grass between the trees—is intimately linked with each person's lineage (Roberts & Mountford, 1971) and, I would argue, their identity. Dreamtime contains not only sleeping-state experiences but also everything we envision, intuit, and conceive. As Jamake Highwater (1982) views it, "The aboriginal *dreamtime* is "the solution to the Western question asked by the late Hannah Arendt: 'Where are we when we think?'" (p. 89).

To offer a second example, Benjamin Whorf (1956) observed that the Hopi language contains no reference to time as it is conceived of in the English language. Durations of time cannot be counted because that aspect of the world is not based on concrete conceptions that one might point to. Neither past nor future exist per se. Instead, everything in the realm of imagined possibility already exists, just in varying stages of manifestation.

Eternal time sits in the ever-changing, yet perpetual, the "perennial reality of the now" (Joseph Epes Brown, as quoted in

Highwater, 1982, p. 118). This is a very old view of time, and one particularly useful to shamanistic cultures. An eternal now combined with a shamanistic worldview means the spirits, gods, and ancestors are always potentially present (e.g., Jones, 1972/1984, pp. 40–41). To use a Western metaphor, the past and future can be just as accessible in temporal terms as the next-door neighbors are in spatial terms. This makes it possible for a skilled practitioner to speak with the dead and future generations (e.g., Eliade, 1974, pp. 355, 487), and for us to influence not only the future through our actions but also the past (Eliade, 1974, p. 171). It seems to me that the eternal view of time holds potential for transpersonal work in healing intergenerational trauma.

Linear Time's Movable Terminus
Linear/terminal time is just one among many ways of viewing time and how humans move through it. Interestingly, there is also more than one way to conceive of linear time.

Contemporary Western society depicts time as moving forward. To navigate it, we draw timelines, looking forward to coming events and to making progress. The future is before us, anticipated, and the past behind us, irretrievable. But such widespread cultural groups as the ancient Greeks (Bortone, 2010, p. 117), the Aymara (Núñez & Sweetser 2006), the Malagasy (Dahl, 1995) and pre-colonial peoples in Kenya (Mbiti, 1970) conceptualize the flow of time in quite a different way. They view the past as being before us, and the future as being behind us. Can you imagine why they might see it that way? It makes perfect sense. People can clearly see what's already happened (as the old saw goes, "Hindsight is 20–20"), but we cannot see what fate might be coming in future. Therefore, the past is in front where our eyes are, and the future is the unknown behind our backs. In these conceptions, time's arrow flies in the opposite direction. So even with linear/terminal time, there is more than one model.

Event-based Linear Time
Many people experience time not as an incremental, evenly spaced "tick-tick-tick" clock sequence but as measured by life events. When telling

stories with the family, for example, people often figure out when something happened by dating it through event reckoning. Looking at photos, one might muse, "Those crazy shoes were only popular right after X graduated from high school, so this must have been [season/year]." The stage of life a person was in at the time that something personally important happened is often much more important to them than the numbered calendric year in which it occurred. So it's easier to determine sequence by recalling the experiences rather than trying to list everything that happened, say, in 2013. This mode of perception is known as *event time* (Levine, 1997), as compared with *clock time.* Both clock and event time are inherent in linear time.

Time on the clock often differs significantly from the psychological experience of time. The duration of an event seems to flex according to our relationship with it. Factors include how interesting and enjoyable the activity is, and the age of the experiencer. The older one gets, the faster time seems to sweep by. This may be due to the relative percent of time the event takes when compared with the person's already-lived lifespan. Time's inner relativity is especially illuminated by how time at the dentist seems to take forever when compared with a picnic at the lake with a beloved.

Cultural Expectations

Cultural expectations abound about the duration of inner cycles. How long should a person take for grieving after a family member's death? At what point does it become necessary to hide that grief due to others' subtle messages that it's time to be done? How long should a person sleep?

New studies show that the chronobiological clock will change over a person's lifespan. Young children are early waking chronotypes, as their bleary-eyed parents will attest. According to Roenneberg (2012), a shift occurs during puberty and adolescence that turns humans into night owls (p. 101). Teenagers who sleep in aren't necessarily lazy; they have a sleep–wake phase delay that causes them to actually get tired later and need more sleep in the morning (American Academy of

Pediatrics, 2014). At around age 20 another turning point occurs, after which people both go to bed and wake earlier for the rest of their lives. This shift in chronotype is now a noted biological marker for the end of adolescence (Roenneberg, 2012, pp. 101–102).

In his excellent chronicles of *temporal misadventures* while traveling in different cultures, social psychologist Robert Levine (1997) observed how modes of relating with time tie in with societal approval. *Monochronic* or *M-time* (Hall, 1959) people like to focus on activities one at a time in a sequence from start to finish. M-time is stringently structured linear time that pays attention to the clock and the calendar. It is favored by countries with industrialized economies because its use enhances ability for individual achievement: "time is money." Contrast this with *polychronic* or *P-time* (Hall, 1959), a cultural mode of relating to time that centers more on people's life events, interactions and connections. P-time dominant people prefer to attend to multiple events or tasks by doing one project until inspiration strikes for another, then returning to the first again, simultaneously progressing a bit on each. They prioritize emotional connection over keeping up with planned schedules. In a P-time-dominant country like Brazil or Burundi, for example, one might make an appointment for noon but not get there until 10 pm, if at all, and this is accepted if something more relationally important came up (Levine, 1997, pp. 96, 194–195).

That drives many North Americans crazy. It's not surprising, given our inherited cultural lens. If time is money, then it is a measurable commodity that should not be wasted by pointless acts like waiting for someone to show up. But contrast this view with that of Jean Traore from Burkina Faso in eastern Africa, an exchange student for whom the concept of wasting time is incomprehensible: "There's no such thing as wasting time where I live....How can you waste time? If you're not doing one thing, you're doing something else" (as quoted in conversation with Levine, 1997, p. 91). Levine concluded that to a responsible person there, "what is truly wasteful—sinful, to some—is to not make sufficient time for the people in your life" (p. 91).

The Commodification of Time

Internalized Time Oppression: Example from Labor History
The length of the work day caused many of the most significant strikes during the early days of the labor movement in Europe and the United States. Employers supported shorter days as well, convinced that fatigue from overwork was counterproductive.

Labor historian Benjamin Hunnicutt (1996) describes a pivotal moment. In 1930, cornflake maven W.K. Kellogg offered all workers at his large Battle Creek plant a six-hour work day instead of eight, with only a minor cut in pay since he believed the shorter hours would mean more efficient work. This visionary program was a huge success for nearly two decades. Workers enjoyed the extra time (and reported using that time for such things as being better parents, doing creative work, enjoying time outdoors, and offering community service), absenteeism and accidents were significantly reduced, and since costs like insurance went down because of the reduced hours, the unit cost of production was so lowered that Kellogg could hire many more people and pay them all as much for six hours of work that he formerly paid for eight (pp. 15, 37, 70). But the workers themselves sabotaged this sweet deal. Following World War II, new management began counterattacking "the threat of leisure" (Hunnicutt, 1996, p. 6) by linking greater productivity to higher wages. And wanting the material advantages of the new consumer culture, workers demanded eight-hour days. The management, workers, and union alike began to dismiss leisure time as "wasted," "lost," or "silly," and to sneer at those who wanted to keep the old six-hour standard as "lazy," "weird," or even "sissies" (Hunnicutt, 1996, p. 145). The last six-hour employee holdouts, mostly women, surrendered to the new regime in 1985 (Hunnicutt, 1996, p. 2).

This trend continues now. External pressures to perform are strong. Corporate employees vying for a higher position might send an email to the boss at 4 a.m. to show what diligent and valuable workers they are. Some people prefer a fast work tempo, finding it stimulating. But for others, such pressures to work more and ever faster can eventually become a form of internalized oppression, leading to chronic or extreme time urgency even in the absence of stimuli.

The Question of Worth

Many people raised under the currently dominant industrial growth model of society have come to conceptualize time as something that needs to be filled by activity in order to gain meaning as valuable and relevant. Taking an ecopsychological perspective, one can see parallels with how wild land is conceptualized as relatively worthless in and of itself until it is developed for human use and potential economic development. The needs of existing vibrant communities of other-than-human beings and are often disregarded when considering use of place; similarly, the rich life of the human soul and what nurtures its thriving is often disregarded as secondary when considering how we should use our time.

In my observation, one root cause of the problem is focusing on our world not as a matrix of living relationships, but as an economic commodity. A person can sell the living body of an ancient tree for lumber or the hours of their own life for wages.

The conception of time as a commodity has direct effects on behaviors that affect not only the individual but also the health of the planet. An example is the common choice not to repair possessions even if the flaw is small, finding that act a waste of time when we can just go buy new ones quickly and cheaply. United States citizens are told that buying more improves the nation's economy. But this act ignores the true costs of these replacement items to both the planet (in terms of raw materials, carbon footprint for transport, packaging, etc.) and to the individual person's empowerment. Repairing or repurposing not only keeps things out of the landfill, it can confer a sense of pride in skill and more—a deeper relationship with each of our possessions as they gain the beloved patina of layered memory, sometimes even across generations.

The cultivation of inner spaciousness—that is, a sense of having enough time not only to complete the tasks of daily life but to feel vast, calm, and fully aware while performing these actions—is therefore not only a path to personal happiness and awakening as described in Buddhism (e.g., Hanh, 1999) but also to pro-environmental behavior that supports the matrix of life on our planet.

Strategies and Interventions

This section contains a few suggested transpersonal and ecopsychological interventions for dealing with hurry sickness in the industrial growth society, mapped onto the three presented modes of time.

Interventions involving Linear Time

Time-urgency symptoms. Review the list of time-urgency symptoms and choose one that you notice in yourself and practice mitigating over time. Interventions can be simple. When eating, allow yourself to prepare and eat some meals slowly with an eye toward full enjoyment of every bite and appreciation for the food, its sources, and the company you are with. Alternatively, you can practice driving more calmly, deliberately leaving early in order to avoid the need to rush and leaving more space between yourself and the car in front of you, even when other cars nose their way in, focusing on the skill of smooth driving rather than speed.

P- or M-time dominance. Experiment with which mode works better for you. If you are happier and more effective while focusing deeply on a single task for a long time, try to set up a schedule with large chunks of uninterrupted time to engage in each task in sequence. Conversely, if you prefer to do one thing for a short while and then switch to another for a time, whether another task, social interaction, or a yoga break, give yourself permission to do that. The only mode that is proven not to work is trying to do two or more things simultaneously, or multitasking.

Pay attention. Vietnamese teacher Thich Nhat Hanh (1999) recommends turning the chore of doing the dishes into a form of meditation. No matter the duration, one thing at a time done well, and with fully attentive presence, can lead to peace of mind. It might even shift your perception of how much time has gone by.

Manage expectations. Henry David Thoreau observed back in 1842, "Nothing can be more useful to a man than determination not to be hurried" (p. 342). One practical way to work toward this is by managing people's expectations about your response time. Email is a particularly egregious time suck, in my experience, and a stressor to boot as it forces frequent task-switching. To keep email from taking over your work life, first turn off the alarm so you can choose when to focus on it. Then simply place a tag line at the bottom of the automatic response that states something like, "In an effort to maintain an efficient and sustainable work life, I will read and respond to emails [however infrequently you can successfully get away with it; I suggest something like once per weekday in the late afternoon or three times per week]. Thank you for your patience." This manages expectations of you. If correspondents know when they can expect a response to their query or request, they will usually relax and accept it even though it is not as fast as they had hoped. And you will have gained hours of your life back to focus more deeply on completing the tasks presented in earlier emails, and perhaps even taking a five-minute walk outdoors.

Appreciate down time. Campaigns are now being waged in both Japan and America to incite exhausted workers to take their earned vacation time, only half of which is actually being used (Levine, 1997, p. 145). Although often frowned upon in the industrial growth society as slacking off, taking time for other aspects of life like fun, relaxation, and regular time with family, friends and nature, as the Kellogg's labor example shows, will actually make people more productive at their jobs in the long run, not to mention healthier and happier. Recognize down time as valuable for renewal, inspiration, calming the nervous system, and increasing mental capacity. Many truly creative breakthroughs have come when resting or even asleep, as in the example of Marie Curie's dreams. They rarely come when the person is exhausted.

Focus on being vs. doing. When stressed with too many tasks and rushing to keep up, I find that I not only make more mistakes but also lose my ability to be gracious—and sometimes even my sense of humor. Further, this unpleasantness is contagious. One strategy that has worked for me in situations of time urgency is to focus primarily on how I am being with others and the task in question that day, rather than whether I can get everything done. It is a mindfulness practice, showing loving-kindness to others through a more pleasant attitude and to myself by allowing myself to slow down.

Ecopsychological Interventions involving Cyclical Time

Sabbath or *screen fast.* The practice of Sabbath, or taking a weekly day of rest, can bring renewal to an overworked mind, soul, and body. Orthodox Judaism and other spiritual traditions recommend not engaging in any form of labor on the Sabbath, following the Biblical creation story that on the seventh day, God's work was finished (Genesis 2:2). This is not just a day off, though; it is a vital part of creation. Generally translated as *rest*, the Hebrew word for what was created on the seventh day is *menuha*. As Rabbi Abraham Heschel (1951/1998) explains, "Menuha is the same as happiness and stillness, as peace and harmony.... the essence of good life" (pp. 22–23). So once per week, the Sabbath offers the soul and the community a refreshing experience of bathing in sanctified time: "The primary awareness is one of our being *within* the Sabbath rather than of the Sabbath being within us" (Heschel, 1951/1998, p. 21).

There are many secular ways to celebrate the Sabbath by choosing to undertake less or no usual work activity one day per week. One contemporary alternative Sabbath is a "screen fast" day or even half day: refrain from going online, watching TV, or engaging with any tech screens aside from voice conversations. It is funny how radical this may sound, considering that ten years ago, neither the iPhone nor Android even existed (Neal, 2014). Give yourself the gift of a regular cycle out of the frantic pace of ordinary life in order to enjoy and celebrate life in simple ways, renew the soul, and experience time as something sacred.

Let the body lead. Consider what would happen if we only ate when the body signaled hunger and slept when we felt tired. A Columbia University study showed that following the clock for eating times tended to lead to obesity (see Levine, 1997, p. 89). It can be both fascinating and useful to discover and align with your own circadian, chronotypical, and other rhythms.

Cycles of nature. One strategy for addressing time pressure is to pay more attention to nature's cycles, which are much vaster and slower. Consciously aligning our own lives with larger planetary rhythms and forces can confer much-needed perspective. Seasonal holidays can remind us of our place in the vast cycle of life and death. Honoring the solstices (the time of year when the daylight is longest or shortest) and the equinoxes (when the length of day and night are equal) as modern Pagans do can enhance such awareness four times per year. Christmas and Hanukkah occur around the winter solstice, and Easter and Pesach parallel the spring equinox. At their heart, these are all ancient celebrations of, respectively, the birth of light at the darkest time of winter and the renewal of returning life and hope in spring—a lovely transpersonal focus to meditate on both without and within. To work with more frequent cycles, observe what phase the moon is in and feelings you may notice changing inside yourself as it waxes and wanes thirteen times per year. Pay attention to all of the changes the seasons bring: differences in length of day and night, cold and heat, moisture, your sleep cycle. Notice which flowers, birds, insects, and animals appear more at these varying times, and the changes they go through. You might opt to deeply observe a single tree or plant over the course of a full year.

A simple practice I do is to go outside for at least five minutes every morning when I first get up, and every evening just before retiring to bed. Five minutes is not long, but it is long enough to remind me about what is going on in the larger world of which I am an embedded part, a world beyond pure human construct. Stars! Changing weather! Birdsong! Neighbors! The practice helps me to both sleep and awaken with a vast, calm, mind and peaceful, appreciative heart. Attending to the more-than-human world offers a way to dwell in deeper awareness of cyclical time.

Transpersonal Interventions Involving Eternal Time

   Contemplative practices. Mindfulness meditation is a proven and wonderful way to slow the self down, particularly the mind affected by too much busyness. Through training people to witness their own internal reactions, meditation can also ultimately alleviate some of the anxiety and behavioral patterns brought on by time pressure and hurry sickness. As Gandhi was reputed to have said about himself, if there is too much to accomplish to include an hour of meditation in our day, we actually need to meditate for two hours. But even fifteen minutes per day is better than nothing, especially if engaged in several times per day. Mindfulness meditation and other presencing practices that exhort us to "be here now" can afford us access to touch the "eternal now," or the chance to at least expand the spaciousness of the moment experienced in the present. So can practices such as shamanic journeying that expand perception into timeless realms. Same with any activity from drawing to athletics to lovemaking that one can immerse in so deeply that the flow state (Csikszentmihalyi, 1990) is induced, wherein the doer becomes secondary to the process of doing and time seems to expand or stand still. As the yoga session ends, do not rush to get up before shavasana. Allow yourself to settle into your newly reset body.

   Cultivate awareness of deep time. Consider time on a longer scale–deep time, as Joanna Macy (n.d.) puts it. For example, the Haudenosaunee people of North America exhort us to consider the impact our decisions might have on seven generations. However, I've heard some say that actually refers not to seven generations in the future as we often think, but to three generations in the future, us now, and three back in our ancestry (see Wheeler & Bijur, 2000, p. 28). What might our elders or our grandchildren yet to be born want to see us doing now? Now consider the possibility that causality is not only one-way or even linear.

   Play with the time scales of other species. To add an ecopsychological component to this meditation, turn also to the elders of other species, all of us stemming from the same Big Bang beginning this galaxy's existence. Consider yourself as a being composed of elements that are shared by all other beings on this planet. Your brain is, at the core, the same as a lizard's; your circulatory system echoes the patterns of branching rivers and trees. What advice might elders like these offer regarding the problem of speed? How does time pass for a tree? For a rock? This thought meditation is another way to potentially touch the vastness of eternal time, and can be particularly useful for offering spaciousness perspective when feeling rushed.

Concluding Wish

The scope of this paper encompasses only a few aspects of relationship with time. However modest, may these thoughts open the door to your becoming a temporal millionaire, with the ability to swim in time's changing flows sleekly, like an otter, and the liberating feeling that you have enough time to fully enjoy this life.

References

American Academy of Pediatrics. (2014, September). Policy statement: School start times for adolescents. *Pediatrics, 134*(3): 642–649. doi:10.1542/peds.2014-1697.

American Psychological Association (APA). (2006, March 20) *Research in action: Multitasking: Switching costs.* Retrieved June 15, 2016 from http://www.apa.org/research/action/multitask.aspx

Ansell, E.B., Rando, K., Tuit, K., Guarnaccia, J., & Sinha, R. (2012). Cumulative adversity and smaller gray matter volume in medial prefrontal, anterior cingulate, and insula regions. *Journal of Biological Psychiatry, 72,* 57–64.

Bortone, P. (2010). *Greek prepositions: From antiquity to the present.* Oxford, UK: Oxford University Press.

Csikszentmihalyi, M. (1990). Flow: The psychology of optimal experience. New York, NY: Harper & Row.

Dahl, Ø. (1995). When the future comes from behind: Malagasy and other time concepts and some consequences for communication. *International Journal of Intercultural Relations, 19,* 197–209.

Dictionary.com (n.d.). "Haste" (definition). Retrieved June 22, 2016 from http://www.dictionary.com/browse/haste

Dossey, L. (1982). *Space, time, and medicine.* Boulder, CO: Shambhala.

Eliade, M. (1974). *Shamanism: Archaic techniques of ecstasy.* Bollingen Series LXXVI. Princeton, NJ: Princeton University Press.

Fitch, V. (1984). The psychological tasks of old age. *Naropa Institute Journal of Psychology 3,* 90–106. Boulder, CO: Nalanda Press.

Friedman, M., & Rosenman, R.H. (1959). Association of specific overt behavior patterns with blood and cardiovascular findings. *Journal of the American Medical Association, 240,* 761–763.

Goodhew, L., & Loy, D. (2002.) Momo, Dogen, and the commodification of time. Retrieved November 20, 2012 from http://joannamacy.net/deepecolog/ intro-to-deep-time/momo.html

Hall, E. (1959). *The silent language.* New York, NY: Doubleday Anchor.

Hanh, T.N. (1999). *The miracle of mindfulness: A manual on meditation.* Boston, MA: Beacon.

Hathaway, B. (2012, January 9). Even in the healthy, stress causes brain to shrink, Yale study shows. *YaleNews.* Retrieved June 15, 2016 from news.yale.edu/2012/01/09/even-healthy-stress-causes-brain-shrink-yale-study-shows

Heschel, A.J. (1998). *The Sabbath: Its meaning for modern man.* New York: Noonday Press. (Original work published 1951)

Highwater, J. (1982). *The primal mind: Vision and reality in Indian America.* New York, NY: Penguin Meridian.

Hornback, K.E. (1992). Socio-economic outlook: Outdoor recreation 2000. *Trends, 28*(2),14–19. Washington, DC: Park Practice Program, National Park Service.

Hunnicutt, B.K. (1996). *Kellogg's six-hour day.* Philadelphia, PA: Temple University Press.

Jones, D.E. (1984). *Sanapia: Comanche medicine woman.* Prospect Heights, IL: Waveland Press. (Original work published 1972)

Kastenbaum, R. (1971, December). Age: Getting there ahead of time. *Psychology Today, 7(5),* 52–-54, 82–84.

Levine, R. (1997). *A geography of time: The temporal misadventures of a social psychologist.* New York, NY: Basic Books.

Loh, K.K., & Kanai, R. (2014). Higher media multi-tasking activity is associated with smaller gray-matter density in the anterior cingulate cortex. *PLoS ONE, 9(9):* e106698.

Macy, J. (n.d.) The relevance of deep time. Retrieved June 15, 2016 from http://joannamacy.net/resources/deepecology/203-the-relevance-of-deep-time.html

Mbiti, J. (1970). *African religions and philosophy.* Garden City, NJ: Doubleday.

Merriam-Webster Dictionary (n.d.) "Haste" (definition). Retrieved June 15, 2016 fromhttp://www.merriam-webster.com/dictionary/haste

Meyer, D.E., Evans, J.E., Lauber, E.J., Rubinstein, J., Gmeindl, L., Junck, L., & Koeppe, R.A. (1997, March). *Activation of brain mechanisms for executive mental processes in cognitive task switching.* Poster session presented at the Cognitive Neuroscience Society, Boston, MA.

Mowen, A., Graefe, A.R., Barrett, A.G., & Godbey, G.C. (1992). *Americans' use and perceptions of local recreation and park services: A nationwide*

reassessment. Ashburn, VA: U.S. National Recreation and Park
    Association.

Neal, R.W. (2014). Apple iPhone to iPhone 6: The 7-year evolution of a game-
    changing smartphone. Retrieved 8/6/16 from
    http://www.ibtimes.com/apple-iphone-iphone-6-7-year-evolution-
    game-changing-smartphone-photos-1533776

Núñez, R.E., & Sweetser, E. (2006). With the future behind them: Convergent
    evidence from Aymara language and gesture in the crosslinguistic
    comparison of spatial construals of time. *Cognitive Science 30,* 1–49.

Roberts, A., & Mountford, C. P. (1971). *The first sunrise. Australian Aboriginal
    myths in paintings by Ainsilie Roberts with text by Charles P. Mountford.*
    Adelaide, Australia: Rigby Limited.

Roenneberg, T. (2012). *Internal time: Chronotypes, social jet lag, and why you're
    so tired.* Cambridge, MA: Harvard University Press.

Schor, J. (1991). *The overworked American: The unexpected decline of leisure.*
    New York, NY: Basic Books.

Thoreau, H.D. (1842, March 22). *Journal VI.* Retrieved from
    https://www.walden.org/documents/file/Library/Thoreau/writings/
    Writings1906/07Journal01/Chapter6.pdf.

Ulmer, D.K., & Schwartzburd, L. (1996). Treatment of time pathologies. In R.
    Allan & S. Scheidt (Eds.), *Heart and Mind: the Practice of Cardiac
    Psychology,* 329–362. Washington, DC: American Psychological
    Association.

Wallace, A.F.C. (2005). The consciousness of time. *Anthropology of
    Consciousness 16*(2*),* 1–15.

Wheeler, K.A., & Bijur, A.P. (Eds.). (2000). *Education for a sustainable future: A
    paradigm of hope for the 21st century.* New York, NY: Kluwer
    Academic/Plenum Publishers.

Whorf, B. L. (1956). An American Indian model of the universe. In J. B. Carroll
    (Ed.), *Language, Thought, and Reality: Selected Writings of Benjamin Lee
    Whorf* (pp. 57–64). Cambridge, MA.: Technology Press of Massachusetts
    Institute of Technology.

Chapter 6
May All Beings Be Happy:
Cultivating Loving Kindness

Judy Lief

If we are to integrate meditation practice into our lives, we need to examine our underlying views of who are we altogether and what it is to practice a discipline such as meditation. We need to ask ourselves: What is the point of sitting practice? We need to explore how we trap ourselves in habitual emotional patterns and mental traps and how we can begin to free ourselves. At the same time, the path of meditation requires a light touch. Otherwise, we will not be able to avoid falling into one self-improvement scheme after another—over and over again.

There are so many self-improvement schemes to choose from. We can buy the latest book—the ten steps to this, or the five ways to that, or the six models to keep us growing and developing. We can try out one scheme for a while, and then we can go on to the next. Yet in the end we are still the same old us in the same old situation. It is endless, and it is also pretty hopeless. Can we work with ourselves in a way that moves us forward but does not bury us in earnestness? Can we begin to appreciate who we are, as opposed to trying to replace who we are now with some new or better model like the hot-off-the-assembly-line car of the year? How can we fully engage in the path of the Buddha or the path of enlightenment?

Meditation is not only about insight and understanding, relaxing and stabilizing the mind, or becoming less distracted and more focused. It is not merely a mental exercise. It has to do with the heart. It is connected with a whole view of reality. Meditation practice springs from the very deepest core of our nature, our feeling of being alive, and our connection with one another. It springs from the heart.

The English phrases "awakened heart, awakened mind," and "enlightened mind" are all used to translate the Sanskrit term, bodhichitta.[1] Bodhi has the same root word as the word buddha: it means "awake" or "enlightened." Chitta is translated as "mind," as "heart," as "essence," and as "heart/mind." In bodhichitta, heart and mind are inseparable. Our way of perceiving the world is not just a mental interpretation; it is a feeling, a vibration, a connection of attraction or avoidance. Our response to the world is heart-based.

For some reason, a big deal is made about this awakened heart, this awakened mind. Book after book is written about this one concept. What is this awakened heart? Why is it such a big deal? Where can we get it? Where does it reside? Does it even exist at all? Those are all worthwhile questions. In trying to give you a feeling for this term, I would like to tell a little story. Imagine for a moment that you are walking down one of the side streets of New York. It is late at night and basically you just want to get to wherever you are headed—say, back home to your apartment, safe and sound, nice and clean. Nonetheless, you have got to go through this walkway to get there. Maybe you are in the meat-packing district. It is a dark night, and trucks have been loading and unloading. There is garbage all around. Maybe the garbage people are coming in the morning, so some apartments you go by have mounds of garbage piled up in front, precariously perched on the sidewalk. You hope they do not fall over and hit you. There are little bits of sides of beef and meat-wrapping paper. A lot of people have been walking down this street. People have been pissing on the walls, and it smells. Maybe you see a rat run across the street and think, "Oh God, what am I doing here?" You watch where you are stepping, because a lot of people have been walking their dogs.

As you are going through all this, something catches your eye. Just outside your peripheral vision, you see a little glittery thing, and you think, "I don't know what that is." You keep walking. But after a while you begin to think, "Well, I wonder what that actually is?" So maybe you go back and

---

[1] There are alternate spellings for bodhichitta.

take a look. You do not want to look too closely because it is in a big pile of junk, but you are intrigued, so you look.

It cannot possibly be anything valuable, but it looks intriguing. Maybe it is a watch or maybe it is a coin. It looks like a diamond. Is it possible that someone dropped it there? You think, "No, it can't be. It's not very likely." Usually you would walk on, but you would feel really bad if it actually was a diamond and you did not pick it up. You think, "It could happen. Someone could have dropped it." So you go back and you look in the garbage and, lo and behold, right on this street there is a beautiful gem.

Of course, what would you do in that case? You would say, "Oh, God, it's my lucky day!" You would grab it, and you would hold on to it, and probably you would look at it every so often to make sure it was true. At first you might think, "It can't be true, I must have been hallucinating. That party was way too wild." But then you say, "No, I'm not hallucinating. It seems to be a real diamond." You get home and tell your apartment mate, "You won't believe what I found on the street just now. I found this diamond, right on Washington Street, way over in that cruddy area there. And I'm going to keep it! I'm going to invest it or something, put it in the stock market in the boom economy."

The discovery of bodhichitta happens just like that. It is exactly this kind of scenario. It is not that we go all over the place trying to find the merchant who peddles this quality of awakened heart, but it is more of a chance encounter, an encounter that we almost miss. It is a surprise encounter. Probably we have walked by other diamonds, but this time we happened to notice it: In just a tiny flicker, we noticed it. At that moment there was some kind of doubt in the mind, or some curiosity of mind, or a little tiny moment of openness in which our peripheral vision actually was in operation for a while. There was a moment—maybe a very fleeting moment—when we were not totally preoccupied with what we were doing, and we saw a little bit beyond our usual boundaries of concern.

Traditionally, it is said that this quality of bodhichitta is as surprising a discovery as it would be to find a diamond in the middle of a garbage heap. It is a surprising and subtle discovery that we do not fully trust it; we do not quite believe it to be true. "This couldn't actually be happening to me—a confused, neurotic, stuck person. Good things don't happen to me. Nothing like this! I don't notice anything. Diamonds don't fall into my lap. Parking tickets fall into my lap."

Bodhichitta is a sudden discovery of something in an odd place. Instead of going to the diamond market, we stumble upon this diamond on the street, in the grit. It is right in the middle of where we do not usually look, the opposite of where we would usually look—right in the middle of the most raw and gritty and potent and urbane section of our being. We come across bodhichitta right in the middle of what we consider all that we would like to throw away—all of our confusion, all of our juicy emotional dramas, all of our conceptual acrobatics, all of our discursive mind rambling, all our aches and pains—mental, physical, and developmental. In the midst of all that we would most like to avoid, when we actually look, when we actually have an open moment, we find a diamond! That diamond is the awakened mind, awakened heart—bodhichitta. And that discovery is considered to be the starting point of the mahayana path, the path of wisdom and compassion.

As you are sitting on your cushion practicing meditation, again and again you may start to think, "Nothing's happening. I'm doing everything right. I keep sitting and I've been coming to meditation classes for the last two months, and still nothing much has happened. I am beginning to notice more and more how nothing much happens. I used to be happy with nothing happening, but now I'm beginning to get irritated." That touch of irritation is provocative. At the point when you notice it, you could ask, "Aha! Who noticed it? Who noticed this quality of mind? From where is this discontent arising? What is it really about?"

One way in which the experience of bodhichitta takes birth is with that little scratch of discontent. Beginning to notice discrepancies between our views, our aspirations, and our actuality is a way of beginning to peek in on bodhichitta. You think, "I know that I could be operating otherwise, but when I actually look, although I know better, I am not. Is that just the way I am?" Bodhichitta does not mean that the skies split open and everything is beautiful. Instead, it could be more like a scratch of discontent or a doubt about what we are doing with our whole life.

Bodhichitta may arise as a suspicion that we know much better, that we actually *know*. An aspect of bodhichitta is that quality of knowing—the suspicion that down below, deep down, we do know. Because of bodhichitta, all the neurotic activity that we typically engage in becomes more and more painful, and in greater and greater contrast to that discovery. Whether you think of bodhichitta as the clarity and purity of a diamond or whether you think of it as an annoyance or as something poking your pretensions from within, it is a fundamental energy and a blessing. Bodhichitta is what makes the spiritual path possible for us, and it is what inspires us to explore what this path is all about.

In Buddhism, you always hear phrases like *letting go, not grasping*. You are told not to hold on to things too tightly, that you should relax and loosen up. However, in discussions of bodhichitta, this awakened heart or awakened mind, the opposite is said. Having had a glimpse of bodhichitta, having had even the smallest suspicion that there could be something in your experience like bodhichitta, you should hold on to that. It is like holding a diamond. If you picked up a diamond, you would not say, "Oh, that was a great experience; now I'll let go of that and go on to the next experience." You would hold on to that diamond and you would tell everybody about it. You would be really thrilled. You would think, "This is a precious thing. I'm going to try to do something with it. It's going to change my life somehow. It's going to change my circumstances."

This glimpse, this discovery of bodhichitta can be held as a beacon to draw one forward. It would be a mistake to discount it. However, I think we do tend to discount our own insight and our own heartfelt connection with other people, and even with ourselves. We tend to discount a lot of things. But when you recognize something that is genuine, something that is real, when you touch the essence of your heart rather than all your more superficial preoccupations, you should hold on to that. When you recognize bodhichitta, you should *not* let that go! It is not that you have had a great experience and you try to recreate it. You grasp onto bodhichitta by exploring what this path or practice is all about and deepening and extending whatever little glimpse you might have had.

Bodhichitta has a lot of different qualities and characteristics. One quality is that it has no birth. It just pops up. It has no mother and father.

Like a virgin birth, it just appears out of nowhere. In your daily lives probably all of you have had this experience many times. Bodhichitta suddenly appears out of nowhere, and for a moment you feel inspired, or for a moment you feel you could be whole rather than fragmented, or for a moment you genuinely care about the world around you, or you have an unstrategized moment of real connection. Because bodhichitta is not produced, we cannot create it. We cannot put the right ingredients together and make it happen. It cannot be produced, and it also cannot be lost. Even when you feel very, very lost, disheartened, and distracted, you cannot get rid of it. You did not create it in the first place, so you cannot dismantle it.

Although we only touch on bodhichitta occasionally, it is an ongoing essential part of who we are. You could say that the very definition of being a sentient being is having this potential for awakening, or this quality of being awake, but not knowing it. There are many different views and philosophical descriptions of bodhichitta, but however you look at it, it did not really arise and it does not really dissolve. Why is that? Because it cannot be pinpointed, you cannot say it is here or there. It is like the Heisenberg uncertainty principle, which says that you cannot pin something down both in space and time at once. Likewise, bodhichitta is not quite graspable. Although you know it is there, when you try to close in on it, you cannot find it. You could ask, "Where is this bodhichitta? Is it in my brain, or in my heart, or in my arm? Is it out there or in here? Is it solid or not solid? Is it a thought or is it an inspiration?" You cannot pin it down exactly, so, it is said to be non-dwelling.

If bodhichitta is an entry, a starting point, an inspiration, how do we nurture and cultivate it? How do we go further with it? Do we just hope for occasional inspiration and forget about it? How we work with that awakened heart is through what is called the open way, or the mahayana teachings. The mahayana path is one of bringing the insight and the shocking quality of bodhichitta together with the actual activities of our daily life. It is about how to bring our brain and our heart together, or how to synchronize our body and mind and emotions into a form that can be of service to ourselves and others.

All of the fuel for that path, all of the understanding, comes from uncovering this quality of bodhichitta from within rather than trying to impose a strategy from without. There are a lot of different techniques and a lot of different meditations in the mahayana, such as rousing our altruistic side and heightening our awareness of the environment and the people around us. But I think a lot of those techniques are circling around the main issue, which is learning how to trust what we have already experienced. We experience bodhichitta, but we do not often trust it. We have a suspicion about it, but we do not accept that suspicion.

It seems as if we are always trying to talk ourselves into something or talk ourselves out of something, but in the mahayana there is a sense that: "Okay, maybe I could trust this experience a little bit and work with it. Maybe I could accept myself a little bit and work from there and cultivate that further. Maybe I could also see this quality in other people." We might be different if we saw people from the viewpoint of this Buddha potential/Buddha seed or awakened heart. It might form a connection prior to what we are trying to accomplish with another person or what we are trying to get out of another person or what we are trying to impress upon another person. That connection might be more fundamental than the this-and-that world, the back-and-forth world, or the get-along world of strategy and struggle.

This starting point of bodhichitta is remembering, or touching back on, over and over again, the basic point: being touched by the world but not being caught in our solid views. Sometimes this is called the bringing together of compassion and openness, or emptiness. How can we act in a moral fashion without being moralistic? How can we benefit others without getting on our high horse about how we are these wonderful beings benefiting others? How can we instead come from a more natural, spontaneous wellspring of energy? And what is that wellspring, what is that force? That real force is bodhichitta.

The hero or the model practitioner within the mahayana tradition is a person who holds and manifests this quality, a person who shines forth with this quality of bodhichitta all the time. These heroes are called the bodhi beings or *bodhisattvas*. Bodhisattvas have made the commitment to bring out this quality of awakened heart and mind in themselves and in others equally. At this point, the path goes past the level of just your own self-improvement. It also goes past the level of trying to forget yourself, to pay no attention to your own path and only work with others. At this level you are going beyond that distinction of self and other altogether. Instead, you are operating purely on the inspiration of bodhichitta and the motivation to manifest bodhichitta in all directions equally, around the clock, day in and day out, in every gesture. Bodhisattvas serve as models or inspiration for regular practitioners such as ourselves. They serve as challenges, wake-up calls, reminders, or helpers.

Bodhichitta is an important concept. People tend to think that Buddhism means just trying to be nice. Of course, there is nothing wrong with just trying to be nice. Some people are already trying to be nice, and if *more* people would just try to be nice, that would be even better! But bodhichitta is much, much more than that.

Bodhichitta provides a whole context or basis of activity that is not conceptually motivated and that is not based on trying to accomplish some scheme—whether the scheme is to be nice or whether the scheme is to be nasty. Without any scheme, it is acting directly from the heart and lets the results arise as they may. It is not based on an attachment to a plan, a scheme, or a result. Instead, over and over we keep coming back to that very simple source. The practice of bodhichitta has nothing to do with solving moral dilemmas or trying to avoid punishment or trying to appear pure or saintly or spiritual. We are simply touching in over and over again with this spark and letting our actions flow from that. On the mahayana path, we are learning to trust the heart and the wisdom it holds.

Chapter 7
No Hidden Corners: Compassion Training in Counselor Education

Dale Asrael
with Paul Bialek

We had been waiting for hours in the freezing mountain air. Hundreds of people huddled together in the thin spots of sunlight as morning came to the Great Stupa of Dharmakaya, its white surface and gold sun–moon spire shining against the deep blue sky. We were waiting for the Dalai Lama, on his way from Denver to Shambhala Mountain Center in the foothills of the Rocky Mountains. Snow had come early—almost unheard of in September in Colorado—and travel was delayed. But we were ready in our down jackets and snow boots, waiting to see this famous spiritual teacher.

Finally, the car arrived. At first, we could barely make out the form of the elderly man, draped in traditional maroon robes with one arm and his head exposed to the cold, as he began to walk the prescribed route. Suddenly, the Dalai Lama turned and began to run, breaking through the line of security men, running into the center of the crowd, his shawl flapping behind him. He stopped in front of a man in a wheelchair, and embraced him. He hugged the paralyzed man for an extended moment. Then, in a stately manner, he arranged his robes and walked slowly back to where his walk had begun. He sat down, and the ceremony began.

I (DA) do not know whether the Dalai Lama and the man in the wheelchair on that cold Colorado morning had met before; but I know that I witnessed a spontaneous gesture of contact and warmth, given without hesitation in a situation in which one easily might have felt constrained by formality. I saw a demonstration of what can happen when one is completely available to the moment of life—not bound by projections and expectations but open and spontaneously responsive to the suffering of others.

After the Dalai Lama ran to hug the man in the wheelchair, he took part in an interfaith panel on compassion. Sakyong Mipham Rinpoche, lineage holder of Shambhala International, was there, as were Queen Noor of Jordan and Rabbi Irwin Kula of New York. Beginning with the Dalai Lama, each speaker presented traditional teachings on the tremendous importance of compassion from the ancient texts of their religions. Each presentation that morning described lessons seen in many world traditions: *Treat others as you, yourself, wish to be treated. Recognize how much all human beings have in common, and act toward others in a way that honors our shared humanity.*

At the end of the panel, the Dalai Lama stood to summarize. Although his main presentation had been in Tibetan, with his interpreter translating his words into English, in closing he switched to speaking English himself. "This has been a very good panel," he said. "We have heard from Buddhist teachers, a Muslim queen, and a *Muslim* rabbi. The interpreter gasped into the microphone, began to whisper loudly, urgently: "Jewish rabbi! Jewish rabbi! Not Muslim! Jewish! Jewish!"

For a moment, I wondered how the Dalai Lama would handle this faux pas, especially at a time of such great conflict in the Middle East. But I saw a big smile on the Dalai Lama's face, followed by his belly-laugh. "Muslim rabbi? Muslim rabbi? Big mistake! Big mistake!" followed by more laughter, now shared by all the panelists. He then continued with his closing remarks.

The Dalai Lama's response to his error—a quite politically incorrect error given the situation and the times—was, once again, compassion. This time the compassion was directed toward himself. It was a demonstration of self-acceptance so immediate and strong that he could humorously draw attention to his error, and even use it to create a fresh opportunity for connection and communication. It was a teaching just as potent as the wise words spoken that morning: The key to compassion for others is compassion for oneself, especially in our own most vulnerable moments.

Compassionate actions of this sort could be easy to idealize. The Dalai Lama would be the first to state that his openness to the suffering of others is the direct result of a long and deep process of training rather than a unique or extraordinary gift that he alone possesses.

Compassion Training

At Naropa University we have been using traditional Buddhist teachings and techniques for cultivating attention, resilience, and compassion as a basis for training counselors for the past 40 years. Research studies have confirmed that the practice of mindfulness meditation has a host of beneficial effects, including lower stress, more focused attention, improved resilience, and greater impulse control (Felton, Coates, & Christopher, 2015; Davis & Hayes, 2011; Brown & Ryan, 2003). Over the past decade interest has grown in studying the effects of compassion meditation and compassion training. A summary of this research (Weng et al., 2013) points out:

> Studies indicate that compassion training can improve personal well-being, including stress-related immune responses (Pace et al., 2009), positive affect (Fredrickson, Cohn, Coffey, Pek, & Finkel, 2008; Hutcherson, Seppala, & Gross, 2008) and psychological and physical health (Fredrickson et al., 2008). Compassion training also enhances responses toward others. Expert meditation practitioners show greater empathic neural responses when listening to sounds of others' suffering during compassion meditation practice compared to controls (Lutz, Brefczynski-Lewis, Johnstone, & Davidson, 2008). Recent work suggests that short-term training can increase prosocial behavior (Leiberg, Klimecki, & Singer, 2011) and increases positive emotions toward

those who are suffering (Klimecki, Leiberg, Lamm, & Singer, 2012). (pp. 1171–1172)

More recent research has found that compassion training increases altruism and alters neural responses to suffering (Gilbert & Chodron, 2014; Weng et al., 2013; Germer 2012), and that compassion meditation increased participants compassion for others while decreasing their fear of feeling compassion for others and being the recipient of compassion (Fulton & Cashwell, 2105; Jazaieri et al., 2013).

In the last ten years there has been a surge of interest in using compassion training as part of counselor education (Bibeau, Dionne, & Leblanc, 2016; Fulton & Cashwell, 2015). A recent review of the effect of loving kindness meditation (LKM) on therapist trainees offers encouraging evidence regarding using compassion training as part of a counselor training curriculum (Boellinghaus, Jones, & Hutton, 2013).

In this chapter we will outline some fundamentals of our approach to compassion training with counseling students at Naropa University. We will focus on the core practices we teach, and discuss some of our findings from bringing these practices into the classroom. Finally, we will make some suggestions about potential avenues for further inquiry.

The Birth of Compassion

Buddhist teaching explains that compassion exists inherently in us as a capacity, or "seed." Using the analogy of gardening, a seed contains all that is needed to produce a full plant, if the right warmth, sunlight, water, and soil are provided. Traditional Buddhist compassion meditation practices, such as metta (loving kindness) and tonglen (taking and sending), are designed to provide favorable conditions for the human seed of compassion to grow and to bloom.

The birth of compassion, however, can be messy. When the seed of compassion begins to germinate, it can feel awful. What students report as they begin these practices is not a straightforward linear path of increasing compassion and decreasing reactivity. Instead, it is a path of discovery that often involves a painful shedding of old assumptions and challenges habitual ways of thinking and behaving.

The first moments of compassionate response may be so tender and exposed that it can be hard to tolerate the feelings. We might feel like all our skin is rubbed off; the sensation of contact is painful and too intense. It can feel embarrassingly intimate, and simultaneously so familiar and so strange that it is hard to even know what it is we are feeling: it just feels raw. Naropa's founder, Chogyam Trungpa, describes it this way:

> Compassion is based on some sense of "soft spot" in us... as if we had a pimple on our body that was very sore—so sore we do not want to rub it or scratch it... That sore spot on our body is an analogy for compassion. (Trungpa, 1993, p. 15)

In this analogy, the embarrassing tenderness we cannot cover up, and that which we often unsuccessfully try to hide from one another, is where compassion begins. It is a vulnerable experience to witness someone suffering. No masks of politeness can soften the edges. Seeing someone in the raw, exposed moment of pain can trigger our aversion to exposure and our fear of pain. We might well feel helpless, wanting to help but not knowing what to offer. Such moments are shocking for counselors in training. They may hold an image of themselves as a compassionate helper; yet, in the naked moment when they are face to face with suffering, this self-image is of no use.

Such a sharp, penetrating moment of disillusionment and challenge to one's self-image is an important aspect of traditional compassion training that we explore in our Naropa classes. It points to the need for a deep kind of experiential learning—and unlearning—in which we become increasingly familiar with the strategies we use to keep both our own suffering, and the suffering of others, at arm's length.

To help students develop the capacity to stay present in the midst of suffering's sharpness and rawness, we teach a series of meditative practices in a classroom culture of acceptance and non-judgment. We invite students to pay close attention to their experience as it arises, and to describe what they notice with as little interpretation as possible. These practices invite students to welcome and investigate their moment-to-moment experience.

The format we have developed, based on years of tracking students' development and receiving their self-reports, includes a two-year sequence of courses, based on traditional mindfulness, awareness and compassion meditation practices. This chapter will emphasize three special techniques that are part of Naropa's lineage heritage, and which students consistently identify as pivotal in their development of compassion both toward themselves and toward others. The three techniques are fresh start, touch and go, and on-the-spot tonglen.

Mindfulness-Awareness: The Ground of Compassion

Mindfulness meditation is a structured method for developing basic presence and the stability and resilience compassion requires. It builds the foundation for learning compassion meditations, and can be considered a compassion practice in its own right.

Mindfulness reveals the need for kind attention toward one's own experience. Students' first gesture of compassion may need to be directed inward, toward their own internal struggles. Mindfulness–awareness practices include traditional sitting and walking meditation, with the most universal technique being mindful breathing. Even being willing to pause and sit still is a gesture of great kindness. Before we can respond compassionately toward others, we have to first stop running away from ourselves.

Stopping and sitting can be a radical act when there is so much to do. The stillness and "non-doing" of mindfulness is revealing. Many new meditators report being distressed, even horrified, to discover what is happening in their unfiltered experience. They notice the speed of their thoughts, the unruliness and pain of their unwanted emotions, and the tension in their bodies. In addition, they notice that they are judging themselves for "not doing it right." In fact, what they are discovering fits in quite well with the traditional descriptions of starting a meditation practice: habitual patterns of the body and mind that were never previously recognized are seen with heightened clarity. The traditional approach in mindfulness meditation is not to try to change what we are experiencing but to learn to hold the difficult experience with compassion. This takes time and patience. Learning meditation in a classroom environment is supportive. As members of the class discuss their meditation experiences, they learn from one another that they are not alone in their struggles. Many of them have historical habits of perfectionism, followed by self-criticism when ideals cannot be met. Discovering how widespread the habit of self-blaming is among their peers can help students become curious about this phenomenon, a much more useful approach than trying to make their judgmental thoughts stop.

Clearly recognizing how persistent and seemingly automatic their habitual self-aggression is, they discover a new possibility: They can have compassion toward the part of themselves that is so deeply conditioned to criticize and judge. Recognizing how they cause themselves unnecessary suffering is the first step. Gradually, students learn to soften the hard edges of self-critique. As they practice the discipline of remaining open and present in the midst of increasingly challenging circumstances, the ability to do so gradually increases. The good news is that we can train in this capacity through simple practices, repeated consistently.

Understanding Mindfulness of the Body and Breath

Mindfulness meditation begins with choosing a specific aspect of direct present-moment experience, called *the object of meditation*, and using it as an anchor, or home base. Traditional instructions begin with body sensations and the breath. Physical sensations provide a tangible experience that can be contacted and recognized, "grounding" attention in the direct experience of the present moment. Bringing attention to sensation provides a powerful shift out of thoughts and into somatic present-moment experience.

Instructions for mindfulness of the body and breath. Feel your feet on the floor. Bring your attention to the sensations of contact where your bottom meets the seat of your chair or meditation cushion.

Feel your body. Notice how being mindful of physical sensations affects you. Be inquisitive about what you are experiencing. What are the distinct sensations you feel in this moment? What can you see in a moment of mindfulness that you had not noticed when you were busy thinking about the past and future?

Notice when your attention drifts away from feeling the body and becomes absorbed in—identified with—thoughts. Gently bring your attention back to the sensations you feel in your body in this moment. Even uncomfortable sensations can be used as the object of attention, paying attention to the distinct momentary details, softly investigating their textures and locations.

Feel the rhythm of your breathing—your natural breathing, shallow or deep, however it may be. What is it like to feel the rising and falling of your diaphragm, the fullness of inhaling, the release of the out-breath? Notice how each breath cycle is unique, occurring in its own time and rhythm. Allow yourself to appreciate the way breathing nourishes the body.

Cultivate a kind attitude by saying to yourself, "I am learning, breath by breath, to be in the present moment. It is natural that I'll forget and that my mind will drift away to thoughts of other places and other times; but I can start again with the next breath, being mindful." As you repeatedly come back to sensations of the body breathing, you are strengthening your capacity to stay in the immediacy of the present.

Understanding Fresh Start

New meditators often describe their practice as a sequence of struggles with physical tension, drowsiness, incessant thinking, mood swings, and the urge to give up. The more they struggle, they report, the worse it gets. The harder they try to make the body and mind match their expectations for meditation, the more physical and mental tension there is. For all meditators, it takes time and familiarity with a range of physical, emotional, and mental phenomena to discover simple presence, allowing each experience to be what it is.

Giving ourselves permission to stop trying to "get it right" is a gesture of great kindness. Chogyam Trungpa taught "fresh start" to address habits of perfectionism and trying too hard, and to introduce the natural awareness relaxation can reveal.

Fresh start encourages us to let go of the whole "project" of meditation; in fact, it is the narrowness of approaching meditation as a project to accomplish that creates much of the struggle. Fresh start is a moment of release—dropping any attempt to control or manipulate practice. Relevant for both new and long-time meditators, it is a gentle reminder with a profound implication: Authentic practice relies on trusting ourselves. "Awakening is not a process of building ourselves up, but a process of letting go" (Chodron, 2012, p. 62). When we let go of overly tight effort and discipline, the mind is spontaneously freed to fall apart into its innate awareness.

Fresh start can be practiced multiple times during a meditation session, alternating short periods of precise engagement in mindfulness techniques with moments of suddenly releasing effort and resting in natural presence. This approach can also be brought into daily life activities.

Instruction for fresh start. If, in the midst of a session of meditation, "your mind is all caught up and driving you crazy, you can stop practicing altogether. Give yourself a break" (Chodron, 1991, p. 50). Maintain an uplifted posture, so that you don't become too loose. Allow the mind to completely relax: there is nothing to do. For a few minutes, rest in non-doing. When you are ready, begin your mindfulness practice again, with a sense of making a fresh start.

Understanding Mindfulness of the Thinking Mind
Thinking is part of the natural activity of the mind. Through meditation, we develop the crucial skill of recognizing thoughts as thoughts. We are not trying to make our thinking stop. Trying to suppress thoughts is like trying to make the ocean waves stop. Waves express the ocean's energy as thoughts express mental energy. Trying to stop them would be a useless struggle. Instead, we change our relationship toward thoughts.

Habitually, we assume that our thoughts are true. Thoughts, however, can never tell us the whole truth. They are always at least one step removed from direct somatic and perceptual experience. Changing our relationship toward thoughts means that we can learn to recognize what they are: conditioned mental activity. With this recognition, we have a choice. We can remain in our thoughts' limited and biased version of reality, or we can return our attention to the present moment. It is actually a gesture of compassion to gently bring ourselves out of the bubble of thoughts into direct experience, where our life is occurring. The key is having an attitude of kindness, curiosity, and understanding toward the human habit of "living in our thoughts."

Instructions for mindfulness of thoughts. Notice when the attention is no longer in the direct felt experience of sensations and breathing and has instead become identified with thoughts. If you are busy thinking a full-blown thought, which takes your attention all the way out of the room, you can label it, saying to yourself, "thinking," as if saying, "Oh, that's a thought; it's not my breathing" (Mipham, 2003). If it is a fleeting thought simply notice it as a thought, non-verbally. Then, gently and consistently, bring your attention back to the direct experience of physical sensations and breathing. Train in approaching all different thoughts—pleasant and unpleasant—with the same unbiased, interested attitude: all of them are thoughts. They perform a function; they tend to lead to more thoughts; they occur in recognizable patterns; and, most important, they come and go by themselves.

Understanding Mindfulness of Feelings and Emotions
Mindfulness of thoughts, as described above, trains students to recognize habitual patterns. Initially, this is quite difficult; but, as they spend more time observing, the patterns begin to stand out. Repetitive thought patterns can be regarded as a clue, or signal, like the tip of an iceberg seen at sea that indicates a massive structure beneath the surface of the water. When a thought pattern—such as planning, worrying, regretting, self-critiquing—comes up repeatedly, it indicates that there is emotional energy underneath it, perhaps unseen.

Understanding Touch and Go
Emotions are important. They are a primary way we connect to ourselves, others, and the world. Emotions color daily life situations in

ways that can lead to communication, appreciation, and gratitude—or to confusion and conflict. For counseling students, emotions have increased importance because they can become the basis of empathy. In addition, much of the students' future counseling work will be to support their clients in looking deeply into conflicting emotions. We have found that counseling students often have both fascination and aversion toward their own emotions. They report historical patterns of either suppressing or impulsively acting out when emotions feel overwhelming.

Learning to meditate skillfully with emotions—rather than mistakenly using meditation as a way to avoid feeling emotions—becomes a crucial aspect of counselor training. Part of Naropa's heritage comes from the Tibetan tantric tradition, which views emotions as containing wisdom. Meditating with emotions, then, is a matter of learning to use their energy as a natural resource for compassionate activity (Wegela, 2010).

"The emotions are composed of energy, which can be likened to water, and a dualistic thought process, which can be likened to pigment or paint. When energy and thought are mixed together, they become the vivid and colorful emotions" (Trungpa, 1976, p. 64). The energy of emotions, the water, is understood to be neutral, almost elemental. It is the accompanying thoughts that direct the energy into beneficial or harmful words and actions. When we habitually believe the conditioned thoughts, it is as if the mind contracts around the emotional energy, looking for a way to dispel it, which only intensifies it. Instead, when thoughts and the underlying emotional energy are clearly recognized, and the mind remains open and aware, the energy has room to move, express its wakefulness without confusion, and dissolve on its own.

The first step in practicing with emotions is to recognize these two distinct phenomena: the somatic sensations (which express the emotion's energy) and the repetitive thought pattern conceptually explaining or managing it. Emotional struggle indicates that the sensations and thoughts are tangled up together, not recognized as separate phenomena. In mindfulness meditation, students learn to clearly recognize thoughts by non-judgmentally labeling their precise patterns ("planning," "worrying," "fantasizing" etc.) and then bringing attention to the underlying sensations.

They "acknowledge the feeling, giving it their full...even welcoming attention and, even if it's only for a few seconds, drop the story line about the feeling.... This allows... a direct experience of it, free of interpretation" (Chodron, 2012, p. 13). They learn to stay with the underlying felt sensations, with curiosity about the details of their textures and qualities, and kindness toward any emotional tension that may be felt.

Many meditators describe long-held habits of avoiding feeling emotions by occupying themselves with familiar thought patterns. The special technique called "touch and go" provides a way to learn a new response to emotions. Touch and go was introduced as both a general approach to meditation—glimpsing but not clinging to—awareness. "You're aware that you're aware...you are in contact, you're touching the experience of being there...and then you let go" (Trungpa, 2015, p. 106). It was also presented in the context of practicing with emotions: "you do not just acknowledge them and push them off. You need to look at them without suppression or shying away...You could experience them, look at them, and *then* come back to your breath" (Trungpa, 2015, pp. 213–214).

Instructions for touch and go. When you find yourself struggling during meditation, turn toward the uncomfortable feeling. For a few moments, let the uncomfortable feeling be the object of attention. "Touch" your present-moment experience with your attention, noting the details of your physical sensations, and noting the thoughts that arise, recognizing any repetitive thoughts. Bring your attention in close to the feeling, gently exploring the textures, just as you might touch a rock or flower with your fingertips. Be curious about investigating the details moment by moment, noticing temperature, location, subtlety, or intensity—even if you find them unpleasant.

After "touching" the feeling for a few moments, shift to "go": Place your attention on a different aspect of the present moment, perhaps something neutral like the rhythm of your breathing or the coming and going of sounds. Bring light awareness to the larger environment. Feel the sensations of contact—your feet on the floor, your body supported by the chair or cushion. Gaze at colors, shapes, light, shadow. "Go" gives you permission to release your grasp on the uncomfortable feeling, to give it space. Then, turn your attention toward the uncomfortable feeling and "touch" again, gently exploring the details. Notice how the sensations differ from your last moment of touching. What is the temperature, texture, movement, or stillness? Remember that it is up to you how far from, or close to, the sensations you may want to be when you "touch." This can help to provide perspective if your experience is intensely uncomfortable. You can softly name the somatic textures of feeling to yourself if you need to stabilize your attention.

After a few moments of exploring the direct experience of whatever you are feeling, shift again to "go," widening the field of attention, gently noticing other sense perceptions, and expanding into awareness of the larger environment.

Over time, with repeated practice of touch and go, you can learn that it is possible to stay with the direct experience of feeling whatever is present, contacting it moment by moment, touching, but not grasping, its texture. You are learning that you can release it by shifting your attention to something neutral.

One of the reasons touch and go is helpful is that we tend to generalize about our feelings. Close observation can shift our attitude from aversion to true inquisitiveness. Instead of relying on generalities, we can learn to explore the details of the feeling. Once we see the details, they are quite interesting in their kaleidoscopic display of texture, intensity, and subtlety.

Noticing the separate elements of feelings automatically shifts our perspective a little bit. We come to see that the edgy sensations, the sense of aversion, the repetitive thoughts are not all tangled up together. It is as if the strands of the tangle become separated, and we can see a bit of space between them. Some of the panic to escape the feeling is naturally released, and it becomes possible to relax and be curious about the details in the midst of discomfort. Touch and go provides a structured way of using attention skillfully, so that we can contact and feel what is arising in our experience with enough precision to note the specific sensations, and with enough distance so that we are not overwhelmed or flooded. In this way we learn to titrate the intensity of experience without avoiding it, following one instant of felt experience with one moment of kind attention. Counselors in training find this is a highly useful skill and one they can apply quite powerfully in session.

One could say that touch and go instruction is a precursor to compassion; but we see it as a compassion practice in itself. It is a way to meet our own feelings with open-ended interest, with kindness and understanding, and with bravery.

Compassion

As we train to be present with our experiences, we gain experiential confidence that we can ground ourselves even in the midst of chaotic situations. The flexibility and resiliency of developing familiarity with our emotions and thought patterns becomes our strength. Then compassion can bloom. The traditional Buddhist image of compassion is a lotus, with its luminous white blossom, its long stem, and its roots deep in the mud at the bottom of the lake. The meaning of this image is that compassion comes from direct contact with suffering. Compassion cannot come from trying to be "a compassionate person." It is only from knowing our own pain that compassion can be discovered. When we know how it feels to lose what we love, we can recognize that pain in others who have lost. Only from knowing the rawness of pain can the healing kindness of compassion arise. That is why the skills of basic presence and bravely abiding with challenging feelings provide such important ground for authentic compassionate response.

Mindfulness Meditation as Compassion Training:
Making Friends with Ourselves
Mindfulness meditation helps us cultivate a kind, attentive attitude toward ourselves. Through simple observation, moment by moment we develop familiarity with the patterns of the body and mind. (In Tibetan, one of the words for meditation is *gom*, meaning familiarity.) We can cultivate the attitude of welcoming whatever arises in each moment.

Every experience is part of human life, and therefore worthy of attention. Recognizing this, we develop a keen interest in the details of the processes of body and mind, and an attitude of trust in our own direct experience, whatever it may reveal. "We develop compassion toward everything that arises in the mind" (Welwood, 1983, p. xiii).

As a result of doing these practices over time, students learn to observe their sensations and the thoughts that arise in conjunction with them. They recognize sensations and thoughts as related, but distinct, phenomena. They begin to notice the difference between having a thought and habitually believing (or identifying with) a thought. This seemingly subtle difference opens up a world of insight that is particularly useful for counselors in training. As they viscerally understand the suffering caused by getting caught in their own negative cycles of thought and feeling, they tend to have less judgment and more compassion for clients who are similarly stuck.

Through repetition, mindfulness meditation can lead to observable changes in attitude and experience. What the Buddhist contemplative tradition discovered and honed with a large repertoire of meditative practices is what neuroscientists now call "experience-dependent neuroplasticity." Paul Gilbert (2009) explains:

> This is called neuroplasticity—cells that are stimulated together and fire together wired up to each other throughout life. So what you focus on, aspire to and practice will make a difference to your brain and that is true for compassion training, too (p. 30).

Eventually mindful awareness and compassion can become new habits, replacing even life-long patterns of denying or rejecting our own suffering and the suffering of others.

Cultivating Compassion

Buddhist practices provide a structure for the seed of compassion to grow strong and resilient. This leads to embodying a new response to pain. Rather than habitually shielding ourselves by contracting away from pain, we can learn to open to the experience of pain and offer warmth, understanding, and kindness in response to suffering.

At Naropa we teach the ancient practices of metta, or loving kindness meditation, and tonglen practice. Compassion meditation techniques traditionally start with reflecting on the suffering of a friend or relative, someone we already care about. In *metta*, the aspirations begin with our own wish for well-being, and then are extended to loved ones and good friends. Gradually, the compassionate response is extended further, to people we feel "neutral" about, those with whom we have conflict, and eventually to "all beings." The fruition of these practices is non-referential compassion, a general sense of radiating compassion in all directions without limit.

Some students, however, hit a wall of resistance as soon as they begin to practice with the aspirations, "May I be happy; May I be free of danger." They report feeling they don't deserve such good wishes, or that just mentioning the word "danger" arouses too much fear. Meditators may experience frustration when such challenges arise, and doubt that they are practicing correctly. Often students tell us that they "aren't good" at or even "can't do" compassion meditation. By this, they mean that they have run into their own resistance: They are experiencing aversion and want to turn away from their discomfort. They are surprised to learn that compassion practices are designed to provoke just these kinds of reactions. Encountering obstacles in compassion meditation is a crucial opportunity to deepen and discover.

In the experience of reaction, we have an opportunity to slow down and contact our fear. Again and again we apply the same logic: as we learn to stay with our fear, we begin to discover our bravery. We can learn to reliably respond to our own fears with understanding and gentleness, and the courage to stay present in the midst of intensity. This is crucial for counseling. If we can't stay with our own discomfort, we won't have much range in offering compassion to others. We will tend to shut down when we, ourselves, feel triggered.

Our challenge as contemplative educators is to create an environment that generally feels safe enough so that these individual experiences of resistance and vulnerability can be openly discussed. Our experience is that to create such an environment the contemplative teacher has to be willing to model the openness and acceptance that we are asking of our students. There is no formula for this kind of pedagogy; rather, it arises as a result of the teachers' practice and the willingness of the students. We find that students are thirsty for this kind of learning environment. It seems to provide enough safety for them to experiment with feeling and tasting aspects of their experience that they might otherwise avoid.

Appreciating what we already have: A self-compassion practice
Many students, even those with years of training in mindfulness meditation, fear attempting traditional compassion practices. They report feeling that they already have too much challenge or trauma in their lives and they don't want to, or cannot, invite more emotional difficulty. In working with this fear we have found it is helpful to begin by first contacting and appreciating the positive aspects of our experience that are available in the present moment.

Rick Hanson (2013) calls this "taking in the good" (p. 62). Hanson points out that we are primed by evolution for a "negativity bias." We recall and pay more attention to negative experience than we do to positive experience. In order to counteract this tendency, we can practice noticing and savoring pleasant experiences and teaching ourselves to take them in. One way to do this is to encourage students to recall moments when they have been the recipients of kindness and compassion. These practices serve to remind students of how powerful it is to receive the kindness or compassion of another person and to motivate them to offer this richness to others.

Instructions for appreciating what we already have. Take a comfortable posture, allowing yourself to feel the sensations of support of your cushion or chair or if lying down, feeling the support of gravity all along your body. Bring to mind an image or memory of something that evokes a positive feeling. For instance, you might think of how good water tastes when you are hot and thirsty; how a child might feel when held by a caring adult; the softness of the fur of your dog or cat; the warmth of the sun on your skin after a cold winter; or how it feels to sit in your favorite spot in nature, supported by the solidity of the earth. Your compassion image might come from your religion or spiritual path: Jesus' love, or Kwan Yin's gaze. Your image might come from your own imagination. Invite your creative mind to freely imagine what compassion might look like, sound like, or feel like. What color is it? Trust the image that arises in your mind.

Allow yourself to relax, opening to and appreciating whatever positive feelings arise. You might imagine healing or love radiating from your compassion image, nourishing you. "As other thoughts or feelings arise, let them be enveloped in this loving luminosity....Trusting this...more than any limiting thoughts of yourself, receive it into your whole being" (Makransky, 2007, pp. 26–27).

Another suggestion is to bring your compassion image to mind during the day, to refresh and remind you of the felt sense of allowing yourself to be nourished by moments of goodness.

Understanding Tonglen

"Tonglen is based on sharing our happiness and accepting pain" (Chodron, 2001, p. 10). It is radical in its suggestion that we can begin to reverse the core process of human struggle. We can question the ingrained habit of trying to hold on to everything desirable, and trying to avoid what is uncomfortable and unwanted. We can observe that, despite the persistence of this habitual way of managing the unpredictability of life, it perpetuates struggle rather than peace.

In tonglen practice, when we encounter difficulty we open toward it, experience it fully for a moment, and feel it as we breathe in. When we experience goodness, we open to and appreciate it, and then we imagine sharing it with others as we breathe out. Breath by breath, we challenge our habitual aversion by expressing our willingness to feel what we normally avoid, and to share the well-being we often try to possess. "In tonglen instead of running from pain and discomfort, we acknowledge them and own them fully....Then the barriers start to dissolve, our hearts and minds begin to open." (Chodron, 2001, p. 4).

At Naropa, counseling students learn the traditional four-stage form of tonglen meditation to gradually train in working with resistance and developing equanimity. They also learn the approach that Pema Chodron calls "tonglen on the spot" (2001, p. 15), bringing the intention of tonglen swiftly and spontaneously into daily life situations.

Tonglen is a challenging but rewarding practice for counselors in training. They often question their willingness to come into relationship with the suffering of their clients, or they may tend to override or bypass their own pain as they try to open to their clients' struggles. This creates an obstacle: Suppressing their own feelings limits their ability to hear and resonate with their clients. When such blockages occur, on-the-spot tonglen can bring them back to authentic connection with themselves and their clients in a single moment.

Instructions for on-the-spot tonglen. Use on-the-spot tonglen in any life situation in which there is conflict, confusion, or suffering. Breathe in any sense of struggle and pain; breathe out, to whoever seems to be suffering, a sense of relief, spaciousness, and well-being. Do this for just one breathing cycle, or many: trust your own sense of what is possible and genuine.

How to include your own struggles in on-the-spot tonglen. Students often report that when they begin to offer compassion to others in their tonglen practice, an overwhelming sense of their own pain arises. Pema Chodron (2001) advises that when our own feelings of grief, fear, and aversion come up in tonglen, it is wise to "shift our focus" (p.38). We shift the focus to ourselves and to anyone else who is struggling as we are. Breathing in, we allow ourselves to feel our own discomfort; breathing out, we extend kindness, understanding, forgiveness, peace toward the struggling part of ourselves. As we continue, we include other beings caught in similar forms of discomfort. In this way tonglen allows us to continually recycle our reactions and use them as fuel for generating compassion. We use own experiences of both well-being and suffering as a link to connect with others. In this sense, compassion does not imply a sense of direction; it radiates wherever it is needed.

Summary of Tonglen

This deceptively simple practice counteracts the ingrained human habit of turning away from what is unwanted. Students regularly report that they surprise themselves by remembering and being willing to apply on-the-spot tonglen, turning toward difficult situations. They find that tonglen makes it possible to stay in contact with their own struggles and their clients' struggles, rather than getting distracted by habits of self-absorption or dissociating.

On-the-spot tonglen gives counselors a tool for cultivating compassion toward themselves and their clients simultaneously. New counselors will, inevitably, make mistakes. Many counseling students describe that the most difficult aspect of their internship year is neither the challenges of the external environment nor their clients; it is their own harsh self-criticism and self-doubt. Their inner commentary, occurring while they are in sessions or later when memories of the day come up, is full of thoughts about their own inadequacy and sense of failure. They report that doing on-the-spot tonglen in their clinical sessions and afterwards helps them to stay engaged, open, and resilient in the midst of pain and struggle. It provides a method for cultivating compassion toward themselves and their clients simultaneously.

The Result of Compassion Meditation Training: What Students Learn

Throughout the semester in the compassion training classes, students write weekly descriptions of their experiences with meditation and contemplative practices. They also keep a journal to record the effects of compassion practice on their clinical work as well as on their mood and behavior in general. At the end of the semester, they write a comprehensive summary about how their relationship to compassion has changed. In 15 years of tracking many hundreds of student responses, we have noticed six overarching themes that emerged from these reports.

Increased Compassionate Response Toward
Themselves in Times of Difficulty

As we mentioned earlier, the intensity and frequency of the students' self-critical thinking is remarkable; most of them report daily occurrences of perfectionist tendencies and the habit of blaming themselves when they make mistakes. As a result of the practices outlined above, many of the students reported increased awareness of their self-aggression during the early learning phases of compassion training. They describe that they see the self-critical thought patterns so clearly that they think at first that they are getting worse. As their compassion practices become more established, however, they describe a gradual increase in self-compassion. The majority of students observed that by the end of the semester they were routinely able to quickly recognize the cycle of self-critical thinking. They reported that following the moment of pattern-recognition, a natural "gap" (moment of cessation of thinking) occurred. In those one- or two-second-long gaps, they were often able to remember to bring their attention to the felt sensations of their bodies. They were able to discern and subjectively feel their uncomfortable vulnerability as direct experience, occurring simultaneously with self-blaming thoughts. They were able to respond with kindness, rather than more self-criticism, toward their own vulnerability. They described themselves as increasingly able to apply the meditative techniques of touch and go or on-the-spot tonglen as methods of holding a compassionate attitude toward their own painful experience. Most significantly, they were able to do so in the midst of challenging situations.

Increased Understanding of the Relationship
between Pain and Compassion

Compassionate response increases when people are able to stay with their experience of suffering, rather than avoiding or rejecting it. Kristin Neff (2011) describes the way that self-compassion leads to emotional resilience.

> The beauty of self-compassion is that instead of *replacing* negative feelings with positive ones, new positive emotions are generated by *embracing* the negative ones. The positive emotions of care and connectedness are felt alongside our painful feelings. When we have compassion for ourselves sunshine and shadow are both experienced simultaneously. (p. 117)

Students described that they first observed this potential in relation to occasional or chronic pain stemming from illness or injuries. They found that the compassion practices made it possible to stay longer with the somatic experience of painful sensations rather than immediately getting absorbed in their repetitive thought patterns of worst-case scenarios, self-doubt, or fantasies. The students reported that as they learn to stay in connection with their pain, a compassionate response often arises without effort. Other students described similar discoveries in relation to emotional pain. In regard to both physical and emotional pain, students reported that when they were able to feel their own pain with compassion, rather than rejecting or denying it, they felt vulnerable but not diminished. They were able think more accurately and creatively about how to handle their pain.

Increased Clarity in Understanding Others

Thupten Jinpa (2015) has observed that compassion training can lead to cognitive reorientation. He and other compassion trainers have repeatedly observed that compassionate responses toward oneself and others, practiced repeatedly over time, become more readily available as spontaneous responses. This can change the way we feel about ourselves and about others. "Changing how we feel about ourselves, about others, and about the world, we reshape the way we perceive ourselves, others, and the world." (p. 207.) Compassion leads to understanding, and understanding increases compassion. Compassion toward oneself liberates compassion toward others and has been shown to positively impact therapy outcomes (Lambert & Barley, 2002; Lambert & Simon, 2008).

Students observe this pattern in their counseling internships. They report that even weekly tonglen-on-the-spot practice directed toward their counseling clients can change their attitudes about their clients. Rather than feeling fear or aversion toward a challenging client, they notice an increase of compassionate responses. This leads to increased inquisitiveness about the clients' experiences and more spontaneity in responding to their clients during counseling sessions.

Greater Sense of Well-being

When we are preoccupied with our own problems—over-thinking and repeatedly strategizing—we feel stressed and burdened. By contrast, when we expand our scope to also caring about others and extending compassion to them, we are no longer isolated in our own personal perspective. Even if we feel discomfort from becoming more aware of others' suffering, we benefit from positive connections with others. We become energized by engaging with others and, when appropriate, working together to address difficult situations.

Jinpa (2015) describes an important difference between empathy—feeling pain in witnessing others' suffering—and compassion—wishing to help relieve suffering.

> Empathy is critical to elicit our compassion, but if we get stuck in the empathy zone, it can be draining, leading to feelings of powerlessness and burnout. Compassion, by contrast, is a more empowered state in which we put our energy into wishing that others be free of suffering, and wanting to do something about it. (p. 189)

Students observe this phenomenon as well. They write that at the end of a day of client appointments they often feel drained or overwhelmed by how much pain they have witnessed. They report that practicing compassionate aspirations for their clients (and themselves) relieves the sense of being overwhelmed. They report that their own state of mind becomes refreshed rather than burdened.

Increased Capacity to Set Appropriate Boundaries

A significant number of students describe being afraid that if they open themselves to compassion, they will become weak. This may be based on the assumption that compassion is a matter of always giving people what they want. This is a misunderstanding of compassion. Authentic compassion arises from seeing a situation clearly and discerning what is needed. With a compassionate outlook, the kindest and most accurate response to a situation may be to say "No." Counselors need to learn how to set and hold compassionate boundaries in order to prevent harm. As a result of compassion training, the students begin to experience the inclusive strength of a compassionate stance. To the extent that we are afraid of suffering, whether our own or the suffering of others, we are controlled by it. When we learn to stay with the experiences of fear and discomfort, we discover a new kind of strength.

Students report that this discovery brings about a deep change in their orientation toward difficult experiences and motivates them to reach out and to help. They describe increasing confidence in setting and holding appropriate boundaries with their clients (Walsh; 2008).

Conclusion

We are delighted to see that compassion training is beginning to be welcomed as a part of counselor training in other programs across the country. Our observation, honed by decades of experience and hundreds of student reports, is that training counselors in this way decreases their stress and increases their willingness to stay in relationship with their clients. We are curious to what extent the effectiveness of these practices impact compassion toward self and other in counselor training. We encourage further research into the various variables, including length of training program, the skill and experience of the teacher, cross-cultural influences, and, specifically, the effects of tonglen. We offer the practice instructions above with the hope that they will be of help to the instructors who take on the challenge of teaching compassion practice to counselor trainees.

References

Beaumont, E., & Martin, C. J. H. (2016). A proposal to support student therapists to develop compassion for self and others through Compassionate Mind Training. *The Arts in Psychotherapy, 50*, 111-118.

Bibeau, M., Dionne, F., Leblanc, J. (2016). Can compassion meditation contribute to the development of psychotherapists' empathy? *Mindfulness 7*, 255–263.

Boellinghaus, I., Jones, F., Hutton, J. (2012). The role of mindfulness and loving-kindness meditation in cultivating self-compassion and other-focused concern in health care professionals. *Mindfulness, 5*, 129–138.

Brown, K., & Ryan R. (2003). The benefits of being present: Mindfulness and its role in psychological well-being. *Journal of Personality and Social Psychology, 84*, 822–848.

Chodron, P. (1991). *The wisdom of no escape: How to love yourself and your world*. Boston, MA: Shambhala Publications.

Chodron, P. (2001). *Tonglen: The path of transformation*. Boston, MA: Shambhala Publications.

Chodron, P. (2012). *Living beautifully with uncertainty and change*. Boston, MA: Shambhala Publications.

Davis, D., Hayes J. (2011). What are the benefits of mindfulness? A practice review of psychotherapy-related research. *Psychotherapy, 48*(2), 198–208.

Felton, T., Coates, L., Christopher, J. (2015). Impact of mindfulness training on counseling students' perceptions of stress. *Mindfulness (6)*, 159–169.

Fredrickson, B. L., Cohn, M. A., Coffey, K. A., Pek, J., & Finkel, S. M. (2008). Open hearts build lives: Positive emotions, induced through loving-kindness meditation, build consequential personal resources. *Journal of Personality and Social Psychology, 95*, 1045–1062.

Fulton C., & Cashwell C., (2015) Mindfulness-based awareness and compassion: Predictors of counselor empathy and anxiety. *Counselor Education and Supervision, 54*(2), 122–133.

Germer, C. K. (2012). Cultivating compassion in psychotherapy. In C. K. Germer & R. D. Siegel (Eds.), *Wisdom and compassion in psychotherapy: Deepening mindfulness in clinical practice* (pp. 93–110). New York, NY: Guilford Press.

Gilbert, P. (2009). Introducing compassion-focused therapy. *Advances in psychiatric treatment. 15*(3). 199-208.

Gilbert, P., & Chodron P. (2014). *Mindful compassion: How the science of compassion can help you understand your emotions, live in the present, and connect deeply with others*. Oakland, CA: New Harbinger.

Hanson, R. (2013). *Hardwiring happiness: The new brain science of contentment, calm, and confidence*. New York, NY: Harmony.

Hutcherson, C. A., Seppala, E. M., & Gross, J. J. (2008). Loving kindness meditation increases social connectedness. *Emotion, 8*, 720–724.

Jazaieri, H., Jinpa, G. T., McGonigal, K., Rosenberg, E. L., Finkelstein, J., Simon-Thomas, E., Cullen, M., Doty, J.R., Gross, J.J., & Goldin, P. R. (2013). Enhancing compassion: A randomized controlled trial of a compassion cultivation training program. *Journal of Happiness Studies*, *14*(4), 1113–1126.

Jinpa, T. (2015). *A fearless heart: How the courage to be compassionate can transform our lives.* New York, NY: Hudson Street Press.

Klimecki, O. M., Leiberg, S., Lamm, C., & Singer, T. (2012). Functional neural plasticity and associated changes in positive affect after compassion training. *Cerebral Cortex*. Advance online publication. doi:10.1093/cercor/ bhs142

Lambert, M. J., & Simon, W. (2008). The therapeutic relationship: Central and essential in psychotherapy outcome. In S. F. Hick & T. Bien (Eds.), *Mindfulness and the therapeutic relationship* (pp. 19–33). New York, NY: Guilford Press.

Lambert, M. J., & Barley, D. E. (2002). Research summary on the therapeutic relationship and psychotherapy outcome. In J. C. Norcross (Ed.), *Psychotherapy relationships that work* (pp. 17–32). New York, NY: Oxford University Press.

Leiberg, S., Klimecki, O., & Singer, T. (2011). Short-term compassion training increases prosocial behavior in a newly developed prosocial game. PLoS ONE, 6(3), e17798. Retrieved from http://www.plosone.org/article/info:doi/10.1371/journal.pone.0017798

Lutz, A., Brefczynski-Lewis, J., Johnstone, T., & Davidson, R. J. (2008). Regulation of the neural circuitry of emotion by compassion meditation: Effects of meditative expertise. PloS ONE, 3(3), e1897. Retrieved from http://www.plosone.org/article/info:doi/10.1371/journal.pone.0001897

Makransky, J. (2007). *Awakening through love: Unveiling your deepest goodness.* Boston, MA: Wisdom Publications.

Mipham, J. (2003). *Turning the mind into an ally.* New York, NY: Riverhead Books.

Mountfield, K. (1979) The Rainbow-Serpent Myth of Australia. In R.. Ira and K. Maddock, (Eds.) *The rainbow serpent: a chromatic piece.* (pp. 23-98). Berlin, Germany: Walter de Gruyter.

Neff, K. (2011). *Self-compassion: The proven power of being kind to yourself.* New York, NY: HarperCollins

Pace, T. W. W., Negi, L. T., Adame, D. D., Cole, S. P., Sivilli, T. I., Brown, T. D., Issa, M., & Raison, C. L. (2009). Effect of compassion meditation on neuroendocrine, innate immune and behavioral responses to psychosocial stress. *Psychoneuroendocrinology*, *34*, 87–98.

Trungap, C. (1976) The myth of freddom and the way of meditation. Boston, MA: Shambhala.

Trungpa, C. (1993). *Training the mind and cultivating loving kindness.* Boston, MA: Shambhala.

Trungpa, C. (2013). *The profound treasury of the ocean of dharma: The path of individual liberation.* Boston, MA: Shambhala.

Trungpa, C. (2015). *Miindfulness in Action: Making friends with yourself through meditation and everyday awareness.* Boston, MA: Shambhala

Walsh, R. A. (2008). Mindfulness and empathy: A hermeneutic circle. In S. F. Hick & T. Bien (Eds.), *Mindfulness and the therapeutic relationship* (pp. 72–86). New York, NY: Guilford Press.

Wegela, K. (2010). *The courage to be present: Buddhism, psychotherapy, and the awakening of natural wisdom.* Boston, MA: Shambhala

Welwood, J. (1983). *Awakening the heart: East/West approaches to psychotherapy and the healing relationship.* Boston, MA: Shambhala

Weng, H. Y., Fox, A. S., Shackman, A. J., Stodola, D. E., Caldwell, J. Z. K., Olson, M. C., Rogers, G. M., & Davidson, R. J. (2013). Compassion training alters altruism and neural responses to suffering. *Psychological Science, 24*(7), 1171–1180.

Chapter 8
Humility and Humanity: Contemporary Perspectives on Healthcare Chaplaincy

Elaine Yuen

Transpersonal theory embraces plurality, complexity, transformation, the known, and the unknown. In this way, almost all of contemporary chaplaincy is a transpersonal endeavor. Our work is filled with individuals and families in transition, miracles and medical realities, the singular person and the larger community: the spirit, the body, and the mind.

While I teach Buddhist-inspired chaplaincy students, we work to be familiar with world faith traditions, as well as to be grounded in Buddhist teachings and practices. We study a wide variety of indigenous and Judeo–Christian beliefs and practices and address contemporary secular positions from agnostic to nihilism.

The story of the Gautama Buddha's decision to seek a spiritual path is a transpersonal journey that occurred millennia before such a word as *transpersonal* existed. When he left the sanctuary of his parents' grounds, he encountered suffering in the forms of birth, old age, sickness, and death. This inspired him not to retreat to the comforts of his home, but rather he set out on a path of investigation. He studied and practiced all the scientific and spiritual traditions of his time, and finally landed on meditation as a way to be with what truly is in the world and inside ourselves. He moved to go beyond himself and extend to transform others and the world. His first teaching, *The Four Noble Truths*, is an investigation of suffering, its cause, cessation, and ultimately, how to work with it in our lives.

While some may think of transpersonal theory as ignoring or going beyond suffering, in truth, the transpersonal view, like Buddhism, is rooted in the realities of our painful existence. We may reach for higher meaning and purpose, but never escape the inevitable pain, sickness, and death of existence. In fact, a large part of chaplaincy practice focuses on the topics of Buddha's teachings: birth, sickness, old age and death; transformation and transition; empathy and compassion; and skillful means for working with others.

This truth of suffering existed long before Buddha and persists well after his death. Our contemporary times allow suffering to be more evident than ever. Consider, for example, the following: Through the internet, which broadcasts worldwide news in an instantaneous manner, we encounter stories of sickness and death, wars, and destruction from conflicts around the globe, replete with pictures, videos, and first-person accounts.

At this time, we might well ask how spiritual and religious organizations can provide service and care that might address this pervasive suffering. In this chapter, I would first like to consider basic values regarding suffering; and then contemplate how a transpersonal, Buddhist-inspired healthcare chaplaincy might provide spiritual care to patients, families, and healthcare staff in our contemporary lives.

Contemporary Challenges to Pastoral Care and Chaplaincy

Chaplaincy, often referred to as pastoral care in Western medical settings, has been framed as an inter-disciplinary practice that bridges religion, spirituality, and human suffering.

> As both insiders and outsiders to health care institutions, professional chaplains reside at the boundary between hospital care and the religious communities we represent. Life at this boundary presents chaplains with a responsibility to facilitate the complex negotiation of religious and spiritual pluralism present among patients, families, health care clinicians, and the wider community. (Beachy, 2013)

Pastoral care draws its imagery from that of shepherds watching over and guiding the sheep that have been entrusted to them for their care and well-being. Similarly, in healthcare settings, chaplains are often the guides of spiritual care and shepherding patients' well-being. This role of guide seeks to lead *from behind* rather than setting an agenda for patients and families to follow. In this context, chaplaincy skills draw foremost upon curiosity and listening to specific needs and longings, sometimes unspoken or hidden in emotions and family dynamics. Patients who are ill must often face difficult clinical decisions with uncertain outcomes. Transpersonal practices have the ability to articulate this uncertainty by providing a context in which anxieties may be faced, felt, and understood. These understandings may support increased clarity about factual and emotional content in clinical decisions. Key to spiritual practice is the inclusion of the *unknown* or *liminal space* within the clinical encounter. In healthcare encounters, we often deny we are standing at the threshold of the unknown (Yuen, 2011).

An additional factor is that the contemporary world encountered by a chaplain is extremely diverse—not only in the sense of racial and ethnic differences but also along dimensions of religious tradition, social and economic status, profession, among others. Individuals who request pastoral care may have many different streams of cultural identities flowing through them: They may be African-American, practice yoga and know Sanskrit, and also attend Christian church services on Sundays. Encounters may be additionally complicated by expectations of what medical care may entail and what goals it strives to achieve. What might this spiritual care-giving look like in the face of diversity? The challenge at hand is to bring the relevance of a transpersonal Buddhist-inspired training together with the needs of an increasingly diverse society.

Traditional Buddhist Perspectives

Educational goals of a transpersonal Buddhist chaplaincy program might include academic study of traditional teachings, as well as a well-grounded personal practice and field training so that theological understandings may be digested and applied to real-world encounters (Kinst, 2012).

The Four Noble Truths' teachings on suffering provide chaplains a ground of understanding for their patient encounters, and in contemplation have the possibility to deepen their theological understanding of what the Buddha himself encountered. The last of The Four Noble Truths is the Eightfold Path, which provides practical guideposts for how a chaplain might navigate this complicated contemporary world (Hirsch, 2012). Each aspect of the Eightfold Path is described as being completely realized (samyak). In particular, the three factors of right, or complete, ethics (speech, action, livelihood) provide a sensibility of how one might contextualize one's position as a chaplain. Right (complete) effort, mindfulness, and concentration support chaplaincy and pastoral care activities and provide the moment-to-moment ability to simply be with whatever is arising.

Developing compassion is also important in the care of self and others in these challenging times. An understanding of compassion acknowledges the fact of an awakened kernel, or Bodhicitta[1] (awakened heart) that is present in all living beings. In a multicultural world, it is this Bodhicitta that allows us to share our humanity and care for one another. In navigating our multicultural differences, Bodhicitta may be discovered (like a seed in the mud), as it is often obscured by our conflicting thoughts and emotions. Acknowledgement of this seed of enlightenment, this kernel of compassion and caring, is in itself a step in the right direction—the ability to nurture this seed through adversity and complexity. The traditional Buddhist analogy is that the seed of enlightenment is nurtured by the manure of experience and grows out of the mud into a beautiful lotus. Similarly, our kernel of Bodhicitta may be nurtured (and composted) by the adversities of our experience to blossom fully into the service of others (Berlin, 2012).

---

[1] There are alternate spellings of Bodhicitta.

Buddhist-Inspired Interfaith Chaplaincy

In the United States, approximately 70% of the population self-identifies as being Christian, and less than 4% percent as Buddhist (Pew Religious Landscape Study, 2016). However in my practice of chaplaincy, a personal understanding of the teachings of Buddhism served as a stable base from which to offer compassion to others in times of crisis, and in these clinical environments, the expressions of compassion and empathetic understandings of suffering were mediated by the context and culture of the 21st century.

The interfaith aspect of the hospital chaplaincy means working with Bodhicitta, the heart of wakefulness, expressed in a myriad of ways: through liturgy, belief systems, and culture. When I first encounter patients in the hospital, they often do not have the inner resources to have a discussion about Buddhism or meditation; for many it seemed exotic. Rather, I use this opportunity to look for the Bodhicitta in the situation, often asking about them, their family, sports, whatever makes them feel open and more relaxed, trying to find what we simply have in common as human beings. A good prayer often grows from that point of connection to basic humanity, emanating from a shared feeling into words that may be framed as a prayer.

I have continued to offer this connection to Bodhicitta to the many people I meet within the different healthcare contexts. I've taught meditation to blind people as a way for them to cope and understand their disability, as well as to appreciate life. In working with them I realized how many of our images and analogies for meditation have to do with sight (clarity, brilliance of mind). One day, after a short meditation session, I asked what it was like for them. One of the young black women enthusiastically responded, "Mm-mm, it was so smooth, just like a peppermint patty!" I also started a meditation support group for the medical students at the hospital. Many of them are interested in meditation as a stress reduction technique, as the medical literature documents the physical and mental health benefits of sitting meditation.

On an inner level, for me as a Buddhist, the chaplaincy training constantly helped me to see *The Four Noble Truths* and appreciate how the Buddha himself was inspired to begin his spiritual path by seeing old age, sickness, and death. It has been very visceral and immediate, and has provided a tremendous ground for my personal practice.

One encounter that embodies both presence and compassion was with an elderly, early-stage Alzheimer's patient who had been admitted to the Emergency Department (ED) for evaluation after a fall. She did not know why she was there, and her body was very tense. It was an unfamiliar environment for her. Her husband had been there earlier, but since it was 11 p.m. he had gone home. She had been admitted in the early afternoon. She did not recognize me as someone from Pastoral Care or even know what that role might be. The doctors and nurses came and went; there was hallway noise outside the ED curtain

I stayed with her, talking in a soothing voice and telling her that "it was okay" as I held her hand. I stayed a long time, about an hour, allowing her body to relax. As I did this, I also explored how my own felt emotional and somatic experience could meet hers, how I could experience her suffering but also experience the potential liberation, or at least relaxation, within the moment.

There is always a recognizable and felt *sacred* moment (Pargament, Lomax, McGee, & Fang, 2014) that I regard as a signal for the completion of a pastoral encounter. Pastoral care providers and chaplains are often called to chaotic situations, be they emotional, physical, or cognitive. In walking with these situations, chaplains seek to uncover the Bodhicitta, the kernel of compassionate heart, that is nevertheless present. Unpacking this aspect is often the simple offering of acceptance and space. In this situation, I was present for and with her, without an agenda. There was also a non-verbal recognition of our shared Bodhicitta—and of the compassion that arose from that connection: I simply stayed and was caring for her.

So What About the Buddhist Patients?

I have been the Buddhist chaplain on call in a large, tertiary care teaching hospital, which meant that the other chaplains called me when patients requested a Buddhist liturgy or could appreciate a Buddhist sensibility. I have been called to attend ethnically Asian Buddhist families, as well as middle-aged Caucasian intellectuals. These different kinds of people reflect the Buddhist demographic in the United States. Although there are an estimated 300 to 360 million Buddhists in the world (6% of the population), over 99% of Buddhists live in Asia. Of the estimated million in the United States, 61% are Asian and 32% white. Buddhism is one of the fastest growing religions in the United States; there has been a 170% increase in the last 10 years, mostly among the educated, middle class (Adherents.com, 2005).

It is not a surprise that many calls I have had as the Buddhist chaplain have been to tend to Asian families. My first call for a Buddhist patient was for a Vietnamese family whose grandmother died suddenly in the medical intensive ICU. Her extended family was in the waiting room, waiting for the monk from their temple to arrive. They kept the picture of the Buddha I gave them with her body as she was transferred first to the morgue then to the funeral home. For another Chinese family, I read the Heart Sutra (in English) aloud before they removed life support from the body of the husband, who had been badly injured and was brain dead since an automobile accident years before.

I have also worked with Buddhists from Western *sanghas*. There was the 22-year-old artist and actress with lung cancer whose funeral at the Shambhala center was attended by a large number of grief-stricken friends as well as her parents. I visited her and her family in the hospital and comforted them as options for medical treatments were exhausted. Her father, himself a Lutheran minister, found solace in a traditional Tibetan Buddhist *Sukhavati* ceremony, and even requested that we perform the 49th day ceremony from the *Tibetan Book of the Dead* as well.

Not all of my Buddhist patients have been near death. I brought Buddhist books to a middle-aged man who had to be treated in the bone marrow transplant unit for several weeks. He died of complications of cancer several years later, after we had shared more ordinary times together such as getting together for a meal with his wife. I was called to his apartment in his last hours, was with him when he died, and officiated his funeral.

A Reflection on Practice

Clinical practice as a healthcare chaplain has demanded a twofold perspective: to allow the felt sense of Bodhicitta to emerge, both in myself and the other, as well as between us, and subsequently to investigate how, through what words, gestures, and intentions, I might address the suffering, concerns, and difficulties at hand. In my years as part of a team of interfaith chaplain-interns at the tertiary care hospital in downtown Philadelphia, I provided support for the spiritual and emotional care of patients. I was on call approximately once a month, responding to calls from the nursing floors as well as to emergencies, and making the rounds in the many intensive care units of the hospital. In addition to our on-call time, we also had supervision meetings where the chaplains in my internship group got together and discussed patient cases, interweaving our discussions with theological perspectives. I was often the only Buddhist in the group of chaplains. Most of the others were Christian and reflected the diverse demographic of a large urban area that ranged from Catholic to black Baptist. Very few of the people there that I cared for were Buddhist.

On an inner level, this activity constantly helped me to understand the basic teachings of Buddhism: *The Four Noble Truths* as vivid reminders of birth, old age, sickness, and death. This reminder was very visceral and immediate, felt within my body and emotions. It also provided a tremendous ground for my personal practice. However, when I interacted with patients, I found it was often not the time to have a discussion about Buddhist teachings or meditation since they rarely had sufficient inner resources to learn about a topic they knew nothing of. Rather I used this opportunity to look for the Bodhicitta, or awakened heart, in the situation and in them—to almost feel it out and then to express with words from that point of connection to Bodhicitta. There was a continual exploration and contemplation of "What is the Bodhicitta that resides in all beings?" and "How can that be expressed in a meaningful way to this particular person?"

When the Buddha achieved enlightenment, he touched the earth, proclaiming the "earth is my witness." Following his example, as

Buddhist chaplains and pastoral caregivers, we too, touch the earth—
this worldly phenomenon of the 21st century, replete with technology,
advanced medications, and many distractions. It is on this earth that we
aspire to serve completely.

References

Adherents.com. (2005). Major religions ranked by size. Retrieved 4/8/2016
    from http://www.adherents.com/Religions_By_Adherents.html
Beachy, J. (2013, Winter). Paging God in the halls of medicine. *The Journal of
    Pastoral Theology 23*(2), 101–105.
Berlin, C. (2012). Widening the circle: Engaged Bodhichitta in hospital
    chaplaincy. In C. A. Giles & W. B. Miller, (Eds.), *The arts of contemplative
    care* (pp. 81–92). Summerville, MA: Wisdom Publications.
Hirsch, T. J. (2012). The Four Noble Truths as a framework for contemplative
    care. In C. A. Giles & W. B. Miller, (Eds.), *The arts of contemplative care*
    (pp. 55–62). Summerville, MA: Wisdom Publications.
Kinst, D. J. (2012). Educational foundations for Buddhist chaplains and pastoral
    care providers. In C. A. Giles & W. B. Miller, (Eds.), *The arts of
    contemplative care* (pp. 9–16). Summerville, MA: Wisdom Publications.
Pargament, K. I., Lomax, J. W., McGee, J. S., & Fang, Q. (2014). Sacred moments in
    psychotherapy from the perspectives of mental health providers and
    clients: Prevalence, predictors, and consequences. *Spirituality in Clinical
    Practice 1*(4), 248–262. http://www.pewforum.org/religious-
    landscape-study/
Pew Religious Landscape Study. (2016,). Retrieved April 8, 2016 from
    http://www.pewforum.org/religious-landscape-study/
Yuen, E. J. (2011). Spirituality and the clinical encounter. *International Journal
    of Human Caring, 15*(2), 42–45.

Chapter 9
Musings on the Connections between Integrative Psychiatry and Transpersonal Psychology

Scott Shannon

Many afternoons of my life I sit in my bright and sunny office while people tell me of their struggles. I listen, ask questions, and listen some more. What is the source of their suffering? What will be their path to healing? The avenues that I explore in this adventure of curiosity and intimacy include: family biological history, developmental trajectory, addictive patterns, experiences of oppression or privilege, current relationships, family-of-origin dynamics, biochemistry, diet, cognitive function, work life, sexuality, distorted belief systems, spirituality, and a range of other topics. The tools I employ in this quest toward increased health might include meditation, medication, supplements, diet, acupuncture, psychotherapy, and plain old common sense. As an integrative psychiatrist, I try to comprehend, as broadly as possible, the whole of a person. No small task.

As conceptualized by most in my profession, my first challenge involves establishing a Diagnostic and Statistical Manual of Mental Disorders (5th, ed.; DSM-5; American Psychiatric Association, 2013) diagnosis. I find the superficial phenomenology of a focus on symptoms and the pathological orientation of the DSM-5 to be much too limiting and crude. I envision the people I am sitting with and my tasks as much larger. Clearly, my assessment must incorporate intrinsic human spirituality. Where are the transpersonal elements? How does all of this link to mental health? What is mental health?

Why, indeed, am I writing this? I hope to deepen the understanding about how integrative/holistic psychiatry connects to transpersonal psychology. First, let us start with the definition of transpersonal psychology. For this chapter I use the well-formulated definition from Hartelius, Rothe, and Roy (2013), that the transpersonal is "a transformative psychology of the whole person in intimate relationship with an interconnected and evolving world; it pays special attention to self-expansive states as well as to spiritual, mystical, and other exceptional human experiences that gain meaning in such a context" (p. 14).

Areas of Further Expansion for Psychology, Psychiatry, and Transpersonal Approaches

Generally speaking, Western psychological thought has been disconnected from the body—the ground of being and consciousness. If we are to consider the whole person, any complete theory must include our understanding about how the protean influences upon the body/brain, and thus mental states, stand as central to how we connect to the world. A psychology is crucial, but not sufficient, to deepen understanding about our context in this world at large. We must fully embrace the physical realm to reach an ecologically sound perspective.

In addition, the transpersonal view attempts to reduce the bias and limitations found in our typical waking egocentric experience of the world. Our shared Western cultural understanding is built on a view of existence that defines each of us as separate, unique, and personal. This helps us to form an identity, develop a personality, hold opinions, experience emotions, and suffer. The transpersonal perspective corrects some of the limitations found in an ego-centric model but could still go further to correct some of our inherent bias.

One could offer an analogy that the transpersonal perspective is similar to the emergence of the ecological model in the 1960s and 1970s. The ecological model in biological science was breaking new ground and represented a major advance on the prior models of biology that did not recognize the primacy of interconnection and interdependence. It dramatically expanded and enhanced our contextual view of the world as an integrated whole rather than as a dissociated collection of parts (for an excellent discussion of this topic see *The Web of Life*, Capra, 1996). However, soon the ecological model recognized some inherent limitations.

The Norwegian philosopher Arne Naess elaborated on the concept of deep ecology in the 1970s (Devall & Sessions, 1985, p. 74). *Shallow* ecology represents a human-centered or anthropocentric conceptualization. *Deep* ecology does not separate out humans (or anything else) from the natural environment. It honors the intrinsic value of all life and recognizes humans as merely one strand in the greater web of life. Likewise, a major shortcoming of some transpersonal models is expressed in the anthropocentric perspective that distracts from and limits our broader understanding.

If we acknowledge this inherent bias, it opens many doors. This may seem like a minor point but it actually creates a wide range of implications for our transpersonal experiences, our spirituality, and ultimately our healing by moving them to the broader web-of-life perspective. It comes as no surprise that transpersonal psychology is based on the primacy of individual consciousness.

In a deep ecological perspective, the primacy of individual consciousness is replaced with a sense of the vast connections that link us to the *all else*. Fritjof Capra (1996) in his seminal book, *The Web of Life*, states it eloquently: "Ultimately deep ecological awareness is spiritual or religious awareness. When the concept of the human spirit is understood as the mode of consciousness in which the individual feels a sense of belonging, a connectedness to the cosmos as a whole it becomes clear that ecological awareness is spiritual in its deepest sense." (p. 7)

Perhaps the greatest implication of this deep ecological awareness lies in how we come to understand an individual's consciousness, brain, or body. We must embrace a radically different understanding of the individual's struggles that cannot be assessed in isolation from the greater context. Holism pushes us to consider the whole person: body, mind, and spirit. The integrative model, in both psychiatry and transpersonal psychology, encourages a broader frame of contextual treatments (social, spiritual, environmental, educational, etc.). As Paul Roy has defined the transpersonal:

> Transpersonal studies is a whole-person, transformative approach to human existence and human experience that includes the spiritual and transcendent as well as the social and community dimensions of human life, all within the context of the global eco-system in which we live. (Hartelius et al., 2013, p. 9)

The ecological model widens our understanding even further to include the vast interconnected and interdependent reality that we are immersed in. The deep ecological model takes the focus off our human experience and importance, instead refocusing on all the nodes in the vast linked system to provide a true context. The ultimate consequence of the deeper perspective shifts the description of a typical transpersonal event from self-expansive and supra-ordinary to one of artificial barrier elimination that is natural and corrective.

> As an integrative/holistic pursuit, transpersonal psychology examines the phenomena of psyche as elements that belong not merely to the ego, but to larger contexts as well: the living body in its entirety, the therapeutic relationship, the social and ecological situation, or the greater-than-human matrix of existence. (Hartelius et al., 2013, p.5)

Issues with Psychiatry

Once we have this operational structure in place, then psychiatry, mental illness, and mental health all take on a radically new meaning in this light. Conventional psychiatry must move beyond its current reductionist model to embrace something that respects the broadest systems of human reality. George Engel's (1977) biopsychosocial model from the 1960s and 1970s provided a reasonable starting place for a true systems approach, but it remains too narrow in scope and mostly ignored in actual practice. Currently, the ecological model that expands on holistic medicine and integrative psychiatry offers us the science of ecology to model our understanding and expand our view about how life connects with the broader universe.

From this ecological viewpoint, mental illness as currently defined seems almost comically limited in scope. We blame the person and blame the brain ("chemical imbalance") by conceptualizing the person in complete separation from their context (ecosystem). The recent findings in epigenetics and neuroplasticity force us to embrace the exquisitely reactive and responsive nature of the person to their environment. Human genetics and the human brain have developed over millions of years as part of the web of life, and these basic operating principles must form our ground. We simply cannot have an honest or scientifically valid view of human functioning (health or illness) without embracing our ecological context.

The current psychiatric perspective of mental illness is based on a narrow phenomenological view that only describes pathology. If you review all of the current psychiatric textbooks, which I have done, you will see that none of them offer any discussions or models of mental health. Conventional psychiatry has no workable model of mental health. This is a grave, grave limitation. Without a workable definition of mental health, a wide range of transpersonal experiences can be, and often are, viewed as pathological and not more accurately seen as health-promoting or evolutionary. Without an ecological perspective, there is no way to grasp the context or meaning of these experiences in our current psychiatric frame. Because transpersonal experiences will often fall outside of the ordinary, they will frequently default to the pathological in an illness-based paradigm such as conventional psychiatry. It is sad, but one of the time-honored sociological imperatives for my profession involves policing threats to our status quo (Francis, 2014; Szasz, 1961; Whitaker, 2010).

Health and Wholeness
We must shift our exploration if we are to discover a deeper and more satisfying understanding of what mental health represents. We must

explore and consider the concept of health if we are to be able to understand mental health. While there are other characteristics of living systems (boundaries, flow of energy, etc.), these four tenets help to create a foundation for the concept of health (and thus mental health):

1.   Seek and maintain balance (homeostasis)
2.   Express the potential within (full expression)
3.   Monitor a flow of information (intelligence)
4.   Move to higher levels of order (transformation)

Homeostasis

Health is a characteristic of all living organisms. Ecosystems also express many characteristics of health as they are but integrated, nesting hierarchies of living systems. Health reflects a tendency to seek and maintain internal order. Health moves against the tendency of the nonliving universe to move to disorder (entropy/thermodynamics). In the physical body, this principle of internal order is called homeostasis. For example, our blood maintains an exquisitely balanced ph of 7.41 in spite of how much highly acidic cola or kombucha we drink. A living system creates and maintains internal order.

While all medical textbooks describe homeostasis on the physical level, this principle occurs on all levels of living systems. We can describe homeostasis on a mental, emotional, or spiritual level as part of our capacity to deal with disruptive challenges, or stresses. This resilience to stress highlights the power of living systems to overcome the disruptive challenge.

Full Expression

Aristotle described the principle of *entelechy*, or self-completion, over 2,300 years ago. Self-completion, according to Aristotle, is the realization of innate potential through development and functioning. Acorns become oaks and tadpoles become frogs. A human embryo matures into an adult. For Aristotle, this drive to self-completion carries such power that only a few things short of death or severe trauma can derail it. Truly, it is nothing short of miraculous that in spite of the forces of entropy and disorder and the many disrupting variables facing development and functioning, life continues to develop and find completion.

Many centuries later, in his novel studies of the psyche, Jung expounded on a principle similar to that of Aristotle's. He called it the process of *individuation*. "In general, it is the process by which individual beings are formed and differentiated [from other human beings]; in particular, it is the development of the psychological individual as a being distinct from the general, collective psychology" (Jung, 2014, para. 757). Jung saw individuation as the innate drive of biological organisms to reach completion on all levels of being—mental, physical, and spiritual. This completion, according to Jung, occurs through self-correcting and self-organizing mechanisms inherent to life, such as healing and maturation. In fact, dreams, for Jung, are the subconscious mechanism by which the mind heals, matures, restores order, and, eventually, reaches completion.

In similar fashion, Abraham Maslow (1971) understood development as the process by which the latent potential of the mental, emotional, and spiritual spheres become a reality This final reality, then, was a mental, emotional, and spiritual wholeness resembling Jung's (2014) individuation and Aristotle's (c. 350 B.C.E.) completeness. According to Maslow, the real work of the clinician is "to help (the patient) to be more perfectly what they already are, to be more full, more actualizing, more realizing, in fact what they are in potentiality" (page). Potential, for Maslow, is essential to the very fabric of the human. And, for that reason, one of the human's most basic drives is to reach its potential.

Whether they call it self-completion, individuation, or the actualization of potential, all of these great thinkers, in their own way, described the process by which humans become complete, healthy, whole people. Often this involves a creative medium to allow the full extent of our inner world to be expressed. *Full-expression* offers another term for how this stands as an integral component of health.

While our drive to express our innate potential is personal and unique, it also extends beyond our person. As an interconnected member of the living universe, we also move to fulfill the needs of the broader system. So, our life purpose is interwoven with the needs of the community of all beings, sentient and non-sentient. The less we are limited by our own narrow needs, the more likely we are able to sense the greatest good served by our talents and skills. This in turn spurs the fullest expression of our being.

Intelligence

All living systems display intelligence; each responds or interacts with their environment to maintain life and survive. Varela, Thompson, and Rosch (1991) described *embodied cognition* as the flow of information within a living system. Consciousness or mind can be viewed as an epiphenomenon created by this flow of information. Mind is process, not a thing. From single-celled protozoa to jellyfish to dolphins to humans, all life creates a flow of information through a reactive living system. The response or change created as part of life reflects the most basic component of intelligence. We are now realizing that many other systems possess intelligence. For example, our immune system displays many elements of intelligence without involving our nervous system. Plants also display a simple intelligence free of any nervous system.

Biologists have described for decades the innate intelligence of the beehive. My wife is a beekeeper, and it is simply staggering to witness 50,000 bees coordinating their work as a unified collective intelligence. There is no central command. Bees simply fill the exact role needed at the time for the survival of the hive. Taken from this hub of activity they are lost; placed back in the hive and they immediately fill a role as needed. The hive operates as a single living organism and is intelligent, but without any descriptor or mechanism to make that happen. Numerous other examples exist of this collective intelligence in other insect and animal communities (Bonabeau, Dorigo, & Theraulaz, 2000).

Transformation

More than simply maintaining order, living systems also move to higher levels of order and complexity. Ilya Prigogine, a Belgian chemist, won the Nobel Prize in 1977 for his description of *dissipative* structures. These are chemical systems that allow for modeling of complex interactions.

When a new source of energy enters an open system, the first response is disorder. Slowly, the system begins to reorganize and ultimately moves to a higher level of order and complexity. These self-organizing systems appear to represent a fundamental process for all living systems, the bedrock for energetic transformations. This is a process we frequently witness occurring in people. Difficult experiences, grief, stress, failures, and the like can compound to create a personal transformation that astounds. Transpersonal experiences can also supply the high level of energetic input needed to disrupt the personal status quo and reorganize the person's very being.

In this model, the disruptive input of information/energy that arises with transpersonal experiences often creates a movement to a higher level of order. The person is radically changed by the experience. Employing the deep ecological conceptualization to this process, the change that occurs is not limited to just the mental realm; the whole being is changed. Rather than viewing this experience as a personal and internal catalyst for change, the deep-ecological model would posit that the opening of awareness to the deeper interconnection significantly increases the flow of information through the system/person, reflective of higher intelligence/order and, more accurately, greater resonance with all that is. This transformative process can also be described as a higher level of health or enhanced ecological connection, and thus greater resilience for the future.

Wholeness

If we examine all four of these principles together, we can begin to see a deeper, more comprehensive model for health. A discussion of health that includes these four elements (homeostasis, full expression, intelligence, and transformation) defines a more complete and full expression of well-being that I have called wholeness. Wholeness integrates the ability to display resilience and resistance to stress. It also incorporates the inner urgency to move to full expression as able, making best use of our talents and skills in our given context. Wholeness mandates the full utilization of our native intelligence, or inner wisdom.

We might have a gut feeling about what our soundest choice would be when dealing with crucial decisions or options. Animals display specific appetite, knowing which food options will correct inherent nutrient deficiencies. Finally, our wholeness moves us in the direction of positive transformation if we allow self-awareness to grow and develop. All of these facets together describe the innate self-healing, self-expressing, and self-transforming capacity that can evolve our well-being—the innate process of wholeness. We are born whole and can recapture this power of healing if we lose sight of it. This is synonymous with transpersonal psychology's concept of inherent wholeness and health (Davis, 2003).

Mental Health and Illness

Once we more deeply grasp the basic tenets of health, it becomes much easier to define mental illness. Mental illness can be described as significant unresolved imbalance(s) within the individual in any, or any combination of, primary realms (environmental, physical, emotional, mental, social, or spiritual). This imbalance could be a toxic load of mercury, a deficiency of iron, a sexual trauma in childhood, social isolation, or oppression, gross materialism, etc. The options for the specific imbalance are legion, but many common patterns exist that we observe commonly as practitioners. This is where training and experience help to support our guiding wisdom as we provide care to another suffering individual. We can also confirm the struggle for mental health when we observe significant limitations in the ability to find full expression, a decrease in the ability to tap into native intuition, or an increased tendency for the person to become stuck in more limited patterns of understanding.

More than by identifying specific symptom patterns, mental health struggles are better defined by the limited ability to grow and move past prior struggles. As long as I see a person evolving in their process with new and different symptoms and a dogged determination to find new awareness, I feel much more hopeful about the prognosis. Health is an active process. Illness is better defined by stagnation and rigidity. Health seeks a balance within an active process or linkages.

In the deep-ecological model, a disconnection from the Source, the creative web of life, becomes a powerful agent for deep malaise that will be unresponsive to a wide range of interventions. One of the basic principles of integrative psychiatry tells us that we must treat the root cause of ecological imbalance. Giving this person who has become disconnected from our source large amounts of fluoxetine (Prozac) is misguided and of limited value in this circumstance because it delays and distracts from the core needs. Ideally, a practitioner might help a suffering individual to develop greater awareness and come to more acceptance to strengthen their resonance with their web of life. This is how I see a transpersonal intervention, as one that will impact through the entire being: body, mind, and spirit. It will support their wholeness and thus their health on all levels. In the frame of integrative psychiatry, we must understand and appreciate the unique person in front of us comprehensively if we are to be of value. Superficial control of symptoms becomes a last resort as it rarely improves health in a deeper sense. Both integrative psychiatry and transpersonal psychology agree that exploring the root causes and establishing strong links creates our best chance for success in our shared work to support mental health.

Transpersonal psychology may align well with integrative psychiatry in another sense. Both paradigms appreciate that expansive, mystical, or spiritual experiences can catalyze deep healing. The mechanism is not psychotherapeutic insight, the interpretation of transference, or remodeling cognitive distortions. The mechanism does not involve dopamine receptors or the correction of a chemical imbalance. One could argue the details, but the model appears to rely on an energetic input elevating the system to a higher level of order/complexity. The inherent intelligence of the living system at its most primal typically operates free of cognitive processing. We do not need to process a transpersonal experience or "understand it" for it to create healing.

In my 30-plus years of practice, I have been profoundly impressed by the power of spiritual/transpersonal events to transform and eliminate "psychiatric illness" or "psychological disorders." This process provides a rough sketch illuminating the nature of healing. While the correction of a nutritional deficit or a cognitive distortion may improve the health of an individual, it will not redirect or reorganize the overall organism on a different path. It does not, by itself, move the individual to a higher level of purpose or order in the greater scheme of things.

The spiritual/transpersonal realm offers the most powerful tool we have available to move someone to a higher level of resonance in the web of life. Actually, using a non-egocentric, non-anthropocentric model, the web of life moves into greater resonance as another individual node achieves greater connection. How do we describe the positive energetic input that carries the links to our web of life and the ability to heal a life so profoundly? We could call it corrective intelligence. We could call it a transpersonal transformation. We could call it the intelligence of the universe. I prefer to call it love—that which connects, heals, and empowers.

This is the nature of healing; this is our task. We all benefit.

References

American Psychiatric Association. (2013). *Diagnostic and statistical manual of mental disorders* (5th ed.). Washington, DC: Author.

Bonabeau, E., Dorigo, M., & Theraulaz, G. (2000). Inspiration for optimization from social insect behaviour. *Nature, 406*(6791), 39-42.

Capra, F. (1996). *The web of life.* New York, NY: Anchor Books.

Davis, J. (2003). An overview of transpersonal psychology. *The Humanistic Psychologist, 31,* 6–21.

Devall, B., & Sessions, G. (1985). *Deep ecology.* Salt Lake City, Utah: Peregrine Smith.

Engel, G. L. (1977). The need for a new medical model: A challenge for biomedicine. *Science, 196,* 129–136.

Frances, A. (2014). *Saving normal: An insider's revolt against out-of-control psychiatric* diagnosis, *DSM-5,* big pharma, and the medicalization of ordinary life. New York, NY: William Morrow.

Hartelius, G., Rothe, G., & Roy, J. (2013). A brand from the burning: Defining transpersonal psychology. In H. L. Friedman & G. Hartelius (Eds.), *The Wiley-Blackwell handbook of transpersonal psychology* (1st ed., pp. 3–22). West Sussex, UK: John Wiley & Sons.

Jung, C. G. (2014). *The Collected Works.* Princeton, NJ: Princeton University Press.

Maslow, A. (1971). *The further reaches of human nature.* New York, NY: Viking

Varela, F. J., Thompson, E., & Rosch, E. (1991). The embodied mind: Cognitive science and human experience. Cambridge, MA: MIT Press.

Szasz, T. (1961). *The myth of mental illness: Foundations of a theory of personal conduct.* New York, NY: Harper.

Whitaker, R. (2010). *Mad in America: Bad science, bad medicine, and the enduring mistreatment of the mentally ill.* New York, NY: Basic Books.

Chapter 10
A Transpersonal Approach to Service-Learning:
A Call to Right Action

Sue Wallingford[1]

The hot Eastern sun descends, giving way to the warmth of the evening's full moon. Lightning etches the night sky, and the stars scatter like a throw of glitter. Taking our hands one by one, our guide, Yorn, ushers us into the turquoise-and-coral-painted boat that will take us to our final destination, where we will pay reverence to our last night together. In quiet anticipation we squeeze together on the weathered wooden bench, holding handmade banana-leaf luminaries.

Water gently laps the side of the boat. It agitates faint glimmers of bioluminescence and reflected night sky. Yorn pushes us from the dock and starts the motor; slowly we putter along the river's edge. In the distance we catch a glimpse of small flickering lights, beckoning to us in a sea of darkness. We draw closer. Yorn shuts the motor off and slowly we drift, until, like pushing through an invisible field, we gently bump the shore. A silent explosion of light fills the sky, disrupting the synchronized blinking we had marveled at only seconds before. Fireflies everywhere. They scatter like a burst of confetti, dispersing and gathering again like one single beautiful organism—that for just a moment we are a part of.

One by one we light the candle in our little luminaries and gently place them on the water's surface. We watch as the river floats them toward the firefly tree. Sitting in silence for what seems like hours, we delight in the wonderment of the moments received.

---

[1] The author would like to thank the many individuals we were able to collaborate with in Cambodia. She would also like to acknowledge students who helped create and participate in this service-learning project, some of whom are included in this talk. Without the passion and vision of these students, this project would have not come to fruition.

Introduction

This night brought to completion a month of service-learning in Cambodia for nine Naropa transpersonal art therapy graduate students, two support staff, and myself. Our team was the third group to participate in this service-learning project since its origination in 2011. The purpose was to work with non-government organizations (NGOs) that advocate for human rights and the elimination of violence against women and children, especially victims of the sex-trafficking industry. The learning goal was to have students gain unique clinical experience as part of their development. Our experience with the fireflies that night could not have been better in authenticating the real meaning behind our work, which in the words of one of my students was "much bigger than we were" (K. Hanczaryk, personal communication, January 2012).

This chapter explores how service-learning can be expanded to include a transpersonal lens. It explores the question, "What makes service-learning transpersonal and how does it look different than other service-learning opportunities?" In our experience, the integration of social justice, art therapy, cultural humility, regular mindfulness practice, and our own art making were the ways we explored this question and deepened our experience. We intentionally brought to light our experiences in discussions and placed them in the bigger context of the transpersonal.

I will share stories from students, examples of art expressions, and peak moments when we were confronted with our limitations, which enabled us to connect beyond our differences and find common humanity with the Cambodian people. I will explore the possibilities of a transpersonal approach to service-learning and how this approach differs from more traditional approaches.

Service-Learning

The pedagogy of service-learning has its theoretical roots in the work of John Dewey (Giles & Eyler, 1994). The philosophy holds that it is the interaction of knowledge, skills, and experience that is key to learning.

Since this early notion by Dewey, the idea that students move beyond the confines of the classroom and books and engage in real-life experiences has been extensively explored by academia (Butin, 2010; Cipolle, 2010; Jacoby & Associates, 2003; Speck & Hoppe, 2007). Generally speaking, service-learning is reciprocal in nature, with the altruistic intention of linking communities and academic study to better serve both interests. When students learn through service, the experience offers opportunities for discourse on personal beliefs, values, and prejudices. Communities can benefit from additional support, new perspectives and energy, and the willingness of the students to help in the ways the community is seeking assistance.

The phrase "transpersonal service-learning" is not seen in the academic literature, although service-learning is often associated with the outcome of an expanded perspective (Daniels, 2013). Some authors have focused on other aspects of service-learning, including the expansion of conscious living and personal transformation (Cress Collier, & Reitenauer, 2005), critical-consciousness development (Cipolle, 2010), and experiential compassion (Balas, 2006).

Service-Learning from a Transpersonal Perspective

Although not clearly labeled, service learning is often a transpersonal experience and pursuit. I suggest a definition: transpersonal service-learning is an opportunity to serve populations in an experientially conscious and compassionate way that brings forth personal, interpersonal, and communal transformation for the betterment of all. The underlying assumption is that transformation occurs from a place of truly experiencing and acknowledging difference, radical self- and other acceptance, and a deep, empathic understanding that leads to deeper appreciation of others and their life circumstances. Where there is intense suffering, we strive to create positive change.

John Davis (2003) describes transpersonal service as:

> authentic service that is non-dualistic, selfless, and oriented to process as well as outcome. Transpersonal service is a natural

reflexive response sparing from awareness, love, generosity and openness. Expressing this reflex requires understanding and working through the barriers of authentic service and developing and integrating capacities to serve in a mature way. (p. 21)

There are specific ways to intentionally enter into service learning with a transpersonal perspective. One way our team did this was to encourage learning with a "beginner's mind," approaching situations with an attitude of openness and curiosity, and a lack of preconceived ideas (Suzuki, 2011), and with the intention of achieving cultural humility rather than cultural competence (Hook, Davis, Owen, Worthington, & Utsey 2013; Tervalon & Murray-Garcia, 1998). Our practices in our own personal art making, writing, meditation, and ritual helped us toward these goals.

The Service-Learning Team and the Call toward Social Justice

Social justice is not always a component of a service-learning project, but participating in a project often results in a new sense and understanding of a need for social change. In many ways this project began as a calling toward social justice.

It was in January 2011 that a couple of my students in the transpersonal counseling art therapy program and I began to muse about taking art therapy services outside the confines of the classroom and focusing on social justice issues. Inspired by the words of Junge, Alvarez, Kellogg, and Volker (1993), who challenge the art therapist to leave the confines of office walls and "take to the streets and view our territory to include the community, society, and the larger world environment" (p. 149), we started thinking about the kinds of populations who might benefit from our services. We wanted to help others and put into practice the teachings of our mentors in transpersonal counseling and contemplative practices. Our hope was to establish a transpersonally based service-learning component for the students' academic journey.

A couple of the students had been researching the impact of the sex-trafficking industry. When they shared the painful stories of the victims, we became intently focused on a plan to make our vision of becoming socially engaged art therapists a reality. Within a few months we had established some connections with an NGO in Cambodia that sheltered girls from the sex-trafficking industry. We created an innovative fundraising plan, designed a culturally informed curriculum of trauma interventions, and explored culturally influenced self-care strategies for the mental health workers to combat their own vicarious trauma (Farley et al. 2003).

The genocide by the Khmer Rouge also added to the complexity of the trauma within much of the current Cambodian populations. To commit to social action, we understood the need to step out of our comfort zone and take on the responsibility of examining our complicity and privilege, as well as address oppressive social hierarchies (Hocoy, 2005; Kaplan, 2007; Levine & Levine, 2011). This blog post by one of the students illustrates this call:

> I imagined a part of myself as an archetypal warrior of justice, in my own way. Privy to the tragedy and suffering of the masses I'll soon encounter, there I stand, silhouetted shield and weapon in hand, survival belt across my waist. There is a flash of light, and with a further look, the sword is rather dull, with fanned bristles, rising triumphantly over my head toward the sky. I'm not here for a fight. Rather than round to deflect bullets, my shield is flat with rectangular geometry, penetrable canvas stretched across wooden framed edges, absorbing the atmosphere. Survival kit is a travel watercolor set, pack of colored pencils, the wisdom to breathe, and the courage to create. Not to mention, there's my band of imaginal allies. My imagination muses a little more and I let out my cry: "May we all have art!"

Service-Learning, Social Justice, and the Transpersonal Connection: Three Vectors of Ego Transcendence

From a transpersonal lens, social justice and engaged activism in the world are part and parcel of the transpersonal movement. The transpersonal is an integrative approach that realizes transcendence is possible once a higher level of consciousness is reached, but not without the opening up of a compassionate heart to the interconnectedness of all beings. Personal transformation cannot exclude the desire for happiness and equal existence among all beings.

Daniels (2009) offers a relevant model for conceptualizing a transpersonal approach to service-learning and social justice. This integrative model considers transpersonal development and transcendence as vectors through which we are able to move beyond the "egocentric concerns with one's own individuation and spiritual development toward full participation with, commitment to and responsibility for, other people, other species, and the world at large" (Daniels, 2009, p. 36). First, the *ascending* current advocates a spiritual path toward transcendence, a refining of consciousness to reach higher states and transpersonal realms and mystical experiences beyond space and time. Second, the *descending* current advocates for an immanent depth perspective where development of empathy and compassion can arise from one's exploration of the unconscious and deepest parts of the self. This current oftentimes involves shadow work. Third, the *extending* trajectory is where the movement from ascension and dissension converge and become a path toward service for others and the world.

Besides providing a model to conceptualize the service-learning project goals we had in mind from a transpersonal perspective, Daniel's (2009) model also illustrates our transpersonal experience while on this service-learning trip. The students' prior training in self-reflection, transpersonal, and contemplative practices laid the ground for the transformation that occurred from this experience. Excerpts from one student's blog post, offers an example:

I felt at a loss entering this service-learning trip. The preparation has proved to be a shadow-illuminating process as I confront my own guilt and shame around owning the unearned privileges that I have. Being stuck with guilt and shame will not serve me. Instead, I seek a way to stay connected and continue to work towards what helps heal the inequalities in the world.

One day, during this learning process, I found myself crying, upset, and wanting to destroy something out of my frustration with feeling powerless in relationship to these systems. My sister, who has been an inspirational devotee of social and environmental justice for me, shared an article about the practice of service. In it was written, "Serving makes us aware of our wholeness and its power. The wholeness in us serves the wholeness in others and the wholeness in life. The wholeness in you is the same as the wholeness in me. Service is a relationship between equals: our service strengthens us as well as others. (Remen, 1999)

White Privilege and Cultural Humility

One of the obvious and most difficult challenges for our team was our own white privilege and the risk of falling into the *white savior complex,* where the results are ultimately not about justice at all but about having a big emotional experience that validated our privilege (Cole, 2012). As a predominantly all-white female group we were ripe, at least unconsciously, to assume this role. Some of our most fruitful and heated conversations centered around this very topic and turned out to be the heart of our work and certainly our learning. We struggled with coming up with answers on the best way to be of service and respectful to the Cambodian people. What do we really have to teach? How much knowledge do we impart? Should we take photos of the work we do? What kinds of photos do we take? What are our blog topics? Where do we stay? How do we dress? How much do we immerse ourselves into the lives of the Cambodian people, and when do we take care of ourselves in the ways we are accustomed? Do we give money to the begging children? Do we ignore them? How do we converse with the Cambodian people?

What can we say and what can we ask?

And there were some other questions that brought about feelings of guilt: How do we meet our dietary needs? Have a comfortable sleeping situation? An air-conditioned environment? A quiet and restful time for contemplation? How do we meet our taken-for-granted comfortable and privileged lifestyle in an environment that is so consumed by poverty, oppression, and disparity? Even with all of these questions, we have not even mentioned the historical and intergenerational trauma so deeply embedded and endemic to the Cambodian people. We are people who come from a culture that values spiritual as well as emotional and physical wellness and a true intention to act from a social justice position. These questions alone froze us at times because we genuinely wanted "to do no harm."

The following excerpt from a student blog post entitled "The Great Divide," gives an example of this struggle:

> After a grueling six-hour bus ride, we drive up to our hotel in Siem Riep and I feel like I have stepped into paradise. The beautiful terracotta tile steps, orchids, and tropical trees lead us to our comfortable air-conditioned rooms and then to an inviting swimming pool. A small pond of blooming lotus flowers, a beautiful covered area with oversized brown wicker chairs and big fans invite us to take a rest from the relentless Cambodian heat. We have access to ice (a NICE delight), drinks and food, tuk tuk drivers on call. It's heaven here. I have a great sleep that night, sans bug nets.
>
> The next morning I take a walk up to the tower located next to the pool. It's the highest point in our neighborhood, and the best view of Siem Reap. Up there I can see the whole town, even parts of Angkor Wat in the distance. I see a large trash pile, which I didn't see before because of the big brick walls surrounding our hotel. A dog sniffs through it, and I see chickens and roosters and really skinny looking cows. I see many people cruise past on motorcycles, sometimes with three or four people riding, usually with baby on board precariously holding on. There are kids in

uniforms going to school, riding bikes that are much too big for them. I smell smog, sewage, gasoline, meat and fish. I sat up there for a while, until the sun came up.

This experience struck a chord deep within me. Here I am, a middle-class, white, American tourist, comfortable in a beautiful hotel, while surrounding and below me is poverty, filth, disease and daily struggle. None of the people I see have A.C., and abundance of food, health care and certainly no pool. It as if I were in a big bubble with thick stone walls, as if to keep all the cleanliness inside and all the filth out.

I am faced now with my own white guilt.

I decided to make this my daily practice, going to the tower for meditation and contemplation so I could see clearly both my privilege *and* my guilt.

The full sense of the deep disparity between our Cambodian friends and our team was impossible to understand until we arrived there. However, we had enough awareness to know that we needed to enter this experience as prepared as possible, so in our preparation we created this mission statement:

Rooted in the principle of collaboration and a belief in the innate wisdom, creativity, and interdependence of all, we, the art therapy graduate students and faculty, seek active engagement with social justice organizations around the world. We will use art therapy practices to help relieve suffering and maintain a vision of unity, as guests and learners in the communities we serve. (Naropa Community Art Studio, 2016)

Essame (2012) advises against assuming that what constitutes art therapy in the West is the same as what constitutes art therapy in the East. Talwar (2010) suggests considering individual differences within specific cultures or groups. In preparing for our trip to Cambodia, the art therapy team was intent upon understanding the culture we would be entering as best we could. With the knowledge that our learning in art therapy theory and practice is primarily rooted in a Western philosophy, we maintained curiosity about our destination in Cambodia. The concept of *cultural humility*, whereby we held the reality that we would not be culturally competent given the complexities of the Cambodian culture, allowed us to maintain a curious stance that was other-oriented, aware of power imbalances, and intent on creating partnerships that could make positive systemic change (Hook et al., 2013; Tervalon & Murray-Garcia, 1998).

Transpersonal Service-Learning: Art Therapy in Cambodia

The Cambodian People and Their History
The Cambodian people's experiences have been marked by years of inexplicable violence, political corruption, and economic despair. The 1965–1972 devastation from the U.S. "secret" bombing of Cambodia during the Vietnam War crumbled infrastructure and contributed to the rise and genocidal reign of Pol Pot and the Khmer Rouge from 1975–1979. The political upheaval post Pol Pot left a grotesque mark on the country. Pol Pot's plan to "purify" the population and return to an agrarian society by exterminating professionals, the educated, artists, musicians, and monks resulted in the loss of nearly one third of the Cambodian population (Chandler, 2007). These atrocities still reside in the minds and hearts of Cambodian people today, as well as in their land.

Because of the genocide by the Khmer Rouge, 70% of the population is under 30 years of age, and the overall literacy rate is 73% (Mundi Index, 2013). With very few elders left to hand down Cambodian traditions and culture, and given young persons' lack of knowledge about or reluctance to discuss Cambodia's dark past, today's generation has the difficult task of resolving the past while simultaneously trying to build the future.

Our Partner Organization
Cambodian Women's Crisis Center (CWCC) is an organization started in 1997 by a group of Cambodian woman with a goal to "help women help themselves," working with survivors and perpetrators of domestic

violence, sex-trafficking, and migration issues (see CWCC website: www.cwcc.org.kh). The group, which has four regional offices in Cambodia, further describes its mission as "to empower women and girls to claim their universal human rights to personal security and to equal participation in community, civil, economic, social, and cultural life." CWCC approaches its work holistically, with community-based, social justice, and empowering programs and projects. Within the Banteay Meanchey office where we worked, there are extensive programs with the intent to address gender-based violence issues from many angles, including providing safe shelter for women and their children, legal assistance, community outreach, anger management for perpetrators, safe migration plans, counseling, reintegration, educational programs, and micro-financing.

The majority of the population served by CWCC are women and children rescued from the ever-growing crime of sex trafficking. There are significant contributors to the prevalence of human trafficking in Cambodia: globalization, an unstable and often corrupt government, a pervasive lack of education, and extreme economic disparity between Cambodia's upper and majority classes. Girls, and even boys, sometimes as young as seven years old, are trafficked by parents, relatives, friends, or partners, often entering the sex trade under the premise that they are to provide for their families as sex workers. To keep victims "compliant," they are beaten, given addictive drugs, tortured, raped, and emotionally manipulated (Tan, 2012; Freed, 2003). Many of the women and children that we worked with were rescued from such situations.

Our work with CCWC was broken up into several components. In the mornings we worked with the staff, which included the clinical team, house-mothers, policeman, lawyers, and the administration, offering basic training in Art Therapy and Trauma-informed Therapy (Steele & Malchiodi, 2012). We collaboratively discussed strategies to heal from vicarious trauma caused by stressful work and the historical trauma endemic to the Cambodian people. The afternoons were spent in the large room where we engaged in lively art-making activities with the whole community, which included children and adults of all ages. We worked closely with the agency's therapists, using art-based assessments and interventions to augment the treatment goals and recovery for their clients.

Transpersonal Art Therapy

Art therapy as taught at Naropa University (Franklin, 2016; Franklin, Farrelly, Foster, Marek, & Wallingford, 2000), is an experiential practice, and naturally leads to the potential unfolding of ego transcendence. Art making and the final product reveal to the maker multiple perspectives on the subject being explored in the image. Insight and deeper understanding resulting from the process also tend toward acceptance and compassion from the maker and those bearing witness to the process. As the art therapist, one is privy to the transformation that comes from the process of creating an image. Because art is a method of working with metaphor and transcends the confinement that words often pose, the truth of unconscious desires and hopes are revealed. Thus, art making in this vein is a transpersonal experience.

The following example draws on the making of art and the resulting story by a 16-year-old girl rescued from the sex-trafficking industry to illustrate the transpersonal nature of working in images. It is a story that tells about her journey of recovery from years of sexual trauma and abuse, her fear and skepticism about her future, and her need for support from others. In trusting others, she was able to move forward and finally be reunited with her family.

She drew a picture of a long road starting in the rocky desert with two little girls. The road curves into a landscape with other people, trees, birds, and houses. When asked to describe the picture, she said that the girl is on a journey. It's a long journey and the path is rocky. She doesn't know where she is going or what is ahead. She is scared but she knows she can't go back. She has to move forward. Another girl shows up on her path and tells her, "keep walking; you will be ok." The girl feels better and so she keeps going. She is still afraid and wants to turn back many times. She gets to this tree and she stops again; she is more scared than ever. She wants to run away. Another girl shows up and tells her, "You have to keep going because your family is waiting for you." She was still afraid but she went on. When she got home her family had dinner ready for her.

I was moved to tears as I witnessed her telling this story while simultaneously illustrating her words. Only after coming to the conclusion did she look at me as if completing something tremendously important. I knew from the story and the way she told it that she would be okay, just like the first visiting girl had predicted in the story. I also knew that had she described her experience in words alone she would not have come to the same conclusion.

This story, besides holding tremendous significance for this young girl in giving her the hope and drive she needed to move forward, also ironically paralleled the journey of the service-learning team. The path was rocky, and we did not know where the path would lead and what we would encounter along the way. We were afraid and needed encouragement to move forward. A lot of trust was required to reach our goal, but in the end we were united and fed, just like this young girl. So in addition to providing the validation the girl needed to keep moving, the gift of the art to the viewer, in this case me, provided the same message.

Words from the Students

As stated earlier, besides art making and meditation practices, blog entries were a form of expression for the team. The students were required to post at least two blog entries during the service-learning experience. Following are just a few excerpts from blog entries by the team over the three years that we participated in this service-learning project. The blog was our way of sharing our experiences with our communities at home as well as a way to bring awareness to the plight of the Cambodian people. These writings brought to light our own personal growth and transformation. They poignantly provide examples of the transpersonal nature of this work.

Example One. When we work with clients, we feel it in our bodies and we carry it with us. When we don't work on that energy, it becomes trapped and can hurt us.

Example Two. CWCC staff members were led in a 20-minute yoga routine, and were asked to create two drawings: one to represent how they felt before yoga, and one to represent how they felt afterward. One staff member depicted a figure whose chest was full of blue dots. In the second drawing, the figure was surrounded by blue dots, with only a few remaining inside his silhouette.

When asked to describe the difference between the two drawings, he responded, "Before, I was very anxious inside. Now, that worry is outside of me. There are some worries that I will always have with me, but those are just a part of me."

In transpersonal psychology, the client often directs the content of the therapy while the therapist holds the context. That is to say, the therapist provides a safe container of walls and a roof, and the client fills the house with life. We understand how image can serve as a metaphor for things that cannot be spoken, and how as images change, the internal experience can be transformed as well.

Mindfulness Practice

Our "beginners mind" approach opened up the possibility for many perspectives to unfold. The practice of "letting in" and "letting go" was essential in helping us to sit with the intense amount of suffering we were confronted with everyday. The art, the social justice cause, and the transpersonal lens from which we viewed our experience would not have integrated in the way it did without our daily mindfulness practice. I believe that sitting with all that we were experiencing allowed the space for deep meaning and transformation to occur, both individually and collectively.

Conclusion

Our mission, to engage actively in helping others from a transpersonal lens with humility and a beginner's mind, was realized. All the experiences, from the great joys we found in personal connections to the deep despair and the unmitigated pain of injustice and trauma, brought home to us the fact that the only way to effect change is to first feel and stay with the suffering of others. Our self-care practices such as art, meditation, and writing helped contain our experiences and were essential for our sustainability. We were able to put words and images to the transpersonal nature of suffering and interconnectedness and come away transformed. Even though the learning was difficult and the emotional terrain uncomfortable and challenging, the experiences garnered in this service-learning experience were key to our learning. Perhaps they fall into the category of what Maslow (1964) described as peak experiences, those in which a person is able to reach the highest state of self-actualization, significance, and fulfillment. That certainly was true of my own experience.

Oftentimes service-learning experiences create a more profound change for the participants offering the service than the ones receiving the service, especially when they are also experiencing a completely different country and culture, and I think this was the case for our group. We, like many service learners, left feeling we had gained more than we were able to give. But there is also the other side of contributing to others: social justice enactment and positive change for the organizations being served. The reports from the CWCC and from those with whom we worked repeatedly told us of the team's impact on increasing hope, lessening isolation and trauma symptoms, and building community. They continue to use the strategies and interventions we shared in addressing their own vicarious trauma. We continue to stay in contact with the team at CWCC and have made life-long connections with the people there. And while we feel positive about our small impact, we are haunted by our privilege of returning to the United States while their suffering continues.

A transpersonal approach to service-learning embodies Daniels' extending trajectory toward service (2009). The paradoxical dance between transcendence and depth work was one we engaged in daily through our meditation practices, art making, and ritual practices. I believe these helped us be more conscious, humble, compassionate, and collaborative.

I would like to finish the story that began this chapter and poignantly speaks to the reciprocal nature of transpersonal service.

Once back at the dock, Yorn held our hands one by one and led us out of the boat to the steady platform of the dock. Other than the gentle sound of water and the boat rubbing the side of the dock, it was silent, as if we all wanted to savor the immensity of what we had just experienced. Silence turned to whispers, and whispers to conversation and laughter as we reentered the ordinary world we had left just hours before. As we made our way toward the covered deck where we would share a bit about our experience, I felt a gentle tug. I turned and Yorn was there, holding his luminary boat. He motioned for us to witness him as he climbed down the wooden ladder that met the river's edge.

"For you," Yorn said, with a smile and slight bow. Yorn then launched his banana boat luminary, and we watched it float away with the gentle wave of his hand.

References

Balas, G. (2006). The lessons of Anapra: International service learning and character education. *Journal of College and Character, 7,* 1–10.

Butin, D. W. (2010). *Service-learning in theory and practice: The future of community engagement in higher education.* London: Palgrave MacMillan.

Chandler, D. (2007). *A History of Cambodia* (4th ed.). Boulder, CO: Westview Press.

Cipolle, S. B. (2010). *Service-learning and social justice: Engaging students in social change.* Boulder, CO: Rowman and Littlefield.

Cole, T. (2012, March 21). The white-savior industrial complex. *The Atlantic.* Retrieved from http://www.theatlantic.com/magazine/

Cress, C., Collier, P., & Reitenauer, V. (2005). *Learning through service: A student guidebook for service-learning across disciplines.* Sterling, VA: Stylus Publishing.

Daniels, M. (2009). Perspectives and vectors in transpersonal development. *Transpersonal Psychology Review, 13*(1), 87–99.

Daniels, M. (2013). Transpersonal roots, history, and evolution of the transpersonal perspective. In H. L Friedman & G. Hartelius, (Eds.), *The Wiley-Blackwell handbook of transpersonal psychology* (pp. 23–43). West Sussex, UK: John Wiley & Sons.

Davis, J. (2003). An overview of transpersonal psychology. *The Humanistic Psychologist, (31),* 6–21.

Essame, C. (2012). Collective versus individualist societies and the impact of Asian values on art therapy in Singapore. In D. Kalmanowitz, J. Potash, & S. Chan (Eds.), *Art therapy in Asia* (pp. 91–101). London: Jessica Kingsley.

Farley, M., Cotton, A., Lynne, J., Zumbeck, S., Spiwak, F., Reyes, M., Alvarez, D., & Sezgin, U. (2003). Prostitution and trafficking in nine countries: An update on violence and posttraumatic stress disorder. In M. Farley (Ed.),

Prostitution, trafficking and traumatic stress (pp. 33–74). Gloucestershire, UK: Hawthorn Press.

Franklin, M. A. (2016). Essence and art: A contemplative–transpersonal view of art therapy. In D. E. Gussak & M. L. Rosal (Eds.), *The Wiley-Blackwell handbook of art therapy* (pp. 99–111). West Sussex, UK: John Wiley & Sons.

Franklin, M., Farrelly, M., Foster, N., Marek, B., & Wallingford, S. (2000). Transpersonal art therapy education. *Journal of the American Art Therapy Association, 17*(2) 101–110.

Freed, W. (2003). From duty to despair: Brothel prostitution in Cambodia. In M. Farley (Ed.), *Prostitution, trafficking and traumatic stress* (pp.133–146). Gloucestershire, UK: Hawthorn Press.

Giles, D., & Eyler, J. (1994). The theoretical roots of service-learning. In John Dewey: Toward a theory of service-learning. *Michigan Journal of Community Service Learning, 1*(1), 77–84.

Hocoy, D. (2005). Art therapy and social action: A transpersonal framework. *Art Therapy: Journal of the American Art Therapy Association, 22*(1), 7–16.

Hook, J. N., Davis, D. E., Owen, J., Worthington Jr., E. L., & Utsey, S. O. (2013). Cultural humility: Measuring openness to culturally diverse clients. *Journal of Counseling Psychology, 60,* 353–366.

Jacoby, B. and Associates (2003). *Building partnerships for service-learning.* San Francisco, CA: Jossey-Bass.

Junge, M. B., Alvarez, J. F., Kellogg, A., & Volker, C. (1993). The art therapist as social activist: Reflections and visions. *Art Therapy: Journal of the American Art Therapy Association, 10*(3),148–155.

Kaplan, F. (Ed.). (2007). *Art therapy and social action.* Philadelphia, PA: Jessica Kingsley.

Levine E., & Levine, S. (Eds.). (2011). *Art in action: Expressive arts therapy and social change.* Philadelphia, PA: Jessica Kingsley.

Maslow, A. (1964). *Religions, values and peak-experiences.* London: Penguin.

Mundi Index. (2013). Cambodia demographics profile. Retrieved from: http://www.indexmundi.com/cambodia/demographics_profile.html

Naropa Community Art Studio-International. (2016). Mission. Retrieved 16 December 2015 from https://ncasi.wordpress.com/about/mission-2/ Remen, R. N. (1999, September). Helping, fixing or serving? *Shambhala Sun.*

Speck, B. W., & Hoppe, S. L. (2007). *Searching for spirituality in higher education: For the worship of code and the service of man.* New York, NY: Peter Lang.

Steele, W., & Malchiodi, C.A. (2012*). Trauma-informed practices with children and adolescents.* New York, NY: Routledge.

Suzuki, S. (2011). *Zen mind, beginner's mind.* Boston, MA: Shambhala.

Talwar, S. (2010). An intersectional framework for race, class, gender and sexuality in art therapy. *Art Therapy: Journal of the American Art Therapy Association, 21*(1), 44–48.

Tan, L.A. (2012). Surviving shame: Engaging art therapy with trafficked survivors in Southeast Asia. In D. Kalmanowitz, J. Potash, & S.M. Chan (Eds.), *Art therapy in Asia* (pp. 283–298). London: Jessica Kingsley.
Tervalon, M., & Murray-Garcia, J. (1998). Cultural humility versus cultural competence: A critical distinction in defining physician training outcomes in multicultural education. *Journal of Health Care for the Poor and Underserved, 9,* 117–125.

Chapter 11
A Longing in the Soul: Healing Sexual Trauma with Equine Facilitated Psychotherapy

Jackie Ashley

There exists countless stories and varying confessions of the unresolved fears and personal triumphs women have discovered under the forgiving and non-judgmental tutelage of the horse. Horses have gained a new prominence as co-facilitators in physical and emotional treatment across the nation. Like all animals with which we form a bond, either in our dreams or from a close relationship, horses appear to be catalysts for growth and self-discovery...that re-inform my belief that the horse is oracle and bellwether for our souls. (Melissa Sovey-Nelson, 2004, p.17)

Why women and horses?

Horses hold a powerful presence in the psyche of women. They have for me and countless other young girls as we stuck pond fronds in our pants as tails and ran through the yard as if it were the Great Plains of the West. And for those women lucky enough to have horses as adults, we have found grooming them, riding them, talking with them, and being informed by them has often saved our emotional lives. Where this obsession comes from is, of course, only speculative, but I concur with many writers on horses and women: that horses are beautiful, powerful, and strong but gentle—all things women long for but often do not experience. On their backs we can fly, we can be free. We can deeply connect, love, and be loved unconditionally. Horses ask us to reside fully in those traditional, feminine realms of intuition, compassion, empathy and care-taking (Kohanov, 2001; Midkiff, 2001; Pierson, 2000; Sovey-Nelson, 2004).

I have been incorporating horses in my work as a somatic psychotherapist–dance/movement therapist since 2001. For the past ten years I have conducted Equine Facilitated Psychotherapy (EFP) groups for women with sexual trauma. I have witnessed profound insight, healing, and growth for many of these women. In this chapter I will explore the foundations of EFP in transpersonal psychology and the influences of somatic psychology and neuroscience as the foundation of my work.

Very limited research exists specifically about working with women with sexual trauma using EFP, aside from some case studies (Trotter 2012). Several professional papers discuss using equine facilitated therapy with other forms of abuse, but this number is also limited (Meinersmann, Bradberry, & Roberts., 2008; Schroeder & Stroud, 2015). The literature also contains some anecdotal writings of women who have used EFP in conjunction with other modalities (Dugard, 2011). More recently, radio station NPR and several newspapers have discussed the use of equine therapy with survivors of military sexual trauma. Hopefully, a growing awareness and interest in this work is emerging.

What is Equine Facilitated Psychotherapy?

Tim Hayes (2015) states that, "Remarkable human psychic breakthroughs originate and are manifested with horses when a person creates that relationship...Not only are the results both transformational and lasting but they occur with amazing speed" (p. 2). Humans and horses have had a healing and transformational relationship both before and after their domestication in about 3500 BCE. Though used for transportation, warfare, and agriculture, their power, grace, and willing nature have held a timeless spot in human mythology (Hallberg, 2008; Oldfield, 1923). While Hippocrates noted the healing power of horses, the first referenced therapeutic use of horses was in a French medical journal in the late 1780s; it stated that horseback riding helped those suffering from neurological damage (American Hippotherapy Association [AHA], 2016). Therapeutic riding and hippotherapy for those with physical and or neurological challenges began in Europe in the 1960s. Hippotherapy means treatment with the help of the horse and comes from the Greek word for horse, *hippos* (AHA, 2016). In 1969 the first professional organization was formed in the United States: the North American Riding for the Handicapped Association. This organization is now known as the Professional Association for Therapeutic Horsemanship (PATH, 2016). PATH recognized that as well as the positive results of riding and hippotherapy, clients created strong emotional bonds with their horses, and through this work, cognitive, emotional, and psychological health improved (Hallberg, 2008). PATH eventually added Equine Facilitated Mental Health training to the curriculum in 1996.

In 1999, the Equine Assisted Growth and Learning Association (EAGALA, 2010) was formed to specifically focus on mental health and learning, not riding. In the EAGALA mode, a mental health professional and an equine professional partner together. EAGALA also focuses on horses as a tool to assist in activity-focused therapy sessions. These two organizations were the first to certify people who wanted to work in the field of equine-assisted activities and therapies (EAAT).

The range of activities in which a horse is used for physical and emotional support and development varies as much as the many orientations and schools of thought that have sprung up. Activities range from handling, grooming, riding, driving, and vaulting to activities on the ground, where the horse is at liberty to move freely within an enclosed area without any halter or rope. In this situation, the person attempts to create a relationship/connection only through body language, energy, and intention. The horse is free to respond authentically without the imposition of any sort of device. This is one of the most powerful ways to fully witness how sensitive horses are to humans (Hallberg, 2008; Shambo, Young, & Madera, 2013; Trotter, 2012).

Equine facilitated psychotherapy is one of the orientations that have sprung up. EFP incorporates the horse as a co-facilitator in the therapeutic relationship, not as a tool in activities. The horse's behaviors, responses, and reactions to the situation are the foundation of the session (Hallberg, 2008; Hayes, 2015; Trotter, 2012). EFP, which requires a licensed professional in the mental health field to be present, is a non-traditional, experiential, body-based approach that can also be considered as group therapy. It takes place outdoors at a ranch or farm, in a barn or a field. It is often used as an adjunct therapy as well as stand-alone psychotherapy when utilized by a licensed counselor (Hallberg, 2008; Hayes, 2015; Totter, 2012).

There are now many organizations with a specific focus outside of psychotherapeutic work with horses, such as coaching, growth and learning, and organizational and corporate development, that do not require a licensed mental health professional.

Transpersonal Roots in Equine Psychotherapy

> We are spirit, the horse and I...essence and substance, specter and apparition...mythological figures empowered with magical gifts and the stuff of childhood tales. Often diaphanous or forced to be in the shadows...We all hunger for the enigmatic, the veiled unexplainable which is beyond human understanding. Some of us satisfy this appetite with the archetypal majesty and power of the horse. (Melissa Sovey-Nelson 2014, p. 50)

In the 1990s articles and books began to appear on the use of horses as part of psychotherapeutic treatment. Many of these seminal accounts parallel and speak to a transpersonal paradigm. Early EFP pioneer, Linda Kohanov (2001) tells her personal story in *The Tao of Equus: A Woman's Journey of Healing & Transformation Through the Way of the Horse.* Her journey began with dreams, premonitions, and listening to body-based wisdom while caring for her injured horse. She emphasized and began to describe the receptive feminine and intuitive capacities that are highlighted in the horse–human interaction. Kohanov shares that horses, as prey and herd animals, are dependent on their instincts to read a situation for safety and survival. When interacting with a human, horses recognize feelings and emotions—including ones denied or hidden—not necessarily words and statements. Horses are looking for congruency in humans and if that does not occur, they respond to that disconnection in ways that inform the relationship (Kohanov, 2001; Shambo, 2013) For instance, if a woman comes up to the herd reporting to all that she "is fine, I just want to be left alone " when actually she is feeling a great longing for connection, fear of relating, or grief for personal losses, I have often seen a horse walk up to that woman, stand there, and just *be with* her. The horse responds to the real, not yet expressed, emotion.

Rupert Issacson's moving equine story is told in his book *The Horse Boy: A Father's Quest to Heal His Son* (2009). Along with his wife and son, Issacson traveled to Mongolia to seek out shamans and the horse culture tribes still found there. He hoped that they could help with his son, Rowan, who had been diagnosed with autism, after traditional methods had limited success. Rowan was barely able to speak, prone to violent fits, and was described as unreachable. One day Rowan ran into a field of horses. His father, assuming the worst, finally found his son at the foot of a big red mare named Betsy. The horse was quiet and relaxed. She stood over Rowan, who lay quietly in the grass gazing up at the horse. Issacson then began to spend time with his son and horses since this was a period when Rowan would predictably be calm. The story of their pilgrimage to Mongolia is one of hardship and eventual healing, of the trust in the ancient wisdom of earth-based cultures and of surrender to ritual as a transformative element in healing.

Other writers have focused on bonding and creativity specific to other ancient traditions, including Celtic mysticism (McCormick, McCormick, & McCormick, 2004); the use of mythology as the basis for EFP work (Broseman, 2007); addressing the subjugation and abuse of women and horses (Pierson 2000); as well as grief, reconnection and personal redemption (Husher, 2005; Richards, 2006). There are numerous collections of the stories of the horse–human relationship and resulting transformation, healing, inspiration, and hope (Farley, 2015; Fitch, 2008; Pike, 2009).

These stories speak to the unique potential horses hold in the transformation of human suffering, the expanded sense of place in the world, and the capacity to connect with other living beings and nature.

Somatic Psychotherapy and EFP

> Somatic psychotherapy operates on the premise that sensation, breath, and movement are the body's form of speech, and that if we listen to this speech we can complete and release stored trauma, relearn how to feel excitement and pleasure, and engage in activities that nourish. (Caldwell 1996, p.4)

Being with horses is a body-based experience. In the presence of these large, potentially dangerous beings, we become embodied. We get pulled into the present moment and our sense perceptions are engaged. In her book *The Listening Heart; The Limbic Path Beyond Office Therapy*, Leigh Shambo (2013), clearly outlines the body-based neuroscience of the horse–human connection and emphasizes the importance of the limbic system in this process.

The limbic system is that part of our brain that mediates between our social and emotional experiences. It is the seat of emotions, feelings, and relational capacity, which in my clients is where much of the damage has been done (Levine & Frederick, 1997). Horses are highly limbic creatures focused on relationships, family bands in the wild, and herd hierarchy and dynamics if domesticated. As prey animals, horses depend on communication for safety for their herd. Herd animals regulate each other just as humans are capable of co-regulating (Baldwin 2014; Shambo, 2013).

Horses respond to perceived danger, which can be anything unknown to them. At first they flee, but in time they return to face the situation with full sense perception. They will fight if fleeing is not an option. This high-arousal state is acute and felt by all in the herd. If one or all escape the predator, within a matter of minutes the nervous systems of the horses regulate and the horses go back to eating or resting.

The experience of body-based violation that is not resolved in the actual event through fighting or fleeing impacts individuals differently, but many fall into a state of unresolved body action or a freeze state (Levine & Frederick, 1997; Levine, 2010; Ogden, Minton, & Pain, 2006). The freeze response, often based on an actual experience of an attempt to survive a life-threatening situation, can become habituated in one's body response to stressful situations. It often can manifest in chronic conditions such as pain, depression, anxiety, relational challenges, and addictions (Levine & Frederick, 1997).

Humans, because of their brain's highly developed frontal lobe, often *think through* the event, trying to make sense of it, frequently resulting in self-blame, denial, or repression. When early childhood sexual trauma takes place before the full brain has developed, the trauma is caught in the experience of the body (Levine & Frederick, 1997). Adult sexual trauma often occurs when the person is under the influence of alcohol or drugs and is not even aware of the event until waking up. Again, the body experiences, but the mind is not cognizant. If someone is sexually assaulted under the threat of violence and potential death, the body goes into the freeze state, since fighting could lead to more harm and fleeing is impossible. The body holds the experience of the chronic inability to resolve the initial wound when it happened.

Women in my groups often state in regard to the sexual trauma, that "No one would believe me anyway," "I was embarrassed, I just wanted to pretend it didn't happen," and many feel confusion about their part in the event. Often these victims blame themselves. Humans have the capacity to think and rationalize, deny or blame. Our bodies are meant to heal and to resolve high arousal in the face of danger and threat to our lives (Levine, 2010), but because of the continued cultural and social attitudes around sexual trauma, victims continue to suffer the effects of these events.

Becoming Part of the Herd

The day is warm, and we feel a slight breeze. The women gather slowly in front of the barn. The table is set with crayons, markers, stickers and stamps. They make their nametags, expressing how they are feeling today. As we sit down on our chairs, I begin a grounding exercise that intends to bring us deeper into our bodies and sensations. We start by imagining energy coming from the center of the earth, up through our feet and through our entire bodies. We bring awareness to the internal sensation of our bones, organs, and muscles. We feel the sensations on our skin and tune into the taste in our mouths, smells, and sounds. I ask the women to check into the area of their hearts and connect with the emotional state they now feel. This is creating a state of embodied self-awareness that helps us establish a relationship with our internal sensations (interoception) feelings, and emotions (Fogel, 2009; Shambo, 2013).

I ask the women to open their eyes and notice shapes, colors, and movements in their peripheral view. We then look up at each other and our surroundings. Looking at each other activates the social relational/engagement network, so essential to healing attachment wounds (Heller, 2015). By observing our surroundings and making eye contact with one another, we begin to create a safe space (Levine, 2010). This grounding work is foundational to the women's experience with the horses. Having a sense of where one's body parts are in space and in relation to other beings (proprioception) is essential to safety when in a herd of horses as they often move quickly and engage with one another. Drawing on the work of trauma-informed body-based therapies, we start with a sense of safety, connection, and choice that will support our emotional work.

We check in with each other, speaking and showing our name tags, our bodies, and our thoughts. How the women initially felt before the check-in, expressed on the name tags, often changes after the grounding exercises and throughout the slowly paced exercise. This is an important learning time for the women. They have the experience of thoughts, feelings, and moods changing and of becoming more authentic and connected to what is actually occurring in the moment, as opposed to what they brought with them. This is mindfulness, a state of present-centered awareness lessening the conceptual thought processes (Fulton, 2005; Seigel, 2010). As each woman practices mindfulness, her ability to return to the present moment becomes stronger. Some share what is going on in their lives, while others pass and choose to stay in a quiet body-centered place. There are some tears and laughter, and also the kind of listening and being seen that many of these women long for and are not really used to.

We move from our chairs to the edge of the paddock and look out on our three horses. I ask the women to tell me what they notice. This is the practice of *bare awareness*, being descriptive, not projective, and it is hard work for many the first few times since we naturally want to project our experience, in some cases our perceived knowledge, onto the horses. We learn how to use our eyes to simplify our experience to really see: color, shade, shape, movement, difference, relationship, and contrast. We deepen even further into ourselves, our sensations, and our sense perceptions.

We then move into the world of horses. This is their home. This is where they spend their days. We are their guests. This is a world of present-moment awareness. Horses are believed to be the most sensitive of all land mammals. With eyes on the sides of their heads, they see panoramically, each eye scanning for predators. Their radar-like ears pick up sounds all around. Their bodies are sensitive enough to feel a fly on their skin, and they are able to twitch their muscles precisely to discard it. Horses are hard-wired for safety and responsive to the least flick of a tail or movement of an ear to communicate to one another their comfort level with closeness, their mood, and where the attention should go. They are a self-regulating entity when in a herd, particularly in the wild.

As the women return each week, their capacity for really seeing these subtleties increases. They begin to pay greater attention and recognize their own body responses to the world around them. They build their intersubjectivity, or "the non-verbal sense of being with another person as a direct result of interpersonal resonance that occurs during coregulation of movements, sensations, and action" (Fogel, 2009, p. 314). As we move into their world, the "morphogenetic field of horses and humans" (Kohanov, 2001, p.69), I ask the women to find a place in the paddock where they feel comfortable and safe. They are asked to tune in to how they feel now, moving in with the horses, becoming part of the herd, intentionally creating space around themselves, and to reconnect, to sense perceptions, emotions, thoughts in the new world, the natural world that includes non-human beings.

We now work with three concepts, initially gleaned from Buddhism: attraction, aversion and indifference. These are called the three *poisons* in Buddhist psychology, but to me they are simply the fundamental ways in which we perceive and move through our daily lives. As we stand in our spots, I ask the women, "Which of these three emotions are strongest?" and "What horse are you attracted to? Why?" Their attraction responses can range from "that one is so beautiful" or "that one seems lonely" to "that one is relaxed, that one reminds me of..." There is often aversion as they report, "one horse is bossing the other horses around" or "that one is so dirty" to "that one wants to be left alone." And also indifference as some women report, "not feeling anything much today," "I don't care really," or "I don't want to pick one over the other."

These statements are explored and discussed with one another from our spots. The women are asked to identify these feelings, if possible, in the body or as sensations in specific areas. The pronouncements and projections are often found to parallel the way we relate in the world to people and situations. Especially with women, there is often the draw to care for one another or the horse, as well as sometimes negative traits reminiscent of perpetrators. When these sensations are explored, there are often newly realized assumptions, and an internal challenge begins. Today we start with attraction and I ask, "Where do you feel the attraction in your body?"

"In my belly," one says. Another adds, "In my heart." And throughout the circle the women check in with their bodies and verbalize their experience. I then ask the women to move from that place in their bodies toward that to which they are attracted.

I may ask them, "How do you move toward what you are attracted to?" and "Do you know how you move toward your attractions? How do you know?" This is slow, meaningful work and there is often much stillness within the group. The question "How do you know" can be very hard to answer. To paraphrase Janet Adler, a pioneer in Authentic Movement, speaking to this place of not knowing encourages us to stay with the not knowing as long as we can because she believes the knowing that emerges will deepen (Adler, 2002). This place we often define as not knowing is that place of intuition, of clairsentience and the power place of shamans. We are moving into the limbic brain and visceral knowledge. It can be uncomfortable and confusing. This is where the horses live. They are always in this place of present-moment, body-informed relationship with their environment and other beings (Kohanov, 2001; Shambo, 2014). In her book *Mind Whispering* (2013), Tara Bennet-Goleman speaks to this: "Horses are always inviting us into the present, always ready to connect with us the moment we attune to them. They live in the moment, waiting for us to find our way there too" (p. 5).

Today some women move toward the horse they are attracted to. One chooses to stay where she is. This is a powerful choice, always offered, made by women in the group with some hesitancy, as judgments, internalized shoulds, and stories emerge in their minds. But knowing when to approach or not is essential for those who have experienced assault. We work to develop a clearer internal sense of what is comfortable. We begin to help each other to listen to and respect those *gut feelings* from the enteric nervous system that connects the gut with emotions and feelings (Fogel 2009).

I remind those who move toward their chosen horse of the horse's *personal bubble* and to notice that impulse to touch the horses. I ask each individual to think of their own experience of people being attracted to them and how were they approached and touched. I advise them to take the time to sense this from the horse and when it feels okay to move into contact. This is a big challenge. Some, new to this instruction, move up into their horse's head and freeze. It then takes a while to decipher one's impulse to touch and to tune into the horse's receptivity to be touched.

When asked for reflection on their own experience of touch, some women withdraw into thoughts and memories. Time is allowed for this, as the thinking part of the brain is beginning to be engaged in the psychotherapeutic process. There are prompts to come back to the sense perceptions, to feel their feet on the earth, and to continue to move toward and sense the horse. Most often, given the time and space, the horses move toward the women. Sometimes this happens for a few. It is a deeply felt honor and surprise to have another being be curious about you. The sensation of the warm breath of a horse on one's hand, chest, or belly powerfully engages these women.

When I finally say, "You can touch them," I encourage the use of body parts other than hands, as horses do not have hands. This is a lovely space to witness, as women explore their own bodies and contact. They are soon offered brushes to groom the horses, and a few pick them up and start brushing. One woman loves to just brush, stroke, comb, and talk to her horse friend, who stands quietly, clearly enjoying the attention. As this horse begins to relax, the head drops, lips quiver, and eyes soften. This kind of nurturing, repetitive movement, or *mindful grooming,* has been shown to co-regulate the heart rates of horses and people (Baldwin, 2014).

After some time with this connection activity, I introduce how to halter and lead a horse. This is another activity of choice, and a few women take me up on it. I talk in the group about how we approach a horse with the intention to halter. There is a practice in natural horsemanship where the human moves toward the horse with the halter through a sequence of steps. These five steps are intention, invite, suggest, ask, and insist. Our first step is to set our intention. We hold the halter, choose a horse, and in our minds say, "I would like to connect with you through the halter and lead rope." We don't even move. Our next act is to walk toward the horse, inviting it to connect through the halter. Sometimes a horse will walk right over. If that does not happen, we walk to the horse and suggest they put their head in the halter. That may be intensified to asking while gently beginning to slip the halter over the horse's head. The horses we work with are very amenable and used to being haltered and rarely move away. If they move away, or are resistant, we have to decide if we go to the last action: insist.

I have integrated these steps into my work as the building blocks to creating awareness about how we form relationships with others and our worlds. Often, particularly with sexual abuse and assault, the intention of the abuser moves into insist. The complicated nuances of intention, invitation, suggest, and ask are there, yet they can result in abuse. Sorting this out is especially challenging in date rape cases involving younger women, or for older women attempting to date again after many years. With the horses and this activity, women connect with their own learned patterns of how they get their needs met, or not. Where do they stop in the process of asking for what they want? Where have others in the family, work, or community overrun their boundaries? How do we get seduced, not just in a sexual way but also in our lives, into doing things we don't want to do? This can be a very powerful and confusing place for the women in their relationship with their horse, as they do not want to insist. But to insist in this activity doesn't just mean force. It can mean, "I insist that you respect my boundaries." Or in a group or family situations, it can signify, "I insist that you let me speak." This is another way of interpreting insist. It means different things in different situations. This can be a rich conversation among the women during the periods of talking about our experiences with the horses.

When I give the instruction for haltering, one woman who has been in previous groups gives me a look. She knows, as I do, that this is something she does not like to do. She has never done it and has chosen not to even try in previous groups. She has shared previously that as a child she was tied to a chair in front of a window while her siblings and parents were out doing chores or playing, including the brother who had repeatedly sexually abused her. This was to keep her "out of trouble" while others were working or enjoying themselves.

She would have nothing to do with tying, restraining, or controlling a horse. She loves horses and has loved them all her life. But when we came to the haltering and leading activity, she would stand off to the side and watch.

As this was the second-to-last meeting of our eight-week scheduled sessions, I decided to challenge her and ask her to halter the horse. I handed her the halter and lead rope, asking if she would at least just carry it around and see what transpired. This was a lot to ask based on her history. Because we have a trusting relationship based on previous work together, we were able to banter back and forth. Despite not wanting to participate, she was willing to try. The other women watched, smiling in support and encouragement. I knew that this was an example of an associated behavior from previous trauma that did not actually pertain to the current situation. We both knew that her issues in life were about taking initiative, being assertive with her needs, and sticking with things.

I had spoken that day and in previous groups about horses being herd animals that look for leadership. There is always a hierarchy in every herd. Horses that are domesticated are used to being haltered and led by humans. The horses that I work with were trained and gentled without force, so when someone comes toward them with a halter they know what is about to happen. They are usually fine with being haltered. Unlike humans, the horses do not really care if it is put on properly. Often horses know that the halter means they get to go out, get fed, and other good things. They also are connected to a leader. They are in a relationship of mutual respect to perform an activity.

As she stood against the fence waiting for the time to run out, I asked another woman to help her. Agreeing, the second woman nicely asked to help. "Nope—not going to happen," she was told. Eventually the woman just stepped back and indicated she was willing to help if needed. The woman who refused the help carried the halter and walked around, not approaching any horse. She ended up leaning against the fence at the top of the paddock, away from everyone and the horses. Another woman came by and offered her help, which was again refused. The woman continued to stand off to the side, holding the halter and waiting for the time to end.

As we watched, we saw one of the horses walk toward the woman planted against the fence. The big chestnut horse with the white blaze came up to her side and stood there. She looked at him. She looked at me. We stood there. I asked her what she thought was happening. Is this horse inviting, suggesting? She fidgeted with the halter, flapping it around, dropping it, making lots of awkward movements—waiting for the horse to move away, get bored, or do something other than stand there. She looked at me and said, "I guess he is waiting for me to halter him?" The horse continued to stand there, now clearly asking.

As all these movements were not going to deter him or scare him away, she fiddled with the halter near his head. She would step away and do everything she could think of to make the horse go away, even shoving the horse gently on the shoulder. The horse waited. She finally put the halter on him. We all quietly looked at her. Tears were seen on the face of the woman who had asked to help. I don't remember what was said. I only know we were all in a world of celebration.

The woman looked up, "What?" she said, in that tone of voice so often heard when someone does something incredible and then seems to think it no big deal. She had been in equine therapy groups many times before and been involved in some incredible healings; this was different. She also did not understand what had happened. "Was he listening?" she asked. "I mean really—how did he know? He was standing behind us. There was no reason for him to come up to me."

She then led the horse down the hill and at the bottom took off the halter. The horse would not leave her side. Later she expressed that she thanked him for the beautiful lesson. She learned that relationships can be partnerships. She was deeply moved by that, "He just stood there and didn't move again. Like he was waiting for me to do it again." But she said she whispered to him, "No—that is enough for me today." The horse looked at her and turned and went up the hill. She picked up a brush and went back to her favorite activity of grooming, but with a different horse and with a different relationship to herself.

It is always hard to leave, but our lives beyond this place of present-moment awareness beckon, and we resolve to bring as much of it as we can into our lives before next week. When the group is finished we usually capture our experiences by creating a spontaneous poem with each women saying one line The following poem is similar to what may be created.

>   The moment expands
>   Learning to be me
>   Learning to feel
>   The wall falls as I let myself be
>
>   Joyful hearts come together
>   Learning to love others again
>   And myself
>   In the healing power of stillness
>
>   Still learning to be in the moment
>   Feel the sunshine and joy inside
>   We hold on together
>   Horses with wings

Conclusion

In the presence of a horse we become embodied. It is hard to be indifferent when around them. We have to pay attention. They are big, powerful, and potentially dangerous. They have a strong smell. And we deeply desire to touch them. We want to sit upon their backs and fly. Horses are deeply relational, curious, and gentle. In my work with horses and women, I have seen profound transformation in those I have worked with. Some of this is written down and documented; some is just felt and spoken of as, "Something has shifted, and I know it was because of that horse."

Equine Facilitated Psychotherapy is a new paradigm, and not always an easy one to access or even accept as a legitimate therapy. Recently, it has acquired a growing body of empirical support, and it is gaining wider interest and acceptance. Horses speak to the transpersonal part of our psyche and our deepest longings. They are deeply bonded with their environment, nature, and other beings. They are mysterious, beautiful, and powerful. They seek safety, play, bonding, and moving into the world of others. It is my hope that more and more horses will find their calling to support and heal us in the many areas of our wounding, and connect us again with our fundamental goodness and natural, innate capacities to heal. I hope they will continue to help and support us to connect with our authentic selves and rekindle our trust and connection with other humans and the world. In the words of the women who have participated in this form of psychotherapy, the horses give them the wings of their lives.

References

Adler, J. (2002). *Offering from the conscious body: The discipline of authentic movement.* Rochester, VT: Inner Traditions.

American Hippotherapy Association (AHA; 2016). Retrieved April 16, 2016 from http//www.americanhippotherapyassociation.org.

Broseman, P. (2007). *Riding into your mythic life.* Navato, CA: New World Library.

Baldwin, A. (Producer). (2014). *Heart to heart communication with horses* (video webinar). Retrieved April 16, 2016 from http//heartmath.org

Caldwell, C. (1996). *Getting our bodies back: Recovery, healing and transformation through body-centered psychotherapy.* Boston, MA: Shambhala Publications.

Bennett-Goleman, T. (2013). *Mind whispering, a new map to freedom from self-defeating emotional habits.* New York, NY: Harper-Collins Publishers.

Dugard, J. (2011). *A stolen life: A memoir.* New York, NY: Simon & Schuster.

Equine-Assisted Growth and Learning Association (EAGALA; 2012). Retrieved April 16, 2016 from http://www.eagala.org

Farley, T. (2015). *Wild at Heart: Mustangs and the young people fighting to save them.* Boston, MA: Houghton, Mifflin, and Harcourt.

Fitch, R. T. (2008). *Straight from the horse's heart: A spiritual ride through love, loss and hope.* Charleston, NC: BookSurge Publishing.

Fogel, A. (2009). *Body sense: The science and practice of embodied self-awareness.* New York, NY: W.W. Norton.

Fulton, P. (2005). Mindfulness as clinical training. In C. Germer, R. Siegel, & P. Fulton (Eds.), *Mindfulness and psychotherapy* (pp. 55–72). New York, NY: Guilford press.

Hallberg, L. (2008). *Walking the way of the horse: Exploring the power of the horse–human relationship.* New York, NY: Universe Inc.

Hayes, T. (2015). *Riding home: The power of horses to heal.* New York, NY: St. Martin's Press.

Heller, D. P. (2015, July 11). *Attachment Theory and Trauma.* Lecture presented at Boulder Marriot in Boulder. CO

Husher, H. (2005). *Conversations with a prince: A year of riding at East Hill Farm.* Guilford, CT: The Lyons Press.

Isaacson, R. (2009). *The horse boy: A father's quest to heal his son.* New York, NY: Little, Brown & Company.

Kohanov, L. (2001). *The tao of equus: A woman's journey of healing & transformation through the way of the horse.* Novato, CA: New World Library.

Levine, P., & Frederick, A. (1997). *Waking the tiger: Healing trauma.* Berkeley, CA: North Atlantic Books.

Levine, P. (2010). *The unspoken voice: How the body releases trauma and restores goodness.* Berkley, CA: North Atlantic Books.

McCormick, A., McCormick, M., & McCormick, T. (2004). *Horses and the mystical path.* Novato CA: New World Press.

Meinersman, K.M., Bradberry, J., & Roberts, F.B. (2008). Equine-facilitated psychotherapy with adult female survivors of abuse. *Journal of psychosocial nursing and mental health services, 46*(12), 36–42.

Midkiff, M. (2001). *She flies without wings: How horses touch a woman's soul.* New York, NY: Random House.

Ogden, P., Minton K., & Pain C. (2006). *Trauma and the body: A sensorimotor approach to psychotherapy.* New York, NY: W.W. Norton.

Oldfield, H.M. (1923). *The horse in magic & myth.* London: William Rider & Son.

Pierson, M. H. (2000). Dark horses and black beauties. New York, NY: W.W. Norton.Pike, K. (2009). *Hope...from the heart of horses: How horses teach us about presence, strength and awareness.* New York, NY: Sky Horse Publishing.

Professional Association of Therapeutic Horsemanship International (PATH; 2016). Retrieved from http://www.pathintl.org.

Shambo, L., Young, S., & Madera, C. (2013). *The listening heart: The limbic path beyond office therapy.* Chelhalis, WA: Human-Equine Alliances for Healing.

Richards, S. (2006). *Chosen by a horse: A memoir.* Orlando FL: Harcourt Books.

Schroeder K., & Stroud D., (2015). Group work for women survivors of interpersonal violence. *The Journal for Specialist in Group Work. 40*(4), 365–386.

Siegel, D. (2010). *The mindful therapist: A clinician's guide to mindsight and neural integration.* New York/London; W.W. Norton & Company.

Sovey-Nelson, M. (2004). *If I had a horse: How different life would be.* Minacqua, WI: Willow Creek Press.

Trotter, K. (2012). *Harnessing the power of equine assisted counseling: Adding animal assisted therapy to your practice.* New York, NY: Routledge.

Chapter 12
Reconciling Identity, Oppression, and the Transpersonal

Kathleen Gregory

Julie A. Kellaway

> If transpersonal psychology is to stand for human wholeness and transformation, it needs to embody what it teaches: there can be no lasting human transformation without inclusiveness, nor holism without diversity. (Hartelius, Caplin, & Rardin, 2007, p. 152)

Nearly a decade ago, a call was made to the field of transpersonal psychology to include voices from all over the world to ensure the continued growth of the field (Hartelius, Caplin, & Rardin, 2007). The call was for transpersonal psychology to extend its current scope beyond the East-West division of first world nations (e.g., Europe, Japan, United States) and be longitudinally inclusive by including (among many others) other Asian countries, South American, African, and indigenous perspectives. In addition, Hartelius, Caplin and Rardin noted the gender gap in the existing transpersonal psychology literature, highlighting the fact that published articles in transpersonal psychology are "still heavily skewed towards men" (p. 152). This despite the fact that most transpersonal psychology programs, like the field of psychology itself, are heavily skewed towards women (Hart, Wicherski, & Kohout, 2010).

Unfortunately, neither of these studies addressed transgendered and non-gendered identifications. The call for transpersonal psychology to embrace inclusivity and diversity was not only predicated on the necessity to ensure that the field remains relevant, but to draw attention to the fact that that the very notion of transpersonal psychology contains a theoretical appreciation for inclusivity and diversity. For example, Fukuyama, Murphy, and Siahpoush (2003) assert that "there is no transpersonal psychology without the multicultural and the spiritual perspectives" (p. 187), while Hartelius, Caplin, and Rardin, (2007) state that transpersonal psychology "opposes specious justifications for the oppression of any person or group" (p.153). However, this vision remains unfulfilled as diverse perspectives remain scarce in the literature; individuals from marginalized backgrounds are dramatically less represented and organized than students, professors, and others in positions of power. As such, sustaining transpersonal social activism remains more theoretical than actual (see Hoffman chapter, this volume; Hocoy chapter in Volume 1 of *Shadows & Light*). The criticism that some transpersonal psychology-oriented clinicians and clinician trainees seek to bypass social injustice concerns to focus on spiritual pursuits is grounded in experiences we have witnessed in the classroom and beyond.

Some current scholars have made the case that the field has made significant shifts in including cultural considerations pertaining to feminist inquiry, ecopsychology, and spirituality within the past decade (Brooks, Ford, & Huffman, 2013). However, in conducting our own search of the literature through PsychInfo in March 2016 we found the term *transpersonal* yielded 1,500 articles. When transpersonal was linked in turn to each of the following terms: gender, African American, gay, lesbian, indigenous, inclusivity, diversity, and multiculturalism, less than 100 articles were generated in total. The PsychInfo results during the same time period jumped to over 500 entries when transpersonal was searched along with the words *spirituality* or *religion*. In addition, it is worth noting that the cross-cultural research conducted in transpersonal psychology is predominantly related to near-death experiences (NDE) in both Western and non-Western countries (Fracasso, Greyson, & Friedman, 2013). While it is expected that the transpersonal psychology field would explore the cross-cultural realms of spirituality, religion, and NDE, given the assertion that transpersonal psychology is rooted in inclusivity and diversity, there is a paucity of published research on transpersonal psychology and multiculturalism. Moreover, there are notable deficiencies in peer-reviewed publications that directly address the principles of inclusivity and diversity applied within the areas of transpersonal psychology theory, clinical practice, and teaching.

Given that both the accrediting bodies for counselors and psychologists—the American Counseling Association (ACA) and the American Psychological Association (APA), respectively—recognize the necessity of multicultural training in counselor and psychologist programs, the dearth of inclusivity and diversity research in transpersonal psychology in particular can leave transpersonal psychology educators vulnerable. This is of concern when the research shows that faculty and instructors who are responsible for teaching inclusively and diversity in a multicultural counseling frame invariably state that the classes are challenging to teach.

Helms et al. (2003) suggest three primary challenges. First, students are often resistant to looking at biased beliefs. When confronted with their biases, they may "act out their resistance by punishing the educator" (p. 4). This may manifest simply as resistance through, for example, not engaging with the material or in-class discussion. However, it can also present more like harassment, including a disrespectful attitude toward the instructor, poor evaluations, or complaints to school administration. A second challenge when teaching diversity and inclusivity involves engaging students who are at different levels of cultural awareness. As our own experience attests, this can cause tension in the classroom since it can lead some students to experience the class as too challenging while other students demand deeper discussions. The third challenge involves student resistance to the material that may reflect institutionalized barriers (e.g., institutionalized racism or sexism), which may hold especially true for faculty with minority status (Helms, et al., 2003). The overarching challenge then becomes managing an emotionally charged classroom setting in which educators attempt to balance class content with class management while potentially enduring harassment, and concern that administration may be unsupportive if a student complains. Again, as

Helms, et al. (2003) reiterate, faculty with minority status may suffer in a disproportionate manner due to unrecognized bias by students, internalized oppression, and institutionalized discrimination.

Discussions from colleagues on this topic have yielded examples over the years that range from subtle to overt bias. Subtle bias from students can emerge as a microaggression (e.g., invalidation of the educator's authority or expertise). Overt bias may emerge directly as student hostility toward the faculty member, which can manifest as walking out of class, verbal aggression (e.g., yelling, utilizing racially charged slurs), and physical aggression (e.g., throwing items).

As a result, educators not only need to ensure that clinical accreditation content is covered, but they also require tools and frameworks to simultaneously manage the emotionally charged nature of the material. In our experience, the impact of unrecognized bias and different stages of development in relation to cultural awareness in the classroom can be significant for educators and students alike. These can cause division between students, and particular pressure may be placed on minority students within the class, especially because their numbers are generally disproportionately low in graduate counseling programs. The most recent figures reported by the APA indicate that full-time, first-year minority graduates enrolled in doctoral programs accounted for between 8% (African-American) and 2% (for both American Indian and multiethnic), whereas the reported number of white students was 71% (Hart, Wicherski, & Kohout, 2010). The rates were similar for masters-level psychology programs (Hart, Wicherski, & Kohout, 2010). No research was available at the time of publication on minority student enrollments in graduate transpersonal counseling programs. In a largely white student body, a student of color may feel they are being called upon to represent "their group." Furthermore, when class discussions include the history, institutionalized practices, and psychological and socioeconomic effects of oppression, students from marginalized locations may experience a sense of diminishment that impacts their sense of belonging in the class and possibly even triggers shame relating to past experiences of oppression and internalized oppression.

That educators strongly address these oppressive dynamics is vital for learning and safety in the classroom. Setting ground rules, narrating the unspoken, and avoiding scapegoating and tokenism dynamics are some of the techniques we employ. We also use a framework to assist in helping students appreciate the fluid and contextual nature of personal identity. That is, when an identity is imposed on another person or when a motif of identity such as race or gender is used to essentialize them in some way, we recognize that these are practices that may enact oppression (Gregory, 2013). Here we understand the word *esssentialize* to refer to the process of attributing natural or essential characteristics to a culturally defined group, such as defined by race, ethnicity, gender, sexual orientation, dis/ability, social class, age and so forth (Razak, 1998). In this way, essentializing is one basis of stereotyping, bias, and prejudice, and thus serves to oppress others. Essentializing is associated with the practices of the traditional rationalist–objectivist view of knowledge. In contrast, contemporary perspectives emphasize that all knowledge is constructed by human beings in social contexts (Mahoney, 2003). As a result, individual identity and its attributes are not perceived as naturally present but as socially created or constructed. Thus, to describe a woman as emotional is to eschew the fact that a "woman's class, race, sexuality, and physical or mental condition combine in history in specific ways to produce her, and the responses to her" (Razak, 2001, p. 157).

Transpersonal research methodologies include a variety of qualitative, phenomenological, heuristic, ethnographic, collaborative, and contextual approaches that fit well with the study of multiculturalism. As Shorrock (2008) outlines, transpersonal psychology can integrate and utilize the views of social constructivism. From this perspective, personal identity is shaped by social context factors in which the dynamics of gender, race, age, ability, ethnicity, sexual orientation and other locations of "difference" from dominant (and often unspoken) cultural norms are "enacted" on individuals (Gregory, 2013).

As previously noted, the foundations of transpersonal psychology and multicultural considerations have been theoretically and intricately woven together, despite the limited literature pertaining to diversity and inclusivity and a lack of engagement with contemporary understandings of identity within the field. This issue is of substantial concern, as the field of transpersonal psychology explores a wide range of experiences that necessarily call for attention to cultural considerations. Outside of the recognition that the nature of transpersonal experiences is intrinsically embedded and shaped by a variety of social contexts, it has also been recognized that the field of transpersonal psychology has not readily embraced the "situated context" of individuals (Brooks, Ford, & Huffman, 2013, p. 612). In fact, transpersonal psychology has historically sought to eschew personality identity "as a problem to transcend" (Brooks, Ford, and Huffman, 2013, p. 612). This creates a tension within transpersonal psychology and raises an important question in relation to inclusivity and diversity: How does transpersonal psychology respond to contemporary constructivist perspectives that recognize the fluid, contrary, and subjective nature of an individual's identity dependent upon social contexts framed by privilege and oppression? This question is pertinent to educators in order to ensure that transpersonal psychology and counseling not only reflect contemporary understandings related to the impact of social context on personal identity development, but also simultaneously seek to present inclusivity and diversity principles and an appreciation for the psychological impact of the social forces of privilege and power.

Gregory (2013) utilized the phrase "floating signifier" from Stuart Hall (1997) to capture the fluid and contextual nature of a person's identity in relation to such motifs as race, gender, and sexual orientation. For Hall, this phrase sought to underscore the "floating" nature of the definition of race; in this case, the aim was to highlight social constructivist understandings of identity and underscore the floating nature of locations of identity in the lives of individual persons. Otherwise, in a given situation, whether in the counseling office or in the classroom, there is danger of an essentialist imposition of "a single, drastically simplified group identity" on a person, in which we deny the reality of "the complexity of people's lives, the multiplicity of their identifications, and the cross-pulls of their various affiliations" (Fraser, 2003, p. 89). For educators, there exists an imperative to reduce student tendencies to embrace overly simplistic versions of the identity of others. This imperative becomes the foundation for class discussion of inclusivity and diversity as students learn to develop a sensitivity to the necessity of refraining from practices that may essentialize another, which can activate assumptions and bias, and lead to oppression.

This imperative thus compels students to critically reflect on their own identity while providing a framework for them to engage skillfully with one another in discussion. To deepen students' appreciation for the floating nature of the motifs of identity in their own lives, we introduce an exercise that invites them to consider elements such as gender, race, sexual orientation, class, ethnicity, age, dis/ability, in relation to their own locations:

> *I am most/least aware of my race when...*
> *I am most/least aware of my gender when...*
> *I am most/least aware of sexual orientation when...*
> *I am most/least aware of my social class when...*

This exercise personalizes the theory of social constructivism and provides an experience of the fluid, subjective, and context-dependent nature of personal identity. It also helps strengthen the movement away from an essentialist notion of identity and serves to undermine the notion that personal identity is a hindrance or problem to be overcome. In fact, experience has demonstrated that this exercise is often a positive turning point for students because they more fully appreciate the floating nature of the motifs of their own identity.

As students deepen their self-awareness and develop an internal framework of the socially constructed nature of identity, they are more readily equipped to explore the ways in which oppression and privilege can be enacted within clinical practice. For this next step, we rely on the distinction made by Hanna, Talley, and Guindon (2000) between two different modes of oppression: oppression by force and oppression by deprivation. The first is in keeping with the social constructivist understanding of identity to which most students have been introduced and have explored in relation to their own identity (Gregory, 2013).

Specifically, oppression by force is described as the act of imposing "on another or others an object, label, role, experience, or set of living conditions that is unwanted, needlessly painful, and detracts from physical or psychological well-being" (Hanna, Talley & Guindon, 2000, p. 431).

In contrast, oppression by deprivation is an "act that deprives another or others of an object, role, experience or set of living conditions that are desirable and conducive to physical or psychological well-being" (Hanna, Talley, & Guindon, 2000, p. 431). In the context of the therapeutic relationship, oppression by deprivation may be enacted when a counselor represses, denies, or avoids raising questions of oppression and privilege with a client, including the common motifs of identity related to oppression such race, gender, social class, sexuality, age, and so forth. To this end, it can be helpful for educators to invite students to consider the ways they as counselors may *benefit* from not addressing locations of oppression such as race and, thereby, may indulge in what Hanna, Talley and Guindon (2000) describe as "secondary oppression" (p. 431). For example, benefits from not addressing locations of oppression may include avoiding discomfort or acknowledging one's own history of either oppression or oppressing (Gregory, 2013). Students should be provided with the opportunity, therefore, to consider their own potential privilege, unspoken bias, prejudice, and fear. In this discussion with students, it is important to acknowledge the essential clinical dilemma to both engage in conversation with clients around potential locations of oppression and thus not deprive them of that opportunity, while simultaneously appreciating the floating nature of these motifs as locations of personal identity. In holding this discussion with students, we seek to ensure that counselor trainees develop an appreciation for the intrapersonal and interpersonal dynamics that may lead to oppression by both force and deprivation.

We have adopted the following set of questions as a means for students to become aware of these realities of clinical practice in accord with their development as transpersonal psychology counselors who are responsive to diversity and inclusivity. Race is used in the following examples; however, it is recommended that other motifs should also be utilized (adapted from Gregory, 2013):

How do I as a psychotherapist introduce locations of identity as a possible motif within a client's life without this itself becoming an incidence of "oppression by force"?

For example, consider how the introduction of race may be presented as an assumption, label, or experience in a way that is imposed on the client that serves to reduce their self-determination and well-being.

How do I as a psychotherapist ensure that by omission, avoidance, or neglect I do not engage in "oppression by deprivation," in which the client is deprived of the opportunity to explore their experience in relation to locations of identity?

For example, how, without it being reduced, denied, or ignored, can race be explored in ways that serve to increase a client's sense of self-determination and well-being?

Do I as a psychotherapist "benefit" from not addressing race and, thereby, am I indulging in "secondary oppression"?

The growing awareness of inclusivity and diversity within the field of transpersonal psychology, along with the need to meet the needs of accrediting bodies to teach competencies in multiculturalism, places importance on laying a strong foundation for counselor trainees. In the contemporary context, educators are called upon to help trainees understand the socially constructed nature of identity, while coupling with it an appreciation for the psychological effects of both oppression and privilege. However, as noted earlier, there is an intrinsic point of stress between transpersonal psychology's emphasis of eschewing individual identity and the reality of the negative psychological effects of oppression and bias. To address this point, it is helpful for transpersonal psychology to include contemporary constructivist perspectives of identity, which are necessarily framed by privilege and oppression. Inherent tensions will continue if transpersonal psychology theorists, practitioners, and researchers stress that personal identity is something to be overcome when contemporary understandings of identity are non-essentialist in nature.

This chapter has highlighted important theoretical and clinical practice issues that relate to the contemporary field of multicultural psychology and counseling and their intersection with transpersonal psychology and counseling. In particular, the incorporation of a social constructivist approach to individual identity has been utilized in the classroom as an antidote to practices of oppression such as essentializing, and as a foundation for the students' future engagement with clients around motifs of identity such as race. In the hope of expanding and creating transpersonal psychology, multicultural psychology, and counselor education, we offer this consideration of including the social constructivist approach to identity and oppression. At the same time, we reject any ideological position that seeks to use such an approach to deny or diminish the reality of the practices of institutionalized oppression and marginalization, and their effects in the lived experience of people. We have sought to facilitate a capacity to address potential locations of oppression with clients in a way that reflects transpersonal psychology's emphasis on human transformation that is whole-person centered and inclusive of an individual's "relationship and situatedness in the world" (Hartelius, Rothe, & Roy, 2013, p. 8).

Furthermore, this chapter presented how to effectively address inclusivity and diversity with transpersonal psychology counselor trainees from a developmental perspective, while also recognizing the reality that students present at different stages of cultural awareness. This requires that we as educators be responsive to the unique individuals in our classroom, rather than imposing a nomothetical developmental structure on students. The techniques described herein help educators move students into greater self-awareness and then to develop a capacity to engage both intelligently and sensitively with the inter-subjective nature of oppression and privilege. In fact, as students deepen their appreciation for the floating nature of motifs of identity, they naturally begin to increase their awareness of the more subtle ways in which oppression and privilege are enacted interpersonally. This serves to enhance self-knowledge and address matters of inclusivity and diversity that are equally as relevant in our personal lives as in our clinical practices.

References

Brooks, C., Ford, K., & Huffman, A. (2013). Feminist and cultural contributions to transpersonal psychology. In H. L. Friedman & G. Hartelius (Eds.), *The Wiley Blackwell handbook of transpersonal psychology* (pp. 612–625). West Sussex, UK: Wiley-Blackwell.

Fracasso, C., Greyson, B., & Friedman, H. L. (2013). Near-death experiences and transpersonal psychology. In H. L. Friedman & G. Hartelius (Eds.), *The Wiley Blackwell handbook of transpersonal psychology* (pp. 367–381). West Sussex, UK: Wiley-Blackwell.

Fraser, N. (2003) Recognition without ethics? In C. McKinnon & D. Castiglione (Eds.). *The Culture of toleration in diverse societies: Reasonable tolerance* (pp. 86-108). Manchester, UK: Manchester University Press.

Fukuyama, M., Murphy, M., & Siahpoush, F. (2003). Bridging the gaps: Weaving multicultural and humanistic perspectives into transpersonal education. *The Humanistic Psychologist, 31*(2-3), 182.

Gregory, K. (2013). The im/possibility of race. *Psychotherapy and Politics International, 11*(2), 152–159.

Hall, S. (1997). *Race, the floating signifier.* Northampton, MA: Media Education Foundation. Retrieved August 10, 2012, from www.youtube.com/watch?v=bMo2uiRAf30.

Hanna, F. J., Talley, W. B., & Guindon, M. H. (2000). The power of perception: Toward a model of cultural oppression and liberation. *Journal of Counseling and Development, 78*, 430–441.

Hart, B. Wicherski, M., & Kohout, J. (2010). 2010 Graduate Study in Psychology. Retrieved August 1, 2016, from http://www.apa.org/workforce/publications/10-grad-study/students.aspx.

Hartelius, G., Caplin, M., & Rardin, M. A. (2007). Transpersonal psychology: Defining the past, divining the future. *The Humanistic Psychologist, 35*(2), 135–160.

Hartelius, G., Rothe, G., & Roy, P. J. (2013). A brand from the burning. In H. L. Friedman & G. Hartelius (Eds.), *The Wiley Blackwell handbook of transpersonal psychology* (pp. 3-22). , West Sussex, UK: Wiley-Blackwell.

Helms, J. E., Malone, L. S., Henze, K., Satiani, K., Perry, J., & Warren, A. (2003). First annual diversity challenge: How to survive teaching courses on race and culture. *Journal of Multicultural Counseling and Development, 31*, 3–11.

Mahoney, M. J. (2003). *Constructive psychotherapy: A practical guide.* New York, NY: The Guilford Press.

Razak, S. H. (1998). *Looking white people in the eye: Gender, race, and culture in courtrooms and classrooms.* Ontario, Canada: University of Toronto Press.

Shorrock, A. (2008). *The transpersonal in psychology, psychotherapy and counselling.* London: Palgrave MacMillan.

Chapter 13
Experiencing Transpersonal Psychology in the Classroom

Diane Joy Israel

Even though I was put in "special needs" classes growing up, I loved learning. I now know that I was "special" because I was different. I learned in ways that were more embodied and more heart-full than memorization and regurgitation. I decided even then that if I ever had the chance to teach I wanted to take a more expansive approach to learning beyond the traditional, one-size-fits-all, logic-based model. In more than two decades of teaching at Naropa University in Mindfulness Based Transpersonal Counseling Psychology, I have found that my "specialties" match my many students' needs for creative and out-of-the box teaching, which includes in-the-moment emotions, relationships, and individual expression.

As a non-traditional professor teaching a non-traditional discipline, I am able to bring together my experience, creativity, and mindfulness to create a container for learning in which students can thrive, learn, and discover the transpersonal in their everyday classroom experiences. The classroom becomes a supportive environment that buttresses the arc of human development and helps students discover new meanings. All learning styles and aspects of student experiences are welcome. The inclusion of personal development, meaning making, relationship, dialogue, and the affirmation of the totality of students' experiences (the good and the messy) is based on transpersonal pedagogies (Clark, 2016; Rowe & Braud, 2013).

I have been lucky to be around many wonderful pedagogical thinkers throughout my life. At Naropa, I have been able to discuss and learn from other faculty such as Judith Simmer-Brown (2009; Simmer-Brown & Grace, 2011) about contemplative education practices, and their application to training in psychology with Peter Grossenbacher (Grossenbacher & Parkin, 2006). In addition, teaching alongside Christine Caldwell's (2013) body-based orientation has always resonated with me as a former professional triathlete.

Other influences include my own mindfulness practices as well as the blossoming emergence of these ideas in counselor training (Bohecker, Vereen, Wells, & Wathen, 2016). As an embodied learner, experiential education has always profoundly impacted me. I draw upon the long history of this tradition, which most recently is being actively applied to developing multicultural counselor knowledge, awareness, and skills (Lee, 2014; Smith & Trimble, 2016). The findings of neuroscience in interpersonal neurobiology and co-regulation remind me to focus on my own well-being as a tool to assist student learning (Cozolino 2013). I also began to see more clearly how my personal experiences, particularly as a student with a learning disability and later as the caretaker of my mother during her death experience, have resulted in an eagerness to understand the human experience of being alive, messy, emotional, and complex. The work of former Naropa president and current faculty Judy Lief (2001; Tulku et al., 2014) on integrating death into one's life experience and contemplative teaching provided support and insight throughout this process. While I draw on these influences, my focus has always been more on engagement with students in the classroom, and less on academic scholarship; thus, this chapter outlines how I approach the classroom.

With personal guidance from Bruce Tift and his book, *Already Free* (2015), I began to integrate these principles into my transpersonal teaching approach, which I call Full-Contact Teaching. The goal is to facilitate growth and nurture the full expression of emotions in my students so that they begin to see all emotions as a universal experience and learn to accept them, whatever they are. Learning to "be with what's already here" builds the skills of self-acceptance and self-regulation in students, which can ultimately be applied to their future therapeutic relationships with clients. The classroom needs to strike a balance between academic rigor and the wisdom of the heart.

Foundational Principles of Full-Contact Teaching

Through adaptation and improvisation, my regular courses (human development, couples and family therapy, and group dynamics and leadership) continue to evolve, as does my pedagogical approach. My goal is to help students appreciate and understand the complexity and impact of human relationships, as well as psychological topics. Our path includes experiential exercises that bring forth students' creativity, interpersonal contact, and contemplation. The class models the therapeutic encounter by being responsive to and finding creative solutions to the students' emerging needs. For example, if students appear tired of the lecture or they seem to fade on me, I'll do an experiential exercise or we stand up and move.

When I am standing before a classroom of students, it is similar to when I am working as a psychotherapist. The books I have absorbed and all the thinkers who have influenced me can only help me so much. Instead of only talking about the theories, I attempt to show, demonstrate, or model them for students. Theories come alive as we are in the present moment with one another. What better way to help students learn how to conduct transpersonal therapy than to experience and practice contact and intimacy, presence and creativity, examining and containing strong feelings, and examining human relationships. This responsive, in-the-moment interpersonal interplay is the first principle that I believe helps psychotherapy students develop as people and eventually as therapists.

A second principle is to stay open to the moment and use creativity and collaboration to keep students involved. Part of my teaching approach is to be open enough to allow me to be creative with students' experiences, turning them into a class and a lesson. Just as jazz musicians might start with a set melody or dancers might start with a choreographed series of steps and then improvise, I have a set sequence—a format really—with which I begin almost every class. But there is no "typical" class. I often abandon the agenda for honoring and being with my students. We create each class together, and what traditional schools have labeled as learning disabilities are not apparent in my classroom, where all styles, modalities, and talents are welcome.

Third, I accept and invite tension and contrast—in me, the students, and the material—as vehicles to practice transpersonal principles of first-person inquiry, authentic connectedness, working with ambiguity, and moving beyond logic and formulas. Bruce Tift recommends that we hold both emotions and processes without choosing sides (personal communication, December 16, 2015). I have found that paradox is the heart of the messiness in each of us. We are not one thing, one way, or one response. If I value one part of you over another, then part of what makes you whole is lost. Valuing it all—and us all—starts to help us appreciate the amazing array of all that it is to be human.

The format is a combination of the experiential and the academic. As an athlete, I love the word *discipline*, and that is what I have to keep track of in the limited classroom hours. It is like training. If you are going to train for a triathlon, you cannot only run. You have to be disciplined to bike and swim as well. Similarly, in classes we still have ground to cover, subjects and theories to get through, a schedule to keep, assignments and a syllabus to follow. By valuing emotions and process as well as mind and content, I feel most grounded to experience wisdom and compassion. It is this fullness that allows students to integrate experiential with conceptual knowledge.

In addition to welcoming emotions, criticisms, and questions, I incorporate students' present-moment experience and responses to the material, which become part of the content of the lesson. In the transpersonal therapeutic relationship, the inner state of the instructor/teacher sets the stage for how the students will learn, and I want my students to be awake, alive, and as messy as they need to be to really learn. Naropa professor Lama Tenpa says, "Classic Buddhist texts at the core are creative models, because they are questioning models" (personal communication, January 11, 2016). Even though students have been taught to be passive receptacles for teacher diatribes, the best learning happens when their minds and hearts wake up!

The three meta-principles that describe Full-Contact Teaching are: a) the experiential, creative and responsive in-the-moment method; b) the students' lived experience as part of the content for the lesson; and c) the fact that paradox is not only tolerated but is invited, explored, and investigated as a teaching tool.

Additional Aspects of Full-Contact Teaching

Several elements help create an environment in which emotions, process, theory, and experience all have a place. Present-moment awareness, embodiment, emotions, and death are in the framework of all the courses. These aspects of the human experience may not be found in traditional university classrooms, but students seem to thrive in this type of exploratory environment.

Present-moment Awareness Guides Class Tempo

Each class begins with a mediation practice derived from Shamatha Vipassana, one of the primary meditation practices at Naropa. *Shamatha* means peaceful abiding and refers to stabilizing one's mind to bring attention into our immediate experience. *Vipassana* stands for insight, the wider view that arises as we stabilize our minds. One aspect of stabilization is the capacity to tolerate our experience of being alive without trying to suppress, pretend, or distract ourselves.

The initial classroom practice allows us to slow down and connect to our breath. Sitting practices ground the pace of life. After sitting, often it feels as if the natural world has made its way into the room. When this happens, it is a breathtaking experience. The hallways and the environment around us—like most schools—are noisy and chaotic. The world just outside the classroom is swirling with busyness.

Everyone races to the next thing, students are on their cell phones, people talk excitedly. To sit down and to be in silence takes discipline and practice, but it is like taking a drink of water in the desert.

Buddhist teacher Pema Chödrön (Chödrön & Lang, 2015) discusses the benefits of taking pauses because it "creates an open doorway to the sacredness of the place in which you find yourself.... pause just long enough, you can reconnect with exactly where you are, with the immediacy of your experience" (p. 38). The beauty of meditation is that it gives us an experience of the value of holding everything. The mind is busy. The hallways are busy. Yet there is a deep peacefulness that arises when we return our attention over and over to our breath. In silence, acceptance is cultivated.

When the class is ready and quiet, we seek to invite open-heartedness, presence, honesty, and healthy boundaries into the classroom. This clarity of structure allows emotions, embodiment, and the *open-now* to be introduced. In this environment, the classroom emerges as an interdependent living system where we effect and influence one another. I see the classroom as a working group. Similarly, Agazarian (1992) suggests,

> Your first job is to get energy contained within the group as a whole system—crossing the boundaries from outside to inside. The clearer the group is about how to bring its outside experience into the group, rather than take flight into outside experience, the more relevant information and energy is available to reach the group goals. (p. 4)

Present-moment awareness practices support students' ability to make contact with themselves and one another, which simultaneously promotes group cohesion. We also use immediate and shared experience to emphasize that we are now ready to begin. In the group-process class, I model how to be in the present moment: paying attention to what is in the room, commenting on how the students enter, and how they seem to experience one another. Then, I invite them to share their visions and impressions of themselves and one another. This way we are all starting together with the same information present to all.

Embodiment: Paying Attention to Emotions and Sensations
In the wider community, people may speak about being or feeling *grounded*. Being grounded is another way of saying being embodied. Full embodiment consists of paying attention to our physical bodies and what we are feeling and sensing on a physical level. Through the body, we can learn how to be in the present moment. This is crucial for transpersonal counselors because when one is highly attuned to themselves, they can be more attuned to what is going on for the client as well as more aware of their own projections. This allows a student or therapist to be embodied, available, and able to more skillfully respond to uncomfortable or challenging situations that arise during sessions. As Tift explains,

> Because our culture is so identified with thinking, we tend to take our concepts as if they are an adequate representation of reality. Embodiment can be a helpful antidote to that tendency. To stay embodied, to pay attention to sensations with no interpretation of this experience invites a dialogue between what used to be true (interpretations) and what is currently true, which is found in our immediate embodied experience. (personal communication with author, December 16, 2015)

To tune into our sensations brings us into our present moment and beyond our thoughts and limiting beliefs. Embodiment is a lifetime journey; as we practice it more, we get better at it and can help others, such as students or clients, become more aware of their bodies and how to stay in the present moment. To sit in the enormity of emotions and the intensity of being therapists, we need to be embodied so we can come home to ourselves, which requires self-care and being present so we can meet whatever emerges.

Sometimes when I see a student's body language change, I may point it out and ask, "What's happening for you in this moment?" Even though much of what is being communicated between people is nonverbal, we have been trained not to see or mention it. In counseling, we need to be attuned to subtle shifts of emotion and awareness in our clients. By teaching students to notice non-verbal cues and by modeling present-moment awareness in the classroom, we help students increase their ability to observe and articulate phenomena, which supports their personal and professional development.

The Valuable Role of Emotions

Inviting emotions into the classroom is not easy because our culture does not teach us how to respond to emotions that are uncomfortable and difficult, such as anger, shame, and anxiety (Miler, 2013). We are more emotional in our nature than we know how to handle. Nothing in our culture currently supports the development of these subtle—or not so subtle—reactions. But as our students go on to become therapists, they will face a wide range of emotions every day with their clients. So I try to model to my students how to live highly attuned and responsive to emotions.

Since I often open a class by telling the students what I'm feeling or sensing, I might then say something to the students like, "Notice any feelings that may be coming up for you right now. See if you can welcome them, expect them, and count on them—for the rest of your messy human life."

Sometimes we go around the room, and everybody shares a word to describe how they are feeling in the moment. One student may say "tired," the next "anxious," the next "grateful." If there is an exam that day, I may openly invite fear, doubt, insecurity—or the common student experience of feeling unprepared or not good enough. At Naropa, we often give a "Warrior's Exam," during which students answer their exam questions orally in front of the class. Once, one of my students came in the day of the exam and said, "I can't take the Warrior's Exam. I'm completely anxious and can't function." I told him I still wanted him to be part of the class and support the other students. Then during a break, this student said he wanted to try to take the test because he saw how so many other students were breaking through their fears and anxieties to complete it. We are practicing the skill of allowing emotions to arise alive and well in the classroom, to be with them, and still participate.

I try not to discriminate against any particular emotions. I teach that anxiety is really aliveness, and joy is not actually better than anger. Social science researcher Karla McLaren's (2010) book *The Language of Emotions* is one of my best resources. McLaren has identified 17 emotions and, as she has so passionately taught, all of them are to be celebrated. McLaren says that in our culture, the "bad emotions" category is large:

> Sadness that lasts too long (or deepens into despair or grief) is definitely bad. Depression is bad but suicidal urges are emergency-room bad. Anger is bad, as are peevishness, righteous indignation and wrath. Rage and fury, then, are extra-strength bad! Hatred, we won't even go into. Jealous is bad bad bad. Fear is so bad, we've got bumper stickers that shout to others that we, at least, haven't got any fear—not a drop! So all the fear-based emotions are bad, too. Anxiety, worry, and trepidation are bad, and panic is call-the-hospital bad. Shame and guilt—they're so bad that we don't even know what they mean anymore! We're persistently trained and implored to express or more often repress our emotions so that other people feel comfortable.... Real joy and real happiness can only exist in relation to all of the emotions; they're a boxed set. We can't just pick and choose our emotions. (pp. 26–27)

For example, when a student feels confused or uncomfortable about issues that come up in the content of the course, we explore them. Then as shame or anxiety or fear arises, we go right into examining those emotions with curiosity. Practicing the experiencing of difficult, complex emotions over and over exercises our emotional muscles.

As students get used to relating to their emotions, they become more adept at identifying, understanding, and having compassion for themselves and their peers. A student recently shared in class that she was very angry at her mother. As she shared her anger, she immediately felt ashamed and embarrassed. As we sat with her feelings and allowed them to be, the anger, shame and embarrassment moved on. In a later exercise when she was with another student who was angry at his father, she was able to sit with his feelings.

Anger is one of those emotions that many students don't know how to handle. McLaren (2010) teaches that anger serves as the protector of our boundaries. So I invite a student to bring their awareness to what their own personal boundaries are. Then I ask if the anger is in response to a violation of their boundaries. Or if a student is struggling with feeling angry at the start of class, I might say, "Why don't you plan on being a messy, unresolved individual for the rest of your life? So what? Is it killing you now?" Of course, none of us wants these uncomfortable feelings, yet somehow given the permission to feel them often helps soften the situation and lets the emotions move through us.

Francis Weller (2015) has said that nearly every day of his practice someone speaks about a feeling of hollowness.

> Many of us are running away from this hollowness. The courage it takes to face this emotional vacuum is tremendous. I have never been so fragile, so out of control, so inundated by wave after wave of grief as I was when I finally faced the emptiness within, but I am grateful that I did so. (p. 61)

We can't be effective counselors if we can't face anger, grief, and ultimately, despair. We need to develop comfort with these feelings *before* we meet with a client.

The practice of facing, and even welcoming, emotions that society deems unacceptable can make for a scary, even terrifying, experience in the classroom but also one that can ultimately be healing and liberating. Are these appropriate words to describe a healthy classroom environment or experience? They are! And they are part of the core teaching principle of letting fundamental tensions co-exist. Tensions are necessary because these are exactly the type of tensions and contrasts that students will encounter in their own lives and as transpersonal therapists in counseling sessions. As Pema Chödrön (Chödrön & Lang, 2015) explains, "Not running away from the pain, learning to accept it as part of the human condition, has taught me everything....the painful aspects of life, the really hard times, have been my main teachers" (pp. 45–46).

Death as a Teacher

Another focus in my teaching—maybe the ultimate one—involves the nature and lessons of death. Death is something that everyone must confront. Every day friends are dying. Every day I grieve the loss of my parents. Every day violence prevails. Without trying to change the pain or the enormity of our suffering, I welcome the topic of death into the classroom. Death is the great mystery of the unknown. It opens a doorway to seek transformation. To live as if we are dying all the time is a component of Full-Contact Teaching.

Naturally, there is a fear of death. If you look at death as a metaphor, whenever a relationship breaks up, when anything ends, whenever we face change, it is a death. Personally, I have been fascinated with death my whole life. In a way, growing up I was living death everyday in the classroom, facing the death of the fairy tale of family and school. With any type of death comes grief, bereavement, mourning, and ultimately, rebirth into something new. That is what I want my students to know and what they will need to teach, that life does not end after death. Life continues in another form. Being fully alive is the contrast to death.

As an adult, going through the dying process with my mother softened and eased my own fear of death and mysteriously gave me permission to be more fully alive and more available and present in the classroom. Through welcoming death, we can experience our deeper inner life. In classes, I give examples of how death is treated in indigenous cultures such as the Navajo or the !Kung and bring the wisdom of multiple traditions to my students.

When there is an opportunity, we "practice" death in the classroom. We practice it with endings, with beginnings, with losses. At the end of the semester, we write our own obituaries. This is a powerful reflection and expression of facing our own deaths. If you live every day as if you are dying, it is a profound practice for embracing the preciousness of life. Bring on the shame. Bring on the anxiety. We know we are alive when we are feeling. The body, nature, our hearts' beating—this is what we have in life.

Full-Contact Teaching Deepens Transpersonal Learning

I teach my students that they are detectives and that each client and each human being is a puzzle. Through exploration and inquiry, I attempt to discover the uniqueness and the brilliance and the specialness of each human being. I live for the moment-to-moment experiences with other human beings in the classroom, and I model how they can do this with their clients.

Full-contact teaching allows students to learn the impact of transpersonal therapy: behavior, body, and mind. When students experience discomfort, they can notice their own judgments. When they realize they are distracted, they can explore the reasons and then leave behind their stories. When they experience pain, they discover how pain is an ally they can explore. These creative learning experiences are humbling and create empathy. What better therapist could you have than one who has experienced all the accompanying emotions that come with being alive?

My wish for students is that when they leave my classroom, they will take away an innate trust in their own intuition, their own authenticity, and their own abilities. Modeling the therapeutic relationship in the classroom, I demonstrate to students what they can do and what may arise with clients. All we have when we are with a client is the present moment and that relationship. You have to be ready to meet the other wherever they are.

Three meta-principles describe Full-Contact Teaching: it is creative, it is responsive, and it uses lived experience and paradox as teaching tools. In addition, present-moment awareness, embodiment, emotions, and death are qualities in the classroom that create a transpersonal environment for counseling students to learn how to be more fully alive. It is inspiring to witness what students are capable of when they get support to break out of the conditioning of their lives.

Students discover how to honor their innate authenticity, passion, and wisdom. This is the transpersonal.

References

Agazarian, Y. M. (1992). Systems centered group psychotherapy: How to develop a working group, p. 4. Retrieved from http://www.systemscentered.com/Portals/113/NTForums_Attach/18 1942136736.pdf.

Bohecker, L., Vereen, L. G., Wells, P. C., & Wathen, C. C. (2016). A mindfulness experiential small group to help students tolerate ambiguity. *Counselor Education and Supervision, 55*(1), 16–30.

Caldwell, C. (2013). *Getting our bodies back: Recovery, healing, and transformation through body-centered psychotherapy*. Shambhala Publications.

Clark, C. S. (2016). Watson's Human Caring Theory: Pertinent Transpersonal and Humanities Concepts for Educators. *Humanities, 5*(2), 21.

Chödrön, P., & Lang, k.d. (2015). Connect with the best of yourself: An evening with Pema Chödrön and k.d. lang. *Shambhala Sun, 24*(1), p. 46.

Cozolino, L. (2013). *The Social Neuroscience of Education: Optimizing Attachment and Learning in the Classroom* (The Norton Series on the Social Neuroscience of Education). WW Norton & Company.

Grossenbacher, P. G., & Parkin, S. S. (2006). Joining hearts and minds: A contemplative approach to holistic education in psychology. *Journal of College and Character, 7*(6), 1–13.

Lee, C. C. (Ed.). (2014). *Multicultural issues in counseling: New approaches to diversity*. John Wiley & Sons.

Lief, J. L. (2001). *Making friends with death*. Shambhala Publications.

McLaren, K. (2010). *The language of emotions*. Boulder, CO: Sounds True.

Miller, J. P. (2013). *The contemplative practitioner: Meditation in education and the workplace*. University of Toronto Press.

Rowe, N., & Braud, W. (2013). Transpersonal education. *The Wiley-Blackwell handbook of transpersonal psychology* (pp. 666–686). West Sussex, UK: John Wiley & Sons.

Simmer-Brown, J. (2009). The question is the answer: Naropa University's contemplative pedagogy. *Religion and Education, 36*(2), 88–101.

Simmer-Brown, J., & Grace, F. (2011). *Meditation and the classroom: Contemplative pedagogy for religious studies*. Albany, NY: State University of New York Press.

Smith, T. B., & Trimble, J. E. (2016). Multicultural education/training and experience: A meta-analysis of surveys and outcome studies (pp. 21–47). In *Foundations of multicultural psychology: Research to inform effective practice*. Washington, DC: American Psychological Association.

Tift, B. (2015). *Already free.* Boulder, CO: Sounds True.
Tulku, R., Chödrön, P., Wilber, K., Wegela, K. K., Lief, J. L., Simmer-Brown, J., ... & Ray, R. A. (2014). *Radical Compassion: Shambhala Publications Authors on the Path of Boundless Love.* Boston: Shambhala Publications.
Weller, F. (2015). *The wild edge of sorrow.* Berkeley, CA: North Atlantic Books.

Chapter 14
The State and Future of Integral

Roger Walsh[1]

Integral Visions

What I would like to do in this presentation is to cover three important questions: The first is the question of how we can optimize the impact of our integral ideas—how we can optimize our impact in the world. The second is to explore what the key ideas are for us to get out there. And the third is how we can apply the integral vision to help and heal our troubled world.

Regarding the first question of how we can optimize our impact in the world—well, of course, there are many different ways. But I want to emphasize two important things. The first is that we do really high-quality work. The second is that we become what we might call gnostic intermediaries.

We need to do high-quality work because we are trying to bring new ideas, a new vision, a new perspective into the mainstream In order to do that, we need to be very effective and skilled in our own disciplines, whatever they are, whether you are a psychologist or philosopher or someone working out in the field or whatever it is. If we are going to impact the mainstream, we have to be really competent in the areas in which we are trying to work.

---

[1] This chapter was originally a talk given at the First European Integral Conference held in Budapest, Hungary, 2014. The speech was transcribed with references added by Carla Clements.

We are called to master a couple of different things: We are called to master not only integral ideas and theory, but also to master our own particular discipline and field so that we can bring them together. To do that we need to do really high-quality work. We need to do careful rigorous thinking; we need to do careful rigorous experiments to test the ideas and applications. We also need to publish our work, get it out in the world and into mainstream outlets. So that is the first important message today: We really need to work at a very high standard, whether it is intellectual or practical.

Part two of how to optimize our impact in the world is that we are called to be *gnostic intermediaries*. Now, a gnostic intermediary is a term that was coined by Carl Jung (2014), used to describe Wilhelm, the translator of the *I-Ching* (1950/1967). It was said that Wilhelm had imbibed the *I-Ching* so deeply into his own being that he was able to transmit its wisdom to the world out of his own direct experience. We are called to be gnostic intermediaries because what we are trying to do in part is bring contemporary modern and postmodern and integral ideas into the mainstream, but we are also trying to bring contemplative wisdom into the mainstream.

We are not just trying to communicate ideas; we are also trying to communicate and transmit a certain kind of wisdom. Integral draws deeply on the contemplative traditions, the perennial wisdom of the world's great philosophic religious and spiritual traditions, and to transmit that requires that we become gnostic intermediaries.

To become an effective gnostic intermediary requires three things. First, it requires that we actually imbibe the wisdom. We cannot just take the ideas; we have to actually marinate ourselves in the ideas. We have to open ourselves to the wisdom of these traditions—whether it is Christian contemplation, Buddhist meditation, the Hindu or Taoist yoga, whatever it is. We have to do these practices and open ourselves to the wisdom that they embody and cultivate.

The second step in becoming an effective gnostic intermediary is to master the concepts and language of the community that we are trying to communicate with. If we are trying to communicate, for example, with psychologists or anthropologists, we need to learn their concepts and conceptual frameworks.

The third thing we need to do is to be able to translate contemplative wisdom into the concepts and language of the community we are trying to communicate with. We want to create an "aha" experience so that these profound, perennial ideas make sense in the language and concepts of the people we are communicating with. So in summary, the two things, then, that we are uniquely called to in order to be effective communicators of the integral vision are 1) to do really high-quality work in both the mainstream and in integral, and 2) to become gnostic intermediaries.

What are the most valuable ideas for us to get out? What are the integral ideas that would be most effective in the world? I would suggest that you take a moment to ask yourself two questions: What do you think are the ideas that are the most crucial for us to get out? And what are the ideas that *you* are called to communicate? What are the ideas that both call you and that you are called to get out into the world? This is a really interesting question—a wisdom question—for each of us to reflect on. And each of us will have our own list.

I want to suggest several ideas we need to get into the world that seem particularly crucial to me. One, of course, we all share is that integral ideas are incredibly important. They are desperately needed at all times, but particularly at this time when we suffer from such an information overload. We are inundated with information and drowning in data. Psychologists talk about the stress from information overload, and part of it is just having more facts than we can process.

But a larger part of the issue is not having a framework that is adequate enough, large enough, deep enough to be able to make sense of and hold all this information (see, for example, Klingberg, 2009). That is where integral comes in. Integral provides an extremely valuable, comprehensive, and integrated framework with which to make sense of the enormous flood of information and competing crosscurrents of ideas in our contemporary culture. So the first idea, which I am sure we all agree on, is that getting the integral vision out into the world and refining it, developing it, and communicating it are essential.

The second idea that I want to suggest is vitally important and that has the potential for real transformative impact is that adult development is possible. This is not new to any of us in the integral world but it is new to the vast majority of people. For the most part, there is an implicit assumption in our culture that development pretty much stops around the time the body stops developing. That is a real tragedy. Yet psychological and spiritual development can continue beyond the conventional level to post-conventional and even trans-conventional levels and this has enormous implications.

Two of them are particularly important. One implication is that what we call normality is not the ceiling of developmental possibilities. We can mature beyond what we thought was possible: There are further levels of developmental maturation that are available to us all; there are further capacities and virtues available to us all if we simply cultivate them appropriately. What we have taken to be normality is looking more and more like a form of collective developmental arrest.

This has enormous implications for each of us individually, for us as a society, and for the planet as a whole. It is quite possible that the recognition that we can mature further is going to be absolutely essential to our survival and sanity as a species. Abraham Maslow (1968) said it well, "What we call normal in psychology is really a psychopathology of the average, but it is so undramatic and so widely spread that we don't even recognize it" (p. 60). This is the first implication of the idea that we can mature beyond conventional levels.

The second implication is that many of our contemporary cultural conflicts are expressions of different levels of development. Conflicts over many social and moral issues such as abortion or religious freedom can be seen as conflicts between people at different levels of development. At the current time our cultures are being torn by conflicts between three major developmental levels: between a pre-conventional or mythic level, a conventional or rational level, and a post-conventional level that is calling the traditional conventions into question. So many of the conflicts in our world—particularly, for example, the conflict with religious fundamentalism—can be seen as expressions of these different developmental levels.

The trouble is that when the different levels are not recognized, then there is virtually no possibility of resolution and peace because people simply assume that those who disagree with them are either wrong or disturbed or deranged. This recognition of adult development has enormous social implications for us. That is the second implication of adult development that I see as vitally important.

The third idea to get out to the mainstream is the idea that contemplative and spiritual disciplines can foster this psychological maturation—not only psychological maturation, but spiritual maturation as well. This, of course, is one of the claims of contemplative disciplines: that they can foster capacities and virtues available to us all, but which remain unknown and undeveloped unless we specifically cultivate them through contemplative practices. The good news here is that the very qualities of heart and mind, the classic virtues that the world so desperately needs at this time—love, compassion, generosity, wisdom, insight, understanding—are not only available to us, but we have time-tested technologies for fostering them.

One of the crucial contributions we can make in our role as gnostic intermediaries is to make sense of these contemplative practices, whether they be Taoist or Hindu yoga or Christian contemplation or Islamic zikr. We can make sense of them, explain them, legitimize them, and demonstrate the benefits so that they become more widespread and cultivate the very qualities that we so desperately need. Thus, regarding the first three ideas that I am suggesting that are really crucial are integral ideas are essential, adult development is possible, and contemplative practices cultivate it.

A fourth idea related to development is that there are two very different kinds of religion. Religion is unique among human institutions in that it has expressions of each developmental level. To simplify I want to focus on two levels: the conventional and the trans-conventional. In our culture we are really only aware of conventional religion. The defining feature of conventional-level religion is that its prime focus is a story or narrative which is to be believed. If you believe it you are saved, and if you do not you are damned. Salvation comes through our faith in a particular story at the conventional level of religious expression.

In the work of James Fowler (1981), this is the mythic literal level of faith development or the synthetic conventional level. Tragically, this is really the only level of religion that our culture and our media recognize; everything is lumped into that, and often dismissed as only that.

But what is important to recognize is that there is a further post-conventional level or trans-conventional level. This level centers not on story, not on a narrative, not on something to be believed, but on a *psychotechnology*—a set of practices to transform the mind and to cultivate the very qualities and states of consciousness—the kind of insights and realizations that the great religious founders and sages throughout the ages discovered themselves. Trans-conventional religion centers on contemplative practices, and one of the most crucial ideas we can get out into the culture is that these practices are effective, that they are expressions of a more mature form of religious expression, and that they help us mature to that level of religious expression.

This brings us to the fifth idea, which is that spiritual disciplines and contemplative practices are psychotechnologies. This is a radically different understanding of spirituality. It is a recognition that these practices are designed to train, tame, transform, and ultimately to transcend the mind. They help us move beyond the mental level into trans-conceptual, trans-rational, intuitive wisdom—the prajna of Buddhism, the jñāna of Hinduism, the marifa of Islam, the gnosis of Christianity. They bring us into the direct intuitive knowing of that trans-rational wisdom that is liberating. It is this wisdom that radically transforms our understanding of who we are, and makes us far more effective instruments of service and contribution in the world.

All of these psychotechnologies and spiritual traditions help us develop for ourselves the very qualities of heart and mind that the great religious founders discovered and which the great saints and sages have kept alive within each of the traditions. These practices, these contemplative disciplines, these psychotechnologies help us cultivate these qualities and transmit them ourselves as part of an unbroken chain across centuries and generations. A special thing about this kind of religion is that it does not require faith. These are practices that we can test for ourselves in our own minds and our own hearts if they work, and find out for ourselves.

The sixth idea that I would suggest is vitally important is that these psychotechnologies, these contemplative practices, the world's spiritual disciplines share common goals and practices. This is the first time in human history we have had all these practices available to us— the first time we can really look at them together and compare and contrast them and do what is called "common factors analysis" to identify the common themes, the common elements, the common practices. I spent a lot of time doing this and writing a book, *Essential Spirituality: The Seven Essential Practices* (Walsh, 2000). I looked across the world's great religions. I was really intrigued to ask, "What is it that the greatest minds in human history—the great sages, the true saints, the most remarkable human beings who ever lived on this planet—what are the qualities that they say are essential for us to develop in order to live full and effective and contributory lives?"

I was struck that across centuries, across cultures, across traditions they all seem to agree that seven qualities of heart and mind are really essential for anyone who wants to live fully, to live effectively, and to understand who and what they really are (Walsh, 2000). Those seven practices are, first, to transform motivation, to shift the motives that move us. The second is to live ethically, to live in a way that is filled with integrity. The third is to develop concentration, the capacity to hold the mind wherever we want it to be. The fourth is to develop emotional maturity. The fifth essential quality is a refinement of awareness. The sixth is wisdom—to cultivate deep insight and understanding of ourselves and the world. The seventh is service, to recognize that we do these practices not just for ourselves alone (because we are not alone), but we do them for the welfare and awakening of everyone. These seven practices seem to be recommended in each of the great religions.

One aspect of spiritual practice that is very relevant to an integral gathering is that consciousness is "catchy." When I was writing *Essential Spirituality*, what surprised me was that the most consistent thing they said to do in order to cultivate each of these seven qualities was to hang out with and be with people who have them. That is why a gathering like this is so valuable and beneficial to us all.

That brings us to the question of what we can do to help heal our troubled world because it is no secret that we are at a crucial time in human history, and the choices our generation makes will really decide the fate of our species and planet. We all know the problems we are facing: overpopulation, injustice, pollution, ecological collapse, weapons of mass destruction. However, what is really important to recognize is that for the first time in human history, each and every one of the major problems we face, and each and every one of our collective crises, is human caused. That means what we call our global problems are actually global symptoms; they are symptoms of individual and collective psychological and spiritual immaturity. What that means is we are in a race between consciousness and catastrophe, and we need to address not just the state of the world but the state of our minds. We are also called to address the psychological and spiritual immaturities and pathologies within us and the pathologies and disrupted social institutions between us. We need to address both the outside problems and the inside problems.

How do we do this? Well, it always comes down to a fundamental question: What can I do? And even more profoundly: What's the most *strategic* thing I can do. In order to answer that question, we need to recognize that this is a wisdom question. There are two kinds of questions: knowledge questions and wisdom questions. Knowledge questions are a one-time question with a one-time answer. Is it raining? Look outside, yes or no. End of question.

Wisdom questions are like koans; each time you ask the question, they have the potential for taking us deeper into the question, into ourselves, and into the reality. The question of "what is the most strategic thing I can do?" is a wisdom question. We will be probably asking ourselves this for the rest of our lives.

What is crucial for us to recognize is that we are trying to do three things simultaneously: We are trying to relieve the external social and global problems, we are trying to heal the internal sources, and we are trying to bring a more integral perspective or way of looking to bear.

We are called to be perspectival therapists; we are called to recognize limiting, partial, destructive perspectives both in ourselves and others. We are called to then recognize and bring to bear more encompassing perspectives—wider and deeper perspectives. And even beyond that, we are called to mature to levels in which all perspectives dissolve into transcendental awareness. Then out of that transcendental awareness, we can allow profound perspectives to re-emerge with the perspectival fullness and the spiritual ground remembered. In doing this we are called to mature; we have to do our own work on ourselves because mature perspectives require mature people. A crucial calling for all of us at this time is to dive into our inner work, our psychological work, our spiritual work as deeply and fully as we can.

That raises the question of how we can work on ourselves and in the world simultaneously, and fortunately there is a practice for that. It is karma yoga, sometimes called spiritual service. Karma yoga is the yoga in which we use our work in the world as our spiritual practice, and it has three primary elements: The first is that before beginning any major undertaking or any project we offer it to a higher purpose, God, or to the service of humanity or community, something beyond our individual ego. The second is that we do our work as impeccably as possible. The third is what makes karma yoga such a razor-edged practice. Along with great effort, we simultaneously try to let go of our attachment to the outcome. These are the three elements that make karma yoga such a powerful and transformative practice. In doing karma yoga, we go into ourselves to go more effectively out into our world; we go out into the world in order to go more deeply into ourselves. And we keep doing this; we keep repeating this cycle until the boundaries between inner and outer dissolve, and it is all one continuous flow.

In conclusion, we live in a time of unprecedented challenge. Never before have we had the power to imperil both our species and our planet, but never before have we had the power to heal our species and to bring all people new levels of prosperity and well-being. The choices our generation makes will decide whether we leave behind us an evolving civilization and a fertile earth or a failed species and a plundered planet. We have the power to do both. It is our remarkable privilege to be able to realize this vision in our own lives, to use it to understand the world, to express it to help heal the world, and to let it use us in whatever ways would be most helpful. Our world is in very deep trouble, and our world is also in good hands because ultimately it rests in yours.

References

Fowler, J. (1981). *States of faith: The psychology of human development and the quest for meaning.* San Francisco, CA: Harper & Row.

Jung, C. (2014). *The spirit of man in art and literature* (Vol. 15). London, UK: Routledge.

Klingberg, T. (2009). *The overflowing brain: Information overload and the limits of working memory.* (N. Betteridge, Trans.). New York, NY: Oxford University Press.

Maslow, A. (1968). *Towards a psychology of being* (2nd ed.). Princeton, NJ: Van Nostrand.

Walsh, R. (2000). *Essential spirituality: The 7 central practices to awaken heart and mind.* New York, NY: John Wiley & Sons.

Wilhelm, R., & Baynes, C.F. (Trans.). (1967). *I-Ching or book of changes* (3rd ed.). Bollingen Series XIX. Princeton, NJ: Princeton University Press. (Original work published 1950)

Chapter 15
Practicing Community: Cultivating Creative Agency Through Improvisation

Mark A. Miller

To begin, I return to stillness. I surrender my need to control and protect. I embrace whatever is given in the moment: the rustle of bodies in seats or on cushions, Bill McCrossen tuning his bass, the squeaky piano bench, the faint electric hum of Khabu's guitar amp, the murmuring expectation of the quieting crowd. Out of the stillness, as the music begins, there is no leader and there are no followers; we move and engage as a single organism, an ecosystem of listening and response. Energies flow through the system like weather. A single sound from the guitar is a balm: calming, healing. Then a blast of fierce emotion tips the system into fiery chaos and I am carried away on a river of sound and feeling. My only concern is the music itself.

Improvisation is a path of self-discovery—an antidote to the traditional hierarchical and patriarchal systems of Western composition and performance in which individual musicians—members of an orchestra or band—serve as technocrats in some distant (or dead) composer's formal scheme. In the old system, the composer or conductor has already asked the important questions and provided all the answers to the musicians and listeners alike. "This is how the music is supposed to go. Do it this way. Do it my way." For the participants, this can be a path of service to the great masters and their works, which is wonderful. But for those who are interested in a creative life, there is little room for exploration and discovery in traditional performance.

Improvisation allows us to tell our own story through our relationships with others. To find authentic agency though community, we have to dig deeper than our traditional roles. We have to develop creative capacities that transcend mere technical competence and theoretical expertise. We need to see clearly who we are, and we have to listen and respond to the creative potential alive and available to us with the arrival of each rich, colorful, full, mysterious, strange, troubling, and beautiful musical moment.

Music Making in Community

In improvisation, the substance and quality of the music is completely dependent on the interaction of the individuals in the ensemble. The contemporary jazz trumpet master Wynton Marsalis calls this interaction a "negotiation" (Burns, 2001), but that term implies willful struggle, and in the end, winners and losers. In true collaboration, there is no struggle; there is only the mutual embrace of possibility: "Yes, I will work with you." "Yes, I can work with that idea." "Yes, we will accomplish this together." Whatever one person plays catalyzes the others in response. Ultimately, our allegiance is not to an individual creative vision—mine or yours—but to the creative output of the whole ensemble. We influence one another, but no individual is consistently in control. Working together, we willingly serve the greater good of the music itself, moment by moment.

Chögyam Trungpa (1988) wrote that "the first principle is not being afraid of who you are" (p. 28). When working with a group of individuals who are unafraid of who they are, we will immediately encounter difference. This is not a problem. The totality of creative possibility is so vast that no two individuals could possibly produce the same creative vision at the same time. The sum of our creative potential—of every rhythmic, harmonic, melodic, textural, and emotional possibility—is uncountable. With so many different possibilities, how can we choose among them? How will we work together?

Far from being problematic, our differences enliven and inspire us. Collaboration is the simultaneous realization of self and other, a seamless integration of the parts and the whole. For the individual, collaboration reveals a paradoxical relationship between our allegiance to personal artistic vision and our commitment to community. This practice is not about compromise as much as it is a willingness to become malleable in support of the collaborative good. On an interpersonal level, this work celebrates both individual integrity and deep mutual appreciation in equal measure. In effect and in practice, I and the ensemble become a single, multicellular whole, complete in our diversity and at one in our differences. The rewards of true collaboration include the joys of honest relationship, of giving and taking freely, of shared risk and mutual responsibility.

> This is an affirmation of life—not an attempt to bring order out of chaos, nor to suggest improvements in creation, but simply a way of waking up to the very life we are living, which is so excellent once one gets one's mind and one's desires out of its way. (Cage, 1961)

Unlike John Cage's aleatoric approach to composition, which relies on randomness or "chance operations," improvisation is a form of spontaneous composition that incorporates the inner lives of the performers. We compose/improvise music according to what we hear, feel, and imagine—sharing with one another what is true and alive for us, and together crafting a work of compositional integrity. Like Cage states, our efforts are not meant to "improve upon creation" but rather to investigate and reveal the richness of our individual creative lives in relationship with one another.

Music as Contemplative Practice:
The Komusō Monks of Japan

Japanese Zen Buddhism features a long tradition of practice and expression in the arts, including ceramics, calligraphy, landscape painting and architecture (Mason, 2005). Music, too, has been a part of this tradition. Active from 1603–1868, the Komusō were mendicant Zen monks who wandered Japan playing *shakuhachi*, the traditional Japanese bamboo flute. Instead of *zazen* (sitting meditation), the Komusō practiced *suizen*, or "blowing meditation" as a path to spiritual awakening. Because the practice of suizen was outlawed after the fall of the Tokugawa shogunate in 1868, the specific techniques of the Komusō monks are not well documented. However, the music itself survives in the form of traditional solo pieces known as *honkyoku*. These haunting works usually refer either to the beauty of the natural world (*San Ya*, "Three Valleys," or *Tsuru no Sugomori*, "The Nesting of Cranes"), or to matters of spiritual significance (*Tamuke*, "Hands Folded Together in Prayer," or *Shingetsu*, "The Enlightenment of Heart and Mind.") What was the relationship between flute playing and the awakening heart and mind cultivated in Zen Buddhism? What practices and principles of Zen are relevant to contemporary music making? Meditation and improvisation foster similar personal and transpersonal qualities, and both require disciplined practice. Within a contemplative framework, both meditation and the arts can be a form of mindfulness/awareness practice. Both can be a path of personal and social transformation.

The Inner Work

Derek Bailey (1993) describes two kinds of improvisation: idiomatic improvisation, which is created according to the guidelines of a particular style or genre, and non-idiomatic improvisation, which is created in the moment, right on the spot, and does not rely on a set of preconceived or culturally derived aesthetic or stylistic constraints. I am interested in the latter. What happens when there are no rules? What happens when anything is possible, when there is no ground, when there is only open sky? How do we orient ourselves in an art form that by definition values unpredictability and freshness over the heavily composed and rehearsed perfectionism of European classical music?

In the Buddhist tradition, groundlessness is both the premise and the practice. The first tenet of the Zen Peacemaker Order is "not knowing," (Glassman, 1998), a rigorous opening to reality as it is. In not knowing, we practice seeing clearly, excluding nothing, embracing *what is* in a spirit of radical acceptance (Brach, 2003). The groundless opening of not knowing allows us to begin fresh, without relying on preconceptions, theoretical constructs, or formulaic thinking. Not knowing cultivates an attitude not of passivity but of "ready mind," as Zen master Shunyru Suzuki (1970) called it. Improvisers know the absolute necessity of starting fresh every time. Otherwise, the music is a re-creation of something that came before, a replication, an imitation creativity.

The second tenet of the Zen Peacemakers is "bearing witness" (Glassman, 1998), taking stock, or waking up to the creative potential of a given situation. For the artist this includes sense perception, emotion, conceptual thought, and imagination— the "stuff" of the music. "Just see what's on your inner radio and play that," jazz pianist Art Lande (1998) recommends. Improvisation is the art of noticing and then working with the real and imaginative world of the present moment without the safety net of a prearranged framework. As Lande (1998) likes to say, "Improvisation is simple. Just play what you hear and when you don't want it anymore, stop." But, as Thelonious Monk (n.d.) noted, "simple ain't easy." The practice requires our complete attention and absolute commitment in each and every moment.

The Vipassana meditation teacher and psychologist Tara Brach (2013) describes mindfulness/awareness as the practice of establishing a sense of personal presence. In addition to the qualities of openness and wakefulness, Brach mentions a third characteristic of authentic presence—that of tenderness toward oneself and others. The quality of tenderness, or simple kindness, allows us to move forward with an open heart to offer patience and compassion in times of confusion or difficulty. These three qualities—openness, wakefulness, and tenderness—help to establish the best possible foundation for making music together in community.

Creativity is the capacity to occupy the present moment in body and mind, and to share that experience with others. In mindfulness/awareness practice, we orient ourselves according to the inner truth of the heart—toward clarity and acceptance, toward what we really need and want, and away from neurosis and ego. These are the characteristics of a good life and of great music making. As legendary jazz saxophonist Sonny Rollins (2015) put it, "Enjoy music and be a good person. Then you have it all!"

To be a good person, we have to take action. Taking action is the third tenet of the Zen Peacemaker Order (Glassman, 1999). When we open to the world and begin to take stock of what is happening around us, we find meaning in our response to others. As a member of an improvising ensemble, I do everything I can to help the other musicians fulfill their creative potential and keep the musical enterprise moving forward. Sometimes I lead, sometimes I follow, and sometimes I am still. Whatever I choose to do is accomplished for the greater good of the music itself.

Working with Others

Underlying the inner practice of openness, wakefulness, and tenderness is an important Buddhist principle, one that Cage pointed to often: the principle of not picking and choosing. Hsin Hsin Ming in *Verses on the faith-mind* says:

> If you wish to see the truth,
> then hold no opinions for or against anything.
> To set up what you like against what you dislike
> is the disease of the mind.
> When the deep meaning of things in not understood,
> the mind's essential peace is disturbed to no avail. (Clarke, 1984)

Our purpose in improvisation is to discover "the deep meaning of things" through the music of the moment. To do this, we cultivate trust in ourselves and our peers and a willingness to extend and expand our aesthetic preferences for the good of the music. In improvisation, we learn to cook with unfamiliar ingredients. Instead of asking, "Do I like this?" we cultivate an open and accepting palate: "I'll try it. Let me see what I can do with this strange new flavor. Maybe we can create a new cuisine together!"

No matter what happens, no matter what strange "ingredients" are placed on the table, when working together in improvisation we don't have time to pick and choose, to analyze, edit, and revise. Every offering, every sound, every note produced by anyone in the group becomes a part of the musical whole as soon as it is played. Each piece of the puzzle has absolute integrity within the greater work. When we abandon our desire for aesthetic perfection and immediate gratification, the improvisational path opens to new possibilities, to mystery and surprise. When we let go of judgment in favor of perception and imagination and embrace difference and diversity as our path, we are free to explore our present moment experience with curiosity and delight, and to share that experience openly with others.

The great jazz soprano saxophonist Steve Lacy said that in improvisation there is only one question: "Is this stuff alive, or is it dead?" (as cited in Bailey, 1993). When we work with awareness as the source of the music, we turn our attention to whatever is alive in the communal field. Perhaps the most important question we can ask is: How can I be of service to this aliveness, right here, right now?

References

Bailey, D. (1993). *Improvisation: Its nature and practice in music.* New York, NY: Da Capo Press.

Brach, T. (2003) *Radical acceptance: Embracing your life with the heart of a Buddha.* New York, NY: Bantam.

Brach, T. (2013). *True refuge: Finding peace and freedom in your own awakened heart.* New York, NY: Bantam.

Burns K. (Director). (2001) *Jazz: A film by Ken Burns.* Wynton Marsalis, performer. United States: PBS.

Cage, J. (1961). *Silence: Lectures and writings by John Cage.* Middletown, CT: Wesleyan University Press.

Clarke, R. (1984). *Hsin Hsin Ming: Verses on the faith-mind.* Buffalo, NY: White Pine Press.

Glassman, B. (1998). *Bearing witness: A Zen master's lessons in making peace.* New York, NY: Bell Tower.

Lande, A. (1998). Improvisation. [Presentation]. *Master class presented at the University of Oregon,* Eugene, OR.

Mason, P. (2005). *History of Japanese art* (2nd ed). Upper Saddle River, NJ: Pearson Education Inc.

Monk, T (n.d). Retrieved May 31, 2016 from http://www.math.wsu.edu/faculty/tsat/quotes.html May 31, 2016.

Rollins, S. (2015). The official Sonny Rollins page. Retrieved from https://www.facebook.com/officialsonnyrollins/?fref=ts

Suzuki, S. (1970). *Zen mind, beginner's mind: Informal talks on Zen meditation and practice.* New York, NY: Weatherhill.

Trungpa, C. (1988). *Shambhala: The sacred path of the warrior.* Boston, MA: Shambhala.

Chapter 16
Transpersonal Psychology, Multiculturalism, and Social Justice Activism

Louis Hoffman

What is the status of transpersonal psychology's relationship with multiculturalism, social justice, and activism? The answer depends greatly upon who is asked. When approaching this question on a theoretical level, transpersonal psychology is poised to be a strong partner with multiculturalism and social justice movements. The values of transpersonal psychology are highly consistent with multicultural psychology and social justice. In some small pockets of the transpersonal movement, this is being actualized. However, the majority of transpersonal psychology is deficient in its engagement with multiculturalism and social justice movements. The overall scholarship on multiculturalism and social justice in transpersonal psychology is lacking, as is representation of marginalized group in the membership of transpersonal psychology. It is important to be honest about this reality. To make the claim of being multicultural and social justice allies lacks evidence and is contrary to the experience of many, including individuals who have confided to me that they, as members of marginalized groups, left transpersonal psychology because of its failures relevant to multiculturalism and social justice. For transpersonal psychology to claim to have adequately embraced these issues is inauthentic. However, worse yet, to claim this when it is not the experience of so many is invalidating the experience of people representing marginalized groups.

Moving into Uncomfortable Spaces

Embracing multiculturalism on a deep level requires a willingness to reconsider even core values of transpersonal psychology (Hoffman, 2016; Hoffman, Cleare-Hoffman, & Jackson, 2014). This is not an easy task—academically or personally. Individuals are often drawn toward transpersonal psychology because of a convergence with its beliefs. Thus, reconsidering core values often brings resistance, anxiety, and even anger at times. This is one of the reasons why discussions about multicultural psychology tend to be uncomfortable for many.

As an example, Daniels (2005) has been critical of Wilber's approach to transpersonal psychology, noting that there is an inherent bias toward Eastern religions and against the Judeo-Christian religions. According to Daniels, "Wilber should be more explicit or at least more cautious about the metaphysical assumptions behind his work, as indeed should all people working in this area" (p. 224). Given that transpersonal psychology deals explicitly and necessarily with metaphysics, it is difficult not to make some assumptions or assertions that, at times, privilege certain spiritual and/or religious traditions. Daniels is not stating that it is wrong to have or write with metaphysical assumptions; however, he does argue that it is necessary to be explicit when these occur and recognize the implications and consequences of these assumptions. If this is not done, it disrespects the beliefs of clients and may lead to the imposition of values. With regard to the bias toward Eastern religion, many in transpersonal psychology have not adequately considered these biases and the implications.

To move to a clinical example, transpersonal psychology tends toward a bias pertaining to emotion that may not be consistent with some cultural values. As an illustration, in supervising many clinicians who embrace transpersonal and/or humanistic psychology, these therapists often have a tendency to encourage "letting go" of emotions. Transpersonal therapy tends to have a bias toward calmness, release, and tranquility. While there may be encouragement to recognize a variety of emotions non-judgmentally, the practice tends to encourage moving toward a more tranquil experiencing of the emotion. For some cultural groups, this is contrary to their culturally preferred ways of relating to, embodying, and expressing emotion.

I am confident that after reading the previous two paragraphs some would object to what I have stated, possibly citing some examples of exceptions. However, I am not speaking to the exceptions but rather to how transpersonal psychology is more generally experienced and represented. To discount the broader experience based on exceptions is similar to arguing that one is not racist because of their "black friend." To become truly multicultural can and should be a difficult process. If the process is too easy or comfortable, my inclination would be to question whether the issues have been engaged with sufficient depth to go beyond the surface and question whether the change has reached a sustainable level.

Transpersonal psychology can build on the exceptions and can be proud of the corners of the movement where it has succeeded. Yet, this should not be used to discount the need for improvement.

Social Justice and Activism

Social justice should not be confused with politics. While we can utilize political systems and processes to help address social justice issues, social justice is deeper than politics. Similarly, while social justice often involves activism, not all activism is aimed at social justice.

Activism should not and cannot be a first step in embracing multiculturalism. It is necessary to first engage in honest self-reflection and work toward a more sustainable embracement of multiculturalism and diversity. This is true on the personal level as well as the collective level (i.e., transpersonal psychology as a whole). To engage in activism prior to "cleaning one's own house" can work against the desired outcomes. Yet, a deep embracement of multiculturalism should naturally lead to concerns about social justice and activism. At the same time, it is important not to include excessive expectations of personal awareness and healing from prior wounds when engaging in activism, although activism is, at times, part of the healing and meaning-making process.

For example, at the time of this writing, one of the more pressing social justice issues of contemporary times is the violence against Black people in the United States and what has been dubbed by Michelle Alexander (2010) as *the New Jim Crow* (i.e., the bias in the legal system that has led to the mass incarceration of Black people). When looking at this issue at a distance, it is easy to discount its importance or validity, or to provide rational counterarguments. Yet, when empathetically hearing the stories of Black people, their experience with the police and criminal justice system, and their experience of loss, it is hard not to be driven to compassion and action. Trayvon Martin, in his death, has become an important symbol of the general disregard for Black lives, and served as the inspiration of the Black Lives Matter movement (Hoffman, Granger, Vallejos, & Moats, 2016). In addressing the issue of multiculturalism and activism in humanistic psychology, which closely parallels the viewpoint of transpersonal psychology in relation to this issue, Hoffman (2016) states,

> If humanistic psychology does not have something to say about Trayvon Martin, I am truly worried about its future. I am not saying what that voice needs to say, but it needs to recognize the deep cultural and personal pain it represents and it needs to say something. It needs to have ears, it needs to have deep compassion, it needs to have a voice, because sometimes silence is the most devastating of all types of speech. (p. 60)

If transpersonal psychology is rooted in compassion and multiculturalism, it, too, will feel compelled to have a voice when witnessing the systematic atrocities that are occurring disproportionally to marginalized groups. Silence will no longer be an option.

Rothberg (2006), writing from a Buddhist perspective, offers a parallel critique of spiritual and religious traditions. He noted that Buddhism has too often focused on personal spirituality and growth while neglecting social issues. He further argued for a socially engaged spirituality in which spiritual individuals are engaged in social issues. For Rothberg, the development of the self should naturally lead to concerns about the collective. The personal and the social are necessarily intertwined. Similarly, in transpersonal psychology, healthy development should not be focused solely on the individual, which can promote an egocentric or narcissistic approach to the world. Rather, the development of the self should lead naturally to a concern for others.

This is not to say that transpersonal psychologists must endorse Black Lives Matter and take to the street in protest. This is one of many ways to act for change. Yet, the struggles of marginalized groups are empowered and sometimes emboldened by silence and complacency. Complacency can occur even in the context of an empathetic relationship when one only seeks to comfort and help one adjust to the experience of oppression. At times, silence does harm. Furthering the critique drawn from Rothberg, critical psychology (Prilleltensky & Fox, 1997) as well as James Hillman (Hillman & Ventura, 1993) have advocated that the field of psychology has too often facilitated people becoming comfortable with situations, such as racism, that should make one uncomfortable. If therapists are concerned about the individual yet ignore their social context and the systemic issues contributing to their situation, then they are failing their clients. To be deeply committed to one's clients, it is necessary to consider more than their role in the current situation.

Transpersonal psychology needs to work toward finding its activist voice, or activist voices. If it is silent on matters that are causing harm to marginalized groups, it will be difficult, if not impossible, to actualize being multicultural.

Implications and Future Directions

The only way forward is to be honest about the present. It is important that transpersonal psychology acknowledge where it has succeeded pertaining to multiculturalism and social justice while also being honest about its failures. Any psychological approach in contemporary psychology unwilling to consider multiculturalism has begun to write the last chapter in its history (see also Hocoy, *Shadows & Light*, Vol. 1). Transpersonal psychology need not suffer this fate.

In this section, I would like to offer a few brief preliminary recommendations of what transpersonal psychology can (or must) do in order to move toward actualizing its valuing of multiculturalism and find its activist voice. First, transpersonal psychology must take an honest look at where there are unacknowledged biases within its theories, research methodologies, and practice. Furthermore, transpersonal psychology must consider where *transpersonal microaggressions* may be occurring. Microaggressions are subtle and often unintentional and/or unconscious communications delivering negative messages directed at marginalized groups or individuals from marginalized groups (Sue, 2010). By "transpersonal microaggressions," I am referring to forms of microaggressions unique to transpersonal psychology. For example, the privileging of certain metaphysical assumptions in accordance only with certain religious or spiritual traditions is a transpersonal microaggression.

Second, related to the above example of a transpersonal microaggression, transpersonal psychology must work to identify aspects of its theory that are biased toward particular religious or spiritual traditions, particularly Eastern religions. Often, the Judeo-Christian and religious traditions originating in Africa are not given as much consideration and may even be viewed with some suspicion at times. I have often heard transpersonal therapists talk about being deceptive with techniques they use with some clients who the therapist fears may be resistant to an approach for religious or spiritual reasons. For example, some Christian clients resist the use of meditation because they associate this with Buddhism, even though there is a rich tradition of meditation within Christianity. Some transpersonal therapists will still use meditation but call it something different to get around this "resistance." This deceptive practice is not good for building trust or therapeutic alliance. It is better, although more laborious, for the therapist to work within the client's religious or spiritual perspective (see also Wickramasekera's chapter, *Shadows & Light,* Vol. 1, for an excellent overview of this issue). While transpersonal psychologists do not need to be experts in all religious and spiritual traditions, they should have a diverse enough awareness of variations to have some recognition of possible sensitivities and adaptations. When working to incorporate aspects of the client's religious or spiritual tradition that one may not be familiar with, such as centering prayer or Vipassana meditation, it is best to recognize one's limitations. It is better to collaborate with or refer to a religious or spiritual professional who can facilitate learning this practice. Recognition of limitations itself is an important aspect of multicultural competence.

Third, from a transpersonal psychology perspective, I would advocate that often the proper foundation for activism is compassion, not anger. Yet, anger has its place, too. Empathy and compassion can facilitate recognizing the need for activism and can also be one source of motivation to engage in activism. What begins with compassion can often draw motivation and sustenance from anger. Too often in transpersonal psychology, and psychology in general, anger gets a bad name. It may be viewed as a secondary emotion, a defense mechanism, an aspect of the shadow, or pathological in itself. While all of these may be true with some forms of anger, there are also many forms of healthy anger. It is important to not be quick to judge anger and, in some situations, to consider how it can be appropriately utilized. Furthermore, there can be consideration of how anger and compassion can work together.

Fourth, transpersonal psychology needs to consider what it means to apply the values and techniques of transpersonal psychology to social activism. For example, how can transpersonal psychology utilize meditation in the service of activism? There have been some examples of meditating for peace or justice; however, I would maintain that for meditation for peace to be an activist endeavor it needs to go beyond meditating in an isolated setting, whether that be individually or communally. It would be better to organize a meditation event in a public place with T-shirts and/or signs that make known what is occurring. When the meditation for peace or justice occurs in a public setting, it incorporates a witness and public stand that can engage others and hopefully lead to dialogues about what needs to change.

Fifth, transpersonal psychology must be willing to learn from others with expertise in multiculturalism, social justice, and activism. In particular, transpersonal psychology should seek out dialogues with multicultural psychology (see also Hocoy, *Shadows & Light*, Vol. 1), peace psychology, and activist/advocacy groups. Similarly, transpersonal psychology needs to be intentional about dialoguing with groups such as the Association of Black Psychologists, the National Latina/o Psychological Association, and Division 45 of the American Psychological Association (Society for the Psychological Student of Culture, Ethnicity, and Race). It is important that transpersonal psychology maintain a humble spirit in these dialogues and first seek what it can learn from these groups before transitioning to voicing what it can offer to the conversation.

Conclusion

Transpersonal psychology maintains great potential to actualize its valuing of multiculturalism; however, there is much work to be done to achieve this, and there are no shortcuts. For transpersonal psychology to become truly diverse, it must be intentional about seeking multiculturalism in its values, theory, and representation. It is not enough to espouse valuing multiculturalism and then hope it will come. The shift must be intentional, and it must be sustained. Once some progress has been maintained, it is easy to rest; however, this often leads to regression. Sustained intentionality is necessary. If this can occur, I am confident that transpersonal psychology will grow, progress, and flourish.

References

Alexander, M. (2010). *The new Jim Crow: Mass incarceration in the age of colorblindness*. New York, NY: The New Press.
Daniels, M. (2005). *Shadow, self, spirit: Essays in transpersonal psychology*. Charlottesville, VA: Imprint Academic.
Hillman, J., & Ventura, M. (1993). *We've had a hundred years of psychotherapy— and the world's getting worse*. New York, NY: HarperCollins.

Hoffman, L. (2016). Multiculturalism and humanistic psychology: From neglect to epistemological and ontological diversity. *The Humanistic Psychologist, 44,* 56–-71.

Hoffman, L., Cleare-Hoffman, H. P., & Jackson, T. (2014). Humanistic psychology and multiculturalism: History, current status, and advancements. In K. J. Schneider, J. F. Pierson, & J. F. T. Bugental (Eds.), *The handbook of humanistic psychology: Theory, research, and practice* (2nd edition; pp. 41–55). Thousand Oaks, CA: Sage.

Hoffman, L., Granger, N. Jr., Vallejos, L., & Moats, M. (2016). An existential-humanistic perspective on Black Lives Matter and contemporary protest movements. *Journal of Humanistic Psychology.* Advance online publication. doi: 10.1177/0022167816652273

Prilleltensky, I., & Fox, D. (1997). Introducing critical psychology: Values, assumptions, and status quo. In D. Fox & I. Prilleltensky (Eds.), *Critical psychology: An introduction* (pp. 3–20). Thousand Oaks, CA: Sage.

Rothberg, D. (2006). *The engaged spiritual life: A Buddhist approach to transforming ourselves and the world.* Boston, MA: Beacon Press.

Sue, D. W. (2010). *Microaggressions in everyday life: Race, gender, and sexual orientation.* Hoboken, NJ: John Wiley & Sons.

Editors' Postscript

Transpersonal psychology remains a vision that influences the contemporary psychotherapy community and beyond. At its best, the transpersonal is dynamic, integrative, and inclusionary. However, it has not always manifested these aspirations. Since its inception, the transpersonal movement has reported to be focused on growth and transformation, and the chapters included within these volumes hopefully bring forth a contemporary vision of how the many contributors see and experience the field. We have sought to highlight what has drawn many to transpersonal psychology, and also bring light to the areas in which we feel it needs to do better. Such dynamism can bring diffuse understandings about what is part of this tradition and what is separate. In this collection, we have provided a collage of theory, research, ideas, practices, and experiences that sprung from the writers' and teachers' connections with their understanding of the transpersonal in contemporary contexts.

Shadows & Light captures many enduring transpersonal themes, such as multiple ways of knowing, varied perspectives to understanding the world and our place within it, and how the spirit moves different individuals in unique ways. Many chapters echo with traditional transpersonal ideas of human potential, individual and community transformation, states of consciousness, and the exploration of spiritual practices. Additionally, this collection purposefully emphasizes the vital perspectives of multiculturalism and social justice, the examination and incorporation of contemporary research discoveries, and the transformative power of creative energy. These are some of the new directions in this field represented in *Shadows & Light*.

In retrospect, we feel that several fundamental approaches to life resonated through the collection. The first is a fearless spirit of openness that includes new experiences, new relationships, and new perspectives.

The second is a focus on respectfully building deeper connections and relationships. These relationships range from connecting more deeply with aspects of our own human experiences and nurturing authentic relationships to building a sustaining relationship with the natural world that holds us. The final theme we discovered is compassion. Each author in their own way reflected on how we can continue to extend ourselves further beyond our bubbles and traps of habits to engage in the work of contributing to the health of our world.

As editors we have felt privileged to work with such wonderful, intelligent, and heartfelt authors, and hope the readers have benefited from everyone's efforts on the project. To the best of our abilities, we have tried to embrace angel Kyodo williams' highlighted call for *Ubuntu* and Charles Tart's appeal for curiosity and humility. As hundreds of thousands of people are increasingly saying everyday throughout the world and at the end of Yoga classes and in other settings—*Namaste*.

Francis J. Kaklauskas
Carla J. Clements
Dan Hocoy
Louis Hoffman

Index

Hoffman, L., 180
Holism, 131-132, 179
Homeostasis, 134, 137
Hope, 53, 78, 155, 157, 166
Human potential, 233
Humanistic psychology, 224, 226
Hurry Sickness, 62-67,

I-Ching, 206
Identity, 30-33, 47, 69, 130, 179-189
Improvisation, 40, 43, 46-47, 49,
  193-194, 215-221
Indigenous, 23, 41, 119, 179-180,
  201
Individuation, 135, 148
Institutional racism, see racism
Integral, 135, 205-213
Interconnectedness, 23, 130-132,
  135, 148, 157
Interfaith, 92, 123-124, 126
Intergenerational trauma, see trauma
Interoception, 168
Intersubjectivity, 165, 169
Introspection, 13-15,
Islam, 92, 209-210

Jazz, 18, 194, 216, 219-221
Jesus, 108
Jinpa, T., 112-113
Judaism, 41, 77
Jung, C., 44, 135, 206

King, M. L., 21, 23
Kuhn, T., 11

Les Miserables, 53
Levine, R., 65, 72
Lief, J., 192
Liminal, 33, 121
Linear time, 67, 70-71,75-77
Love, 2, 21-24, 25, 36, 55, 108, 140,
  146, 162, 176, 209

Macy, J., 33, 79
Malcom X, 21
Marginalization, 21, 180, 188

Martin, Trayvone, 226
Maslow, A., 135, 157, 208, 223-224,
  226-228
Mass incarceration, 226
Mayan calendar, 68
Meaning, 29, 74, 120, 156, 171, 191-
  192, 220-221, 226
Meditation, 1, 14-15, 18, 35, 50-51,
  75-76, 79-80, 83-84, 86, 89, 93-114,
  119, 123, 126, 129, 146, 151, 155-
  157, 195-196, 206, 218-219, 228-
  229
  metta, 94, 106
  zazen, 218
Mental Health, 42, 50, 123, 130, 132-
  134, 138-140, 147, 163-164
Mental Illness, 132-133, 138-140
Microaggression, 182, 228
Mindfulness, 19, 41-42, 47, 77, 79-80,
  93, 96-101, 104-108, 122, 144, 156,
  169, 191-192, 218-221
Monk, T., 220
Multiculturalism, 20, 23, 26, 30-31,
  122, 144, 180-183, 187-188, 192,
  223-230
Music therapy, 40, 43
Myth, 69, 162-165, 208, 210
Mystics, 33
Mysticism, 26-27, 34-36, 130, 139,
  165
  mystical experience, 148

Naropa University, 43, 50, 93, 95-96,
  106, 144, 154, 191-192, 195, 198,
Near-death experiences, 180
Neuroplasticity, 105, 133,
Neuroscience, 105, 162, 166, 192
Nondual (non-dual), 145-146
Numinous, 25-26, 35

Oppression, 20, 25, 30-31, 73-74,
  129, 138, 150, 180-188, 227
Out of body experiences, 3-4

Parapsychology, 3-8
Patriarchy, 25, 32, 215

Notes on Editors

Carla Clements, PhD, has been chair of Transpersonal Counseling Psychology at Naropa University for 10 of the last 15 years, where she has mentored professors in transpersonal pedagogy and personally taught hundreds of this generation's transpersonal psychotherapists. She has published several articles on transpersonal psychology and has worked as a transpersonal psychotherapist for 30 years in Denver and Boulder, CO. In addition, she is currently the independent rater for the MAPS-supported study of MDMA-assisted psychotherapy for chronic, treatment-resistant PTSD. She is a long-time yogini, musician, and naturist who published a CD entitled *Creationship*. Her daughter, Cate, is the delight of her life.

Dan Hocoy, PhD, is Chief Strategy Officer (and Past President) of Antioch University in Seattle and also serves as Associate Vice Chancellor of Advancement for the Antioch University System. Dan failed in his efforts to become a Catholic priest and settled for being a licensed clinical psychologist instead, so that he could at least serve souls in psychiatric hospitals and private practice. He is author of numerous publications that intersect culture, social change, and psychology. Dan is particularly obsessed with the transformative power of art as well as the notion of synchronicity and spends an inordinate amount of time trying to get the universe to conform to his personal interests.

Louis Hoffman, PhD, is a faculty member at Saybrook University and director of Existential, Humanistic, and Transpersonal Psychology Specialization. He is a fellow of the American Psychological Association (APA) as well as three APA divisions (10, 32, & 52). An avid writer, Dr. Hoffman has eight books to his credit, including *Existential Psychology East-West*, *Brilliant Sanity*, and *Journey of the Wounded Soul: Poetic Companions for Spiritual Struggles*. He serves on the editorial boards of the *Journal of Humanistic Psychology, The Humanistic Psychologist, PsycCRITIQUES: APA Review of Books,* and Janus Head. Dr. Hoffman is also a licensed psychologist in private practice. He lives with his wife and three sons along with their dog in beautiful Colorado Springs, CO.

Francis J. Kaklauskas, PsyD, facilitates the Group Psychotherapy Training Program at the University of Colorado, Boulder and is core faculty at Naropa University Graduate School of Counseling and Psychology. He is a fellow and past board member of the American Group Psychotherapy Association. Dr. Kaklauskas' other publications include being the primary psychological consultant and on-screen presenter for the three-part video series, *Hooked: The Addiction Trap*, and co-authoring the Group Psychotherapy chapter in *The Handbook of Clinical Psychology*. He has co-edited three previous volumes: *Brilliant Sanity: Buddhist Approaches to Psychotherapy, Existential Psychology East-West,* and *The Buddha, The Bike, the Couch, and the Circle*. He is passionate about music and feels fortunate to have studied under Milt Hinton, Chuck Rainey, Bill Douglas, and Mark Miller. He regularly tries to recruit his wife, Elizabeth, and son, Levi, to be his rhythm section partners.

Notes on Contributors

Jackie Ashley, MA, is Senior Adjunct Professor in the Somatic Counseling Psychology Department at Naropa University, teaching body-based meditation practice, creative arts therapies in addition to supervising graduate students in their internships. She is a Somatic and Dance/Movement Psychotherapist specializing in working with those challenged by severe and persistent mental illness, personality disorders, and trauma. She has been utilizing horses in her private practice, Wild At Heart LLC, since 2001, where she works with individuals and leads groups for women with sexual trauma, those with psychiatric disorders, and those in recovery from addictions. Through the use of movement, body awareness, contemplative practice, and the creative process, she supports her clients and students to further integrate their emotional and physical experience to enhance their lives and well-being.

Dale Asrael, MA, is an *Acharya* (master teacher) in the Buddhist and Shambhala lineage of Chogyam Trungpa Rinpoche and Sakyong Mipham Rinpoche. She has trained in meditation for over 45 years, and teaches and leads retreats internationally. She is Core Faculty (Associate Professor) at Naropa University in MA Clinical Mental Health Counseling: Mindfulness-Based Transpersonal Counseling. She founded, and is the principal instructor for, Naropa's Mindfulness Instructor Training program.

Paul Bialek, MA, is a core professor in the MA Contemplative Psychotherapy & Buddhist Psychology program at Naropa University and a Counselor in private practice in Boulder, CO. He has trained in meditation for over 35 years and currently studies in the Shambhala Buddhist lineage with Sakyong Mipham Rinpoche. He is dedicated to exploring and refining contemplative approaches to counselor education in courses such as Buddhist Psychology and Psychology of Meditation. He feels privileged to work with remarkable students and colleagues that take contemplative teaching and learning to heart.

Jeanine M. Canty, PhD, is a professor and chair of the Environmental Studies department at Naropa University. A lover of nature, justice, and contemplative practice, Jeanine teaches courses in Ecopsychology, Deep Ecology, Multicultural Perspectives for Environmental Leaders, and an eight-day Wilderness solo. She is the editor of and a contributor to the collection *Ecological and Social Healing: Multicultural Women's Perspectives.* Selected works have been featured in *The Wiley Handbook of Transpersonal Psychology, International Journal of Transpersonal Studies, Sustainability: The Journal of Record and World Futures,* and *Journal of New Paradigm Research.*

Tina Fields, PhD, is associate professor and chair of the Ecopsychology MA program at Naropa University. She has taught about the psychological, cultural, and spiritual dimensions of sustainability issues since 1999, including five years of living and learning fully outdoors. She is co-editor of *So What? Now What? The Anthropology of Consciousness Responds to a World in Crisis.* Tina also enjoys calling contra dances and caring for her beloved 99-year-old father.

Kathleen Gregory, PhD, is an Associate Professor in the Graduate School of Counseling and Psychology at Naropa University. Previously she convened the Master of Counseling program at La Trobe University in Melbourne, Australia. She was a student of the late Ven. Traleg Kyabgon Rinpoche for over 20 years and teaches his instruction on the intersection of Buddhism and psychotherapy. She has published in the areas of Buddhism and health, contemporary Buddhism, and race and psychotherapy.

Diane Joy Israel, MA, is a psychotherapist, entrepreneur, end of life coach, educator, and athlete. She was the executive producer of the award-winning film *Beauty Mark*. Diane serves on the boards of PassageWorks Institute and the Grief Support Network. She is an adjunct professor and on the Board of Trustees at Naropa University.

Julie A. Kellaway, PhD, received her doctorate in counseling psychology and certification in ethnic studies from Colorado State University. She is a licensed psychologist and teaches transpersonal counseling and psychology at Naropa University in Boulder, CO. Julie's research interests include gender roles, ethnic bias, and assessing clinical outcomes.

Judy Lief was a close student of Chögyam Trungpa Rinpoche, who trained and empowered her as a teacher in the Buddhist and Shambhala traditions. She is the author of *Making Friends with Death: A Buddhist Guide to Encountering Mortality* and numerous articles that have appeared in *The Shambhala Sun, Tricycle, O Magazine, Buddhadharma,* and *The Naropa Journal of Contemplative Psychotherapy.* She edited several of Trungpa Rinpoche's books, including the recently published three-volume set, *The Profound Treasury of the Ocean of Dharma.*

Mark A. Miller, MFA, has won and been nominated for many prestigious awards as a musician. He has toured and recorded with Art Lande, Paul McCandless, Peter Kater, R. Carlos Nakai, David Friesen, Tuck and Patti, and Bill Douglas, among others. Mark's recordings with jazz pianist Art Lande include "The Story of Ba-Ku," "Prayers, Germs and Obsessions," "World Without Cars," and two award-winning children's albums featuring Meg Ryan and Holly Hunter. With pianist Peter Kater, he has recorded eight albums including "Migration," "Honorable Sky," and "Illumination" (nominated for a Grammy Award in 2013), as well as sound tracks for television and Off-Broadway.

Laurie Rugenstein, EdD, MT-BC, is a professor in the Transpersonal Counseling and Psychology Program at Naropa University. She founded and directed the Music Therapy Concentration in this program for 13 years. She then served as Coordinator of the Mindfulness-based Transpersonal Counseling Concentration for 9 years. In addition to her work at Naropa, Laurie served as a music therapist with hospice for 22 years. Laurie has a long interest in music and voice and has studied voice work with members of the Roy Hart Theatre for many years. She is a primary trainer in the Bonny Method of Guided Imagery and Music and uses this transpersonal approach in her private practice. Laurie is a mindfulness instructor at Naropa University, and her current spiritual practice is caring for her husband, who has advanced Parkinson's disease.

Scott Shannon, MD, has been instrumental in the creation of a holistic and integrative perspective in psychiatry. Scott joined the American Holistic Medical Association in 1978 as a founding member and served as President from 2000–2001. He is an Assistant Clinical Professor of Psychiatry at the University of Colorado and Past-President of the American Board of Integrative Holistic Medicine. Scott is the founder of the Wholeness Center in Fort Collins, CO. His books include *Handbook of Complementary and Alternative Therapies in Mental Health, Mental Health for the Whole Child,* and *Parenting the Whole Child.*

Charles T. Tart, PhD, is internationally known for his psychological work on the nature of consciousness, particularly altered states of consciousness, and as one of the founders of the field of transpersonal psychology. His two classic books, *Altered States of Consciousness* and *Transpersonal Psychologies* were widely used texts that were instrumental in allowing these areas to become part of modern psychology. His most recent book, *The End of Materialism: How Evidence of the Paranormal is Bringing Science and Spirit Together,* integrates his work in parapsychology and transpersonal psychology to show that it is reasonable to be both scientific and spiritual in outlook. He was a Professor of Psychology at the Davis campus of the University of California for 28 years and has had more than 250 articles published in professional journals and books, including lead articles in such prestigious scientific journals as *Science and Nature.*

Todd Thillman, MDiv, is currently enrolled in the Mindfulness Based Transpersonal Psychology graduate degree program at Naropa University. In 2004 he received his Master of Divinity degree from Naropa University. He spent the next 11 years working as a chaplain for a local non-profit Hospice program. He has been involved in mindfulness-based meditation practices since 2001. In addition to his work with others, his main passions are his beautiful wife, Karlene, his 12-year-old son, Gavin, and his brand new son, Declan.

Sue Wallingford, MA, is Chair and Associate Professor in the Mindfulness-Based Transpersonal Counseling Program at Naropa University. She is founder and director of the Boulder Art Therapy Collective, which offers a variety of art therapy services to the community, including individual and group art therapy, open studios, workshops, and trainings.   In 2011, Sue spearheaded the creation of the Naropa Community Art Studio-International (NCAS-I), a sustainable service-learning project with the mission to bring art therapy practices into international populations, working toward social justice and human rights issues. In her spare time, you can find her in her studio creating art. She is currently preparing for her next art exhibit, comprising mixed-media assemblages on the theme of transpersonal passages and portals.

Roger Walsh, M.D., PhD, is one of the most influential individuals in contemporary transpersonal psychology and has won a number of international and national awards. He is on the faculty of the University of California at Irvine, where he is a professor of psychiatry, philosophy, and anthropology, as well as a professor in the religious studies program. His books include *Paths Beyond Ego, Meditation: Classic and Contemporary, and Essential Spirituality: The Seven Central Practices*, as well as several co-authored books with his wife, Frances Vaughan.

angel Kyodo williams is an author, activist, one of three black women Zen "Senseis" or teachers, master trainer and founder of the Center for Transformative Change. She has been bridging the worlds of transformation and justice since her critically acclaimed book, Being Black: Zen and the Art of Living With Fearlessness and Grace. She applies wisdom teachings and embodied practice to intractable social issues at the intersections of climate change, and racial and economic justice. Her 27 Days of Change online program and 3rd Way Leadership supports changemakers in inner meets outer change worldwide. Her newest book collaboration, Radical Dharma: Talking Race, Love, and Liberation was released this year on Juneteenth -- a day that symbolizes and holds forth the promise of Black Liberation. Rev. angel notes, "Love and Justice are not two. Without inner change, there can be no outer change. Without collective change, no change matters."

Elaine Yuen, PhD, is an Associate Professor of Religious Studies and Chair of the Department of Wisdom Traditions at Naropa University in Boulder, CO, where she teaches courses on spirituality and ritual, Buddhism, and pastoral care. She has taught national and international programs exploring the interfaces between Buddhism, meditation, creativity, and contemplative care-giving. Dr. Yuen is cross-trained as a social science researcher, and is particularly interested in the relationships between meditation and the creative process. A Senior Teacher in the Shambhala Buddhist tradition since the early 1970s, she continues her exploration of contemporary life through many activities as a teacher, parent, and artist.

www.ingramcontent.com/pod-product-compliance
Lightning Source LLC
Chambersburg PA
CBHW061956090426
42811CB00006B/951